MICHAEL
BALLACK

EUAN REEDIE

MICHAEL
BALLACK

THE BIOGRAPHY

JB

JOHN BLAKE

Published by John Blake Publishing Ltd,
3 Bramber Court, 2 Bramber Road,
London W14 9PB
England

www.blake.co.uk

First published in hardback in 2007

ISBN 978 1 84454 375 5

British Library Cataloguing-in-Publication Data:

A catalogue record for this book is available from the British Library.

Design by www.envydesign.co.uk

Printed in Great Britain by Creative, Print & Design

1 3 5 7 9 10 8 6 4 2

Papers used by John Blake Publishing are natural, recyclable products
made from wood grown in sustainable forests. The manufacturing processes
conform to the environmental regulations of the country of origin.

Contents

Introduction

Anew year is supposed to herald fresh starts, bright beginnings and engender burgeoning hope and optimism for the future. However, for Michael Ballack and his beleaguered manager and faltering club, the start of 2007 was imbued with a severe sense of foreboding, as worsening fortunes spiralled ever downwards. Internal strife involving reports of Jose Mourinho at odds with owner Roman Abramovich over the club's transfer policy, a rash of injuries to key players and Ballack's protracted failure to live up to a rapidly fading reputation seemed to suggest to many pundits that the west London football juggernaut was on the verge of disintegration.

Still, if this was a blip, it is one most football clubs would be delighted to suffer given that Chelsea, despite this catalogue of misery, were still in contention in every competition they had entered. When you have enjoyed a period of untrammelled success, however, even the slightest misfortune is magnified and portrayed as a disaster.

Conversely, Michael Ballack could be thankful for his team's suffering, as it served to mask his own persistent weakness when wearing a blue shirt. The fact that Chelsea's calamities were discussed so feverishly by the media were not due to the German's listlessness, but owed much to the uncharacteristic behaviour and comments of their manager.

Jose Mourinho, hitherto the alpha-male, authoritative force of nature in management terms was appearing abnormally pervious to criticism, decidedly wayward in his selection policy and astonishingly outspoken and critical about his own players. What remained constant, however, was his resolute and inexplicable defence of Michael Ballack, who was beginning to arouse consternation among Chelsea supporters and attract unfavourable reviews from football pundits.

His fourth goal for his new club, against Everton in December 2006, was a false dawn for the struggling German as he turned in two uninspiring performances in Chelsea's successive 2–2 draws at home to Reading and Fulham respectively. Fulham's late equaliser through Carlos Bocanegra highlighted the malaise afflicting the normally unruffled champions. Shorn of the galvanising presence of injured captain John Terry, Chelsea were defensively quite simply a mess – horribly illustrated by Ballack hideously mistiming an attempted clearance in the box allowing the ball to go straight into the path of grateful Bocanegra who prodded it home past the Blues' reserve goalkeeper, Hilario.

After the match, Jose Mourinho, who often seems to revel in

mischievously delivering juicy and jaw-dropping soundbites for the press, was a picture of misery, pouring out his heart in a torrent of negativity rather than showering praise and plaudits on himself and his players. Unbelievably, he castigated his own managerial abilities and the commitment of his players, making particular mention of the contributions of Andriy Shevchenko, Shaun Wright-Phillips and Saloman Kalou.

Avoiding censure from Mourinho was, however, Ballack, who remarkably continued to be stubbornly shielded by the defiant Portuguese.

It was an extraordinary show of faith for the German; perhaps early in the season such praise was acceptable, but if the likes of Shaun Wright-Phillips were targeted for their under-performance when afforded a paucity of first-team starts, why was Ballack not being publicly rebuked for failing to live up to his world-class reputation? Suddenly the self-styled 'special one' seemed to be losing his touch and appeared to be suffering from the unremitting pressures of Manchester United's vigorous and vibrant chase for the title.

It was then alleged in the press that both Didier Drogba and Claude Makelele had had to be restrained in the dressing room after the Fulham match when the pair attempted to remonstrate with Mourinho over his unwavering support of Ballack. The duo's revolt was, it was claimed, motivated by Ballack's failure to pull his weight, perform defensive duties and contribute to Chelsea's attacks. Their unrest was further fuelled by Mourinho's steadfast refusal to publically acknowledge such failings. According to the *Sunday Times'* Duncan Castles, these failings were clear to see in the statistics of Ballack's performances to date: 'Ballack's critics among his teammates could point to statistical analysis of his contribution to back their case. According to figures from the ProZone system – used by many clubs to assess the contribution of their players in terms of running, tackles, passes and shots – in his first five months as a Chelsea player Ballack has been on par with the "benchmark" for a domestic central midfielder. He is nowhere near the élite Champions League level, which has been attained in England only by his teammate Frank Lampard, Manchester United's Paul Scholes and Gilberto Silva of Arsenal.'

Castles added that 'Premiership scouting reports on Chelsea's number 13 are hardly more flattering. While they talk of an individual whose physical presence and sense of timing in the penalty area is a threat when his team has the ball, they also highlight his sluggishness over the ground and an apparent reluctance to support the back four. Defensively, Ballack is regarded as a weakness to be exploited. Privately, an opposing coach admitted his team had found Chelsea "not as dynamic as they used to be" when lined up in a 4-4-2 formation, in which Mourinho has accommodated the German at the head of a midfield diamond.'

Despite this damning assessment of his expensive recruit, Mourinho was bullish and continued to stand by his man. He admitted in an interview with a German radio station that Ballack had 'not done anything amazing yet', but still paid tribute to Michael's willingness to play for the team. The coach went on to say: 'Reports about problems in the dressing room are not correct. Do we want more from him [Ballack] in terms of performance? Not from him, from everybody. And if the objective is to put some kind of pressure on me, then no chance because I pick the team, nobody else does it. Press opinions, other player opinions are not for me.'

However, despite Mourinho's attempts to paper over the cracks that were insidiously appearing in his hitherto impregnable empire, Chelsea and Ballack's ills had not gone unnoticed at Michael's former club, Bayern Munich. In a three-pronged, opportunistic attack, the German club's chief executive Uli Hoeness, president Franz Beckenbauer and chairman Karlheinz Rummenigge seized the chance to voice their views about the man who had famously scorned them.

Hoeness fired the first salvo when he questioned Jose Mourinho's wisdom in bringing in a host of stellar talents, one of whom was, of course, Ballack, and then being unable to assemble them into a coherent and cohesive team unit. He added: 'It's difficult for Ballack to be at his best because he is such a such a similar player to Frank Lampard. They need to decide where his best position is. Both like to attack and get forward, but one of them also has to get back and defend. I think there is a lot of confusion as to what people's role is.'

Beckenbauer, meanwhile, suggested that Ballack would have enjoyed more prosperous fortunes if he had joined Manchester United. Finally, Rummenigge completed the critical assault on Ballack by insisting Bayern had done the right thing in allowing him to leave on a free transfer.

Given the often rancorous relationship he had endured with the pair at Bayern and the acrimony his transfer to Chelsea had engendered for both parties, Ballack was stirred to respond. In an interview with *Die Welt*, he said, 'Nobody escapes the criticism, which can be very hard here in England. I have already caught the attention of the critics. But I am happy that

I made this move. My decision was right and I don't regret the transfer for a second. It has been the right step, both personal and professional. It is not only a challenge, but a pleasure to be part of a team with so many outstanding players.'

Ballack also said that Chelsea's narrow playing system and subsequent lack of crosses into the box were blunting the cutting edge he could provide. He explained that he was missing the service provided by Bayern's rampaging wing-backs, Philipp Lahm and Willy Sagnol. And Ballack also responded with a riposte for Rummenigge, saying, 'Herr Rummenigge should simply tell the truth and accept the fact a player decides to go to another club. His comments just make me laugh.'

Ballack was rested for Chelsea's first two games of 2007 – a 0–0 draw at Aston Villa and a 6–1 thumping of Macclesfield in the third round of the FA Cup at Stamford Bridge. However, any notion that he would return reinvigorated and ready to prove his doubters wrong were soon dispelled.

He looked overwhelmed by the frenetic football played in Chelsea's 1–1 draw at Wycombe in the first-leg of the League Cup semi-final. Perhaps he could be excused failing to impose himself against lower league opposition whose hustle and bustle can often stymie the finesse and class of even the greatest of players.

However, when you are earning in excess of £100,000 a week, there are no excuses when you are impotent in one of the season's seminal matches against one of Chelsea's closest rivals, as was the case when they travelled to Liverpool in mid-January, the day before Arsenal hosted Manchester United.

Naturally, the significance of this double bill was not lost on Ballack, who realised this was 'a defining weekend' of the campaign and that Chelsea could not afford to lose further ground to Manchester United by slipping up at Anfield. But cometh the hour, and cometh another thoroughly miserable day at the office for Ballack, who was ineffectual in Liverpool's convincing 2–0 win. To make matters worse, he was ignominiously involved in a comical mix-up with Didier Drogba. As the two stood over a free-kick on the edge of the Liverpool box, Ballack was not alert to Drogba's quick-thinking desire to pass the ball, which ended up dribbling through the German's legs in a nutmeg to forget.

At least Michael could console himself with the realisation that, in spite of his and Chelsea's dismal fall from grace, the tantalising prospect of securing his first silverware in England remained on the horizon. He was again rested when Chelsea comfortably disposed of Nottingham Forest 3–0 in the FA Cup fourth round, and was present in a blue shirt when the Blues eased to a 4–0 win over Wycombe at Stamford Bridge to secure a meeting with Arsenal in the League Cup final.

At the start of February 2007, the bittersweet nature of his Chelsea career to date was encapsulated in a game against Blackburn at home. As Chelsea produced a rousing display worthy of their champions' status to cruise to a 3–0 win over Mark Hughes's gallant outfit, Ballack showed glimpses of the continental class which had first attracted Jose Mourinho's gaze. Ballack's vignette included a delightfully-driven left-foot cross for Andriy Shevchenko and a subtle headed flick-on for Saloman Kalou to score Chelsea's third goal. Ballack was sadly denied a fifth goal for his new club when his diving header was parried by Blackburn goalkeeper Brad Friedel. *Match of the Day* pundits Alan Hansen and Alan Shearer welcomed Ballack's stylish contributions, but suggested that the German was capable of much, much more.

Echoing the criticism that had dogged Ballack while he was in Germany, the pair attacked Michael's casual, ambling style which could easily be interpreted as insouciance and lack of effort. Shearer noted: 'Sometimes he lives on easy street, but he has a bit of quality.'

Chelsea's frustrated supporters were not as forgiving about their midfielder's maddening inability to grasp a game by its neck and exhibit fight and fire. The *Guardian*'s Jon Brodkin described the growing disquiet at Stamford Bridge vis-à-vis Ballack, who was barracked by the home fans throughout the Blackburn match. He wrote: 'When a disgruntled Chelsea supporter wanted his feelings about Michael Ballack relayed to the midfielder on Wednesday, his choice of emissary was revealing. Jose Mourinho, sitting nearby in the dug-out, was ignored. So, too, were Ballack's team-mates in action against Blackburn Rovers. Instead the fan turned towards an injured player watching from the bench. "JT [John Terry]," he bawled, "Tell Ballack to show some balls."'

It was a pertinent request given that Ballack clearly required to add some of John Terry's grit and determination to survive the hurly burly of English football and escape the wrath of an increasingly discontented Chelsea public. So, did Jose Mourinho endorse the exhortations for Ballack to incorporate the qualities of an Anglo Saxon artisan into his game? Was he also losing patience with the German's unwillingness to track back assiduously à la Michael Essien, or bomb forward like the barnstorming Frank Lampard? No, the Special One was sticking to his guns and chiming out the trite and tired messages of support for his under-fire midfielder. He told reporters: 'Michael Ballack makes a big contribution to the team. Because I pick the team, not the press or the supporters, if he makes me happy and gives me what I want, then he is OK.

'It's obvious this football in England is faster than anywhere else in the world and it is not easy to adapt. But he gives everything for the team.'

Giving everything for the team was simply not enough for Michael Ballack to justify his wages. It was perfectly reasonable to expect Ballack to produce world-class performances commensurate with his status as the highest paid footballer on the planet. But, despite mounting criticism of his form, Ballack mounted a defiant defence in an interview with a German news agency, as reported in the *Daily Telegraph*: 'As far as I am concerned, I have integrated well into the team. I feel very happy, I've found my role in the team and I have had plenty of confirmation of that, above all from my coach, Jose Mourinho, with whom I talk a lot.' Ballack added: 'There are a load of tabloid newspapers in England which always need something to write and it doesn't particularly bother me. Naturally, in a team like Chelsea it takes time to perfect your game and play an outstanding role.'

The Chelsea faithful were unlikely to be appeased by Michael's insistence that he was satisfied that he had fitted in well. They would no longer tolerate pallid performances from the German and were demanding he, like fellow players John Terry, Michael Essien and Frank Lampard, would give everything for the blue shirt rather than appear to blithely stroll through games.

The second-half of Ballack's first season in English football were set to say much about Michael's personality and standing in world football. Can he summon up more of the courage and sprit that were hallmarks of his time at Bayer Leverkusen, who suffered a series of devastating failures?

The worst-case scenario is that if he continues in the current mediocre vein and, if perceived wisdom is to be believed and Jose Mourinho opts to move elsewhere, any new manager could quite conceivably consider Ballack an unwanted luxury and jettison him and that other under-performing import, Andriy Shevchenko.

Do not count out on a radical reversal of Ballack's fortunes, however, something which has typified Michael's memorable career.

Silverware on several fronts is still a realistic goal and as the spring takes place, perhaps Ballack will emerge from a winter of discontent and blossom into the player his reputation suggests.

When your name is Michael Ballack and you have on the one hand, suffered a torturous last-day championship loss, a devastating booking to prevent you from playing in the World Cup final, and on the other hand celebrated glorious goals for your club on its unexpected journey to the final of the Champions League and played a starring role in your country's two-legged play-off triumph to progress to the World Cup finals, you are prepared for anything to happen. Watch this space, for football is a capricious beast as Michael Ballack knows only too well.

1

A Brave New World

Joining one of the biggest and richest clubs in Europe, earning a mammoth salary and living in one of the trendiest and most vibrant cities in the world with the love of your life and two adoring sons sounds simply heavenly.

How could Michael Ballack possibly fail in the latest chapter in his footballing career when he was set to enjoy an untrammelled existence, full of opportunity and garlanded with riches, one might ask? Surely as one of the best footballers in the world, he would effortlessly adapt to life in England and take the Premiership by storm, inspiring Chelsea to glory at home and abroad?

It is often easy to speculate on such an apparently perfect life when contemplating the luxurious lifestyle of a star footballer. Indeed, Michael Ballack may be massively wealthy and festooned with the trappings of fame, but a burgeoning bank balance would not shield him from the harsh realities of life. He is not immune to the unpredictability of the human condition, nor is he impervious to the demands of a move to pastures new.

Having never lived outside of Germany before, Michael initially – and inevitably – experienced what the anthropologist Kalvero Oberg described as 'culture shock'. The phenomenon, which Oberg coined in the 1950s, described the anxiety of adjusting to a new cultural or social environment when people move to a different country, and are forced to adapt to its language and culture.

The five stages or 'hurdles' he identified involved the traveller experiencing a wide range of emotions, from euphoria to depression, as he or she strives to integrate into an alien environment. Michael Ballack would certainly identify with these feelings during a tumultuous first year at Chelsea.

The country proved to be a startling contrast to his homeland, as would the football; the blistering speed of the game in the English Premiership, the merciless and unrelenting fixture schedule and the testing tactical requirements of his new team would at times combine to leave him in a bewildered haze.

However, he knew that if he eventually succeeded in arguably the greatest league in the world like other imports before him – think Gianfranco Zola, Eric Cantona and Thierry Henry, to name but three – he would earn respect and plaudits from both his team's supporters and followers of rival English clubs. The fact that he is German, and therefore invidiously associated with World War II, ruthless, robotic efficiency, and a charmless lack of humour, is no barrier to achieving legendary status in the Premiership.

His former German national coach, Jürgen Klinsmann, enjoyed a brief yet highly memorable stint at Tottenham in the mid-1990s, impressing with the excellence of his play and self-deprecating goal celebrations where he mocked his reputation as a serial diver by plunging to the ground with his team-mates. Yet for every Klinsmann, there is a Karlheinz Riedle – a German who, for whatever reason, never set the Premiership on fire à la Dennis Bergkamp or David Ginola.

Yes, in many respects footballers have it easy, but they are paid to perform in a climate where constant brilliance is demanded and the feats of past masters are a burdening benchmark. Welcome to England, Michael...

Indeed, in addition to the maelstrom of past and present pressures Michael encountered even before he had kicked a ball for his new club, misgivings and quibbles flew around both the Shed End and Fleet Street. His staggering salary was, as we shall see in a future chapter, the main thrust of many an anti-Ballack discussion.

Sniping sections of the media also obsessively raised concerns about the German's ability to dovetail with fellow midfielder, Frank Lampard. Recurring sentiments expressed by sceptical scribes centred on the fact that the pair were considered too similar and both were fuelled by attacking ambitions.

It was widely claimed that Chelsea would be faced with a conundrum on a par with that which England had encountered in trying to accommodate Frank Lampard and Steven Gerrard. There were even fleeting reports that Jose Mourinho planned to dispense with the services of Lampard, who had been hugely disappointing during the World Cup, with Barcelona the likely destination. And then there was the additional headache for Mourinho of choosing between the all-action dynamo that is Michael Essien and the redoubtable Claude Makelele, who had been an immovable force in the defensive midfield holding role since joining the Blues in the summer of 2003. *The Times'* Gabriele Marcotti crystallised the reservations of many pundits about Chelsea's wisdom in acquiring Ballack when he wrote, 'sometimes things happen that do not quite make sense and that raise more questions than they answer. Chelsea's signing of Michael Ballack, the Bayern Munich midfield player, falls into this category.

'Ballack simply does not appear to be the kind of player that Jose Mourinho would sign. The Portuguese has avoided bringing in big-name veterans on massive wages. Then there is the tactical issue. Ballack is something of a tactical anarchist and it has taken Bayern three years of fiddling with a variety of formations to find his best position on the pitch. It is hard to see Mourinho experimenting with various tactical schemes just to suit Ballack.'

Marcotti described the Bayern formation and Ballack's role at the top of a midfield diamond, a role that did not exist in Mourinho's system. He foresaw problems for the player, who – neither a centre forward nor a winger – would have to slot into Chelsea's midfield three.

Marcotti's mystification about the prospect of adding Ballack to an already successful formula at Chelsea certainly seemed well-founded in the context of Jose Mourinho's previous tactics. For the pragmatic Portuguese had favoured a 4-3-3 formation in his first two seasons with the club – and swept imperiously to two Premiership crowns in the process.

In deploying the lone striker Didier Drogba, who was supported either side by a tricky winger – Damien Duff, Arjen Robben, Joe Cole or Shaun Wright-Phillips – the Londoners became a formidable force. At times during the 2005/06 season, however, Mourinho had preferred to dispense with his wing wonders, opting for a more narrow and compact formation during the FA Cup Semi-Final against Liverpool, for example. The experimentation emulated the diamond formation which had served the Portuguese so well when he managed Porto. In light of Chelsea's 2–1 loss to Liverpool, Mourinho explained his thinking by pointing out that his wingers were luxury players who could, although capable of match-winning brilliance, equally be liabilities and squander possession which could cost his side dearly.

He had every faith in Lampard and Essien, meanwhile, safe in the knowledge that the pair had shown themselves to be pillars of consistency and security. But by adding Michael Ballack to the mix, Mourinho could add another ultra-reliable performer to the midfield. The German maestro was habitually assured in possession, crisp in the tackle and capable of supporting his forwards with perfectly timed incursions into the box.

And then there is his pièce de résistance. Ballack possesses a rare commodity among top-flight footballers that even Diego Maradona did not have – he is adept with either foot and therefore able to switch with ease from left to right while Lampard and Essien patrol the centre of the pitch.

Ballack had, during his career in Germany and particularly latterly with Bayern Munich, proved himself the consummate midfield performer – swaggering from one side of the pitch to the other, sitting deep and fulfilling the anchor role or, his favourite tactic of all, rampaging forward with smouldering authority and to lethal effect.

Former Chelsea winger Pat Nevin quelled doubts that Ballack's arrival represented tactical folly on Mourinho's behalf and insisted that it could, in fact, add a dash of panache to the champions' play. He explained to BBC Sport, 'When Chelsea beat West Ham 4–1 in April, I think they started with a 4-2-2-2 formation. That's a system which I don't think anyone in British football has tried yet.

'It's the Brazilian system, which their national team uses all the time. I think if he gets Ballack in, it's a system he might consider because it's one you need intelligent footballers to use. You can't play it with average players. Ballack can play behind the front two with Lampard. He tends to come in from the left, and Lampard is quite happy coming in from the right. Mourinho has won the championship twice in a row, so he will be thinking, what is there to add?'

Jose Mourinho was also naturally bullish about Ballack's possible role in the team and dismissed fears that his similarity to Frank Lampard would prove problematic. 'How can Michael's arrival affect Lampard and the team?' he asked. 'It will affect the team because Lampard wants top players to play with him and as a coach I am looking forward to playing them together and extracting the best.'

The man at the centre of the tactical quandary, Michael Ballack, was also insistent that he would add an extra dimension to Chelsea rather than cause disruption to the Blues' midfield.

'I am quite flexible,' he said. 'I can play at the back, the front of midfield, and that flexibility is in the side as well. Jose knows my strengths and the goals I score from midfield positions. Frank Lampard and myself play in roughly the same position. Frank has a great responsibility at Chelsea with the number of goals he scored and I think I can help him share the burden.'

He added: 'Frank is a great player but just like at any other team I have really enjoyed playing with my team-mates. This is not going to be a problem for me and we both want to be successful, which is what will drive us on.'

However, there were lingering doubts in some quarters that such confidence, which was borne of an over-sized ego according to some critics, could cause dissension in a hitherto harmonious Chelsea camp. How would Ballack – like most players on the continent used to speaking his mind to both his manager and his team-mates – get on with strong characters within the Chelsea dressing room, in particular John Terry and Frank Lampard, the Blues' two on-the-field lieutenants?

If the cynics were to be believed, there was already trouble ahead for Ballack and Lampard, whose similar style would apparently be problematic on and off the pitch. As for John Terry, well, Ballack had nearly come to blows with him while at Bayern Munich.

During Chelsea's 4–2 first-leg win during the Quarter Final of the Champions League in 2005, Terry had accused the German of diving to win a penalty, which Ballack duly converted. Before the second leg, Terry was apparently barged by Ballack and Bayern goalkeeper Oliver Kahn in the players' tunnel as tensions reached boiling point.

However, one year on and Ballack launched a concerted charm offensive in order to defuse any possible feud with Chelsea's hugely popular and inspirational captain. On signing for the Blues, he lavished fulsome praise on Terry, remarking, 'You have to remember that he is Chelsea's captain and represents the club so, therefore, I've got a lot of respect for him. He is a world-class player as well. But the game is about winning; he wanted to win, I wanted to win and going down 4–2 against Chelsea was hard.

'These sort of things happen,' continued Ballack. 'It is like mind games in the tunnel. Look at Arsenal and Man United last season, when Roy Keane and Patrick Vieira were involved in an incident. I'm sure they weren't exchanging pleasantries, but it's all part of football. John Terry is a great player and a fighter. That type of spirit is what made me realise I would like to play in England.'

Terry was also keen to play down any talk of a potential problem between the pair and reciprocated Ballack's compliments effusively, saying, 'Obviously he's a great player and I've played against him a few times a couple of years ago. I'm looking forward to playing alongside him. He's a massive player – you just have to look at his goal record for Germany and Bayern Munich.

'He scores great goals, similar to Lampard. He's looking forward to playing with him too. We did once have a little square-up in the tunnel, myself, him and Oliver Kahn. That's what football is all about in the tunnel before a game and I'm excited about him coming to Chelsea and it's looking good for us.'

So, Ballack was happy, his team-mates were happy: harmony and bonhomie reigned on the King's Road.

Well, not quite – there was major dissent within this all-prevailing mood of mutual backslapping: Chelsea's French defender, William Gallas. It was nothing personal against Ballack, it was the disparity between their respective wage packets which infuriated the Frenchman.

The *Daily Telegraph*'s Mihir Bose alleged that Gallas was already considerably irked by his failure to profit from the millions of Chelsea's owner, Russian tycoon Roman Abramovich, prior to Ballack's arrival. He explained: 'While new players came in on lavish salaries and existing players received new contracts – some, like John Terry, will even discuss their third deal – Gallas remained on the terms he had been given in 2002, a year before Abramovich arrived.

'Originally bought in May 2001 from Marseilles by the then manager, Claudio Ranieri, he earned around £16,000 a week. His original contract included a get-out clause, stating that he could leave if another club offered around £6 million for him. This clause was removed in 2002 when he was given a new five-year contract and a salary of £25,000 a week. At that time several clubs were interested in him, including Arsenal.'

Bose added that while Abramovich's arrival in 2003 heralded new deals for some existing players, such as Frank Lampard, Gallas continued to be both underrated and under-paid despite his unstinting excellence for the club. The arrival of Michael Ballack on wages massively dwarfing his own was the final straw for Gallas, whose misery was compounded when the German was handed the Frenchman's cherished number 13 shirt.

Sacré bleu!

Gallas, who had already failed to join the rest of the Chelsea squad on their pre-season tour of the United States claiming he needed more time off, had worn the shirt throughout his career with the London club. He was understandably not best pleased that a German interloper was to be entrusted with his prized property. His agent, Pierre Frelot, fumed, 'It is not possible for them to give Ballack the number 13 shirt without talking to William first. William has been wearing that shirt for five years and it is the shirt he expects to be in. As far as we are concerned, William's absence is still a misunderstanding.'

Ballack protested his innocence in the whole unsavoury affair, admitting he had requested the number 13 shirt when he had first joined Chelsea – only to be told it was not available.

'I had accepted the number 19 shirt. But two days ago the coach came and said "Okay, it's fine for you to have the 13." There was no particular reason behind the decision.'

Cynics can draw their own conclusions about Mourinho's sudden u-turn. As for Gallas, he had had enough – and left in acrimonious fashion for Arsenal, in a transfer deadline-day switch involving England left-back, Ashley Cole, joining the star-studded ranks of the Stamford Bridge club.

Meanwhile, other Chelsea players said to be ever so slightly unsettled and uneasy about a newcomer in their midst were wingers Shaun Wright-Phillips and Arjen Robben. The pair would have been forgiven for fearing for their chances of first-team football given the wingless, narrow system Mourinho was set to implement.

Even before Ballack arrived on the scene, Wright-Phillips'

game time was limited, so what chance would he have of dislodging the German captain from his seemingly intractable place in the Chelsea team?

West Ham certainly recognised that the irrepressible youngster craved a starting spot to showcase his scampering runs and mazy dribbling and expressed interest in Ian Wright's adopted son near the end of 2006.

Arjen Robben was also destined to become a David Fairclough-esque, supersub, another victim of Jose Mourinho's preference for midfield mastery over wondrous wing-play. Yet the confident Dutchman insisted before the start of the season that he was not threatened by Ballack's prospective perpetual presence in the Chelsea first-team line-up, saying, 'I'm never concerned because I always know my own qualities. I have a lot of confidence in myself and I'm not afraid for my place. Of course you know at Chelsea that you can't play every game because it's a world-class squad and with extra world-class players coming in, it's going to be even harder. But I'm very confident.'

While his move had so far created quite a commotion inside and outside the club, at this point there was no reason for Ballack to panic as he had yet to kick a ball for his new side. And while the chill winds of uncertainty about his transfer blew gustily back in England, the German could bask in the comforting warmth of the American sunshine and its people during Chelsea's pre-season training camp in Los Angeles. He was comforted by his coach's confidence, unbreakable optimism and unyielding self-belief.

In recruiting Ballack, Andriy Shevchenko, John Obi Mikel, Salomon Kalou, Ashley Cole and Khalid Boulahrouz, offsetting the departures of Eidur Gudjohnsen, Damien Duff, Asier Del Horno and Hernan Crespo, among others, Jose Mourinho was convinced he had assembled a squad capable of fulfilling his ultimate aim: winning the Champions League. He had purchased proven quality that could facilitate an assault on all fronts, including Chelsea's quest to join Huddersfield, Arsenal, Liverpool and Manchester United in winning the English championship three times in a row.

After watching his team's first training session during pre-season, Mourinho crowed, 'The hunger is there, the new players make it more difficult for the other ones to keep a place but at the same time the motivation is big. For Ballack and John Obi Mikel there is also the motivation to get into this group. The group is getting stronger, the friendship is amazing, the way we are building – I am very happy with what I have in hand.'

Mourinho would afford welcome encouragement and sustenance to Ballack throughout what was to be an occasionally troubled season for the German. The colourful Portuguese had shown he had wanted Ballack from the outset, pursuing him doggedly while he was at Bayern, and then confirming his admiration in a series of text messages to Michael during Germany's memorable voyage during the World Cup.

Mourinho even emulated Ballack's decision to sport a close-cropped haircut, extolling the merits of a soilder-style short-back-and-sides by declaring he was getting ready 'for war' when the new season commenced. It now remained to be seen whether new recruit Michael Ballack was equipped for life in the trenches with the pugnacious Portuguese or would go AWOL as the impending football campaign infolded.

Relaxed in the knowledge that he had won the trust and confidence of his coach, Ballack made his début for Chelsea in a 1–0 loss against a Major League Soccer all-star team, displaying his range of astute passes in Illinois at the beginning of August 2006. He played the first half of the friendly encounter before being replaced by the young Norwegian, John Obi Mikel. In Chelsea's next friendly, a 1-0 win over Feyenoord, Michael played the full 90 minutes and asked for people to be patient with him as he steadily got to grips with his new club. He said, 'It was the second match – you cannot be at the level where you want to be. Lots of players were at the World Cup and had a long season followed by some time off.

'You just need time to get back. We just need games to grow together. We are not used to each other yet. I don't really know the team yet, and the team doesn't really know me. It still takes some time, but it will improve from game to game. We've just been together for one week, whereas it normally takes weeks and months for a team to reach a top level – even a team like Chelsea.'

A 1–1 draw with Celtic at Stamford Bridge provided few clues as to how Ballack, who came on as a second-half substitute against the Scottish champions, would adapt to his new surroundings as it was another friendly encounter. A truer indication of his potential for greatness in arguably the world's greatest football league would come in the white-hot atmosphere of competition. The FA Community Shield may not satisfy these criteria, but in recent years it has clawed back its former status as a competitive fixture. Essentially, it still represents a piece of silverware and, when the opponents are

Liverpool and Chelsea – whose recent intense rivalry yielded crucial victories for the Anfield Road side in both the FA Cup and the Champions League – it is a clash not to be sniffed at.

And it was the men from Merseyside who continued their supremacy in one-off fixtures to win the Community Shield 2–1. For Ballack, meanwhile, it was a miserable afternoon when he was forced off with a bruised hip after only 24 minutes. Prior to that, he had found the Liverpool midfielder Mohamed Sissoko an uncompromising player who stymied his ability to dictate matters. Michael and Sissoko would clash again later in the season in similarly unhappy circumstances for the German.

It was a rude awakening to the rigours of English football for Michael, who faced the jarring realisation, if it had not been apparent already, that he would not be afforded the time and space he had enjoyed in Germany. Michael was now facing a race against time to be fit for Chelsea's opening match of the Premiership season, at home to Manchester City at Stamford Bridge.

He told Germany's *Bild* newspaper, 'The injury is a painful bruise, entailing a swelling and a haemorrhage. The hip periosteum has become inflamed. I have to wait and see what happens over the next few days, but I'm hoping it'll be okay for the Manchester City game on Sunday.'

However, Jose Mourinho struck a more realistic and pessimistic note when he expressed doubt about his midfielder's prospects of recovering in time to make his first start in English football. He revealed, 'My opinion is that Michael will not be fit to play. His improvement since last Sunday has been very small and he has not trained with the team. He trained on his own on Thursday so I don't believe he can play unless he improves a lot.'

As he so often is, Mourinho was proved correct in his assessment and Ballack missed a comfortable 3–0 win for Chelsea. He was also unavailable for his side's trip to Middlesbrough, which ended in a shock 2–1 defeat for the champions, for whom Ballack's fellow Blues' new boy, Andriy Shevchenko, netted his first goal in the Premiership. For once, even though it was ridiculously early in the season, Chelsea were playing catch-up in the championship race to Manchester United, who had already notched up two wins from two games.

It was therefore a timely boost for the Blues when Michael was passed fit for Chelsea's trip to Blackburn, where he took his place in a formidable midfield comprising Frank Lampard, Michael Essien and Claude Makelele. After a quiet opening 45 minutes, this imposing quartet seized the initiative and helped Chelsea to a hard-fought 2–0 victory. Ballack could reflect with some satisfaction on a pleasing début and, as the *Guardian*'s Kevin McCarra described, 'had some nice touches.' The *Daily Telegraph*'s Henry Winter was even more complimentary, commenting on Ballack's 'impressive appetite. He almost engineered a chance himself midway through the half, but it lacked the power to trouble (Blackburn goalkeeper) Brad Friedel.'

Even more encouraging for our man was the glowing praise he received for his performance from his manager and one of his team-mates. Jose Mourinho enthused, 'I think at Blackburn, Ballack, Lampard and also Essien, they had a very important game for us. They were very powerful in midfield and in the second-half had complete control of the game by passing. Ballack was very intelligent when the team was winning. Instead of playing in the diamond, he was playing 10 metres behind, very close to Makelele. In the second half they controlled the game well.'

Frank Lampard added, 'I enjoy playing with Michael Ballack. Blackburn was his first full game and there is a long way to go, but when you are playing with players who want to move the ball and look for you when you are running into space, and expect the same of you, then it's great. I think we can get a really good combination together. I think we are on the same wavelength and hopefully we can be successful for the team.'

Michael Ballack, given his love of the team ethic, was more concerned with Chelsea's procurement of three points to ensure Manchester United did not increase the gap at the top of the table than his own satisfactory performance. He remarked, 'It was a very important triumph for us because before the game we had only three points and United had nine. Yes, maybe we were a little nervous because we had lost the previous match and United won on Saturday. As a result, we made too many mistakes in the first half. But then we improved and we made enough chances to get the victory.'

In his home début for Chelsea against Charlton, which resulted in a 2–1 win for the champions, Ballack turned in an even more noteworthy display, showing glimpses of the skill and invention that had shaped his reputation as a world-class performer. Firstly, he delivered a sumptuous 40-yard pass for Didier Drogba and secondly, he performed one of the most memorable tricks in the history of football, the Cruyff turn, before firing a left-footed strike just wide. On six minutes, it was from his header, blocked by a Charlton defender, that Drogba opened the scoring for Chelsea. This was a moment that epitomised the message on the back of one Chelsea supporter's shirt: 'The Drog's Ballacks'.

The confident German also hinted that he was not prepared to play second fiddle to the darling of the Bridge, Frank Lampard, in the penalty-taking stakes. After Lampard had missed his third penalty in four attempts, including an infamous failure in the 2006 World Cup for England, Ballack said, 'Maybe I will take the next penalty because Frank didn't score, but I'm not a player who has to take every free-kick or penalty. Frank took the penalties last year, so maybe we will take turns.' As it transpired, he would not have long to wait to demonstrate his penalty-taking prowess.

The Times' Russell Kempson was in awe of the German genius who rose above the hurly burly of English football to exude elegance and class in abundance. He wrote: 'Michael Ballack strolls through the midfield like an emperor. Head held high, tracking back, thrusting forward, casually transferring the ball from left foot to right. He may be a stranger to the Barclays Premiership, but already he is lording it, the master of all that he surveys.' High praise indeed, which could be considered hyperbole given that Ballack had not scored and was not yet significantly superior to any other players on the pitch.

However, this tribute and other comparable platitudes were tangible evidence that he was impressing English audiences with a Teutonic trait that they normally despise when it is displayed by a player wearing the white shirt of Germany:

supreme confidence. Ballack's strolling, upright playing style, so often the focus of derision in Germany, had found favour in his new home. However, if his cocksure strutting was not combined with workrate and an end product, his perceived casual indifference would be decried as vociferously as it had been in his homeland. He had made an impressive start to his Chelsea career, yes, but to paraphrase football pundits' parlance, the championship season is a marathon and not a sprint, and he therefore needed to prove he had the stamina to maintain such exalted standards over a protracted period rather than in short-term spurts.

In addition to being considered integral to Chelsea's hopes of cementing their domestic dominance, he and Andriy Shevchenko were seen as key players in Jose Mourinho's bid to capture one prize that had remained irritatingly elusive for the West London club: the Champions League. After being paired with old foes Barcelona, Werder Bremen and Levski Sofia in Group A, when asked to assess his side's qualification prospects, Ballack struck the right balance between confidence and caution, given the quality of the group from which Chelsea were expected to qualify. He said: 'We are not worried about getting through, but we know how strong the other teams are and respect them. Barcelona was the strongest team last year. Not only in Spain but in Europe they played very well. They are a big team. I know how strong Bremen are. Some people say we have been drawn against the strongest teams from the first seeds and third seeds. That is good because it is a big challenge for us to play against these teams.'

Chelsea opened their Champions League campaign with a

3–1 win in Bulgaria against Levski Sofia, before hosting a team with which Ballack was well-acquainted, Werder Bremen. He was able to easily assess the strengths and weaknesses of one of his former rivals in the Bundesliga, saying, 'I remember games where they lost badly because they were playing so offensively. They want to score every game. But sometimes they give chances to the other team and make mistakes in defence. At Munich, we lost three years ago at home. They won 3–0 and they won the title too. This was not good. But I remember games where they lost badly because they were playing so offensively. In the Champions League they lost 7–2 at Lyon, two years ago. They were not very stable.'

'But Miroslav Klose has, for the last six months, had the best performances he has ever produced. He is scoring regularly. He can change a game on his own.'

Chelsea were superior to their German opponents from the outset, but their domination of the match lacked the reward of a goal until Michael Essien struck on 24 minutes. Werder upped their game in the second half, with the irrepressible Miroslav Klose hitting the bar with a header, before Michael Ballack seized the headlines with a single shot which embodied skill, courage and swaggering self-confidence in one fell swoop.

On 74 minutes, with an increasingly competitive game looking likely to swing either way, Chelsea were awarded a penalty when Clemens Fritz clumsily blocked Didier Drogba in the box. Given that Chelsea's regular penalty taker, Frank Lampard, had missed the Blues' last effort from 12 yards a few days previously, Ballack decided that he should shoulder the burden bestowed on a player by the ultimate test of nerve.

Up he stepped and *wham!* smiting the ball with ferocious force and speed – of more than 74mph – he bludgeoned the ball into the top right-hand corner of the net beyond the reach of the despairing Werder goalkeeper, Andreas Reinke.

Granted, Germans traditionally do not miss penalties, but to strike a ball with such unerring conviction and prodigious power at such a crucial juncture of the match was simply awe-inspiring.

With one swing of his cultured right boot, he had silenced – temporarily, at least – the cries of derision from his doubters. For once, a German footballer's penalty kick, which secured a 2–0 win for Chelsea, was greeted with uncontained enthusiasm rather than abject misery by the English media. The Press Association's Frank Malley wrote, 'If ever a footballer demonstrated confidence in his own talent it was Michael Ballack when he lashed home the penalty which clinched Chelsea's 2–0 win over Werder Bremen in the Champions League on Tuesday night. It was emphatic. It was Germanic. It was the sort of strike which announced here was a man who could handle responsibility, a man comfortable at the heart of the action, a player for the crucial moments.'

Shaun Custis of the *Sun*, the newspaper that had drummed up anti-German sentiment during Euro '96 by picturing English players in army helmets prior to the England-Germany semi-final, could perversely not help but wax lyrical about a German footballer. 'Chelsea have found the cure for the English penalties disease – give the kicks to a German,' enthused Custis, who added, 'Ballack is the Michael Schumacher of football. He struts around like he owns the place, but he has the skill and the power to justify his arrogance.'

Former Chelsea striker Jimmy Floyd Hasselbaink, himself an excellent exponent of thunderous shooting, observed in his role as television pundit for Sky, 'If the goalkeeper had gotten a hand to that ball he probably would have broken his arm.' German sportswriters were also purring at the masterful way Ballack had conducted Chelsea's play from midfield.

The German wire service DPA suggested, perhaps prematurely given that Michael was still a newcomer at Chelsea, that Ballack had taken over the role of 'team leader' and 'wields the sceptre in midfield.'

Meanwhile, former German international Matthias Sammer believed Ballack had hammered out a statement of intent with his penalty strike. He explained, 'His penalty was impressive. It was great to see how he took the ball and converted it. It was a signal.' Sammer felt Ballack was now with a club which had a wonderful opportunity to win the Champions League, adding, 'I just wish him a major title. I am sure he will because that is what he is still missing. On a national level Chelsea are always favourites. He is almost 30 years old and does not have to play football every day. He should train and play, and it's not too bad to get a break if it is too much. It will do him good.'

While Ballack basked in the acclaim of the football world, Frank Lampard was anxiously clinging to his role as Chelsea's premier midfielder and penalty-kick taker. A defiant Lampard, who had been asked to pass the penalty-kick duties to someone else by Jose Mourinho after his miss against Charlton, insisted, 'Yes, I will take more penalties for Chelsea – and for England too, I hope. We did speak about it before the Werder Bremen game and decided it was the right time for Michael to take one.

'I will take them in the future but there is nothing wrong, I don't think, with mixing it up. It gives us an advantage that the opponents don't know who our penalty taker is going to be. In the future we'll see what happens. But, yes, the Germans are good at taking, as we know.'

For his part, Ballack was more concerned that Chelsea continue their winning ways in the Champions League with a win than the plentiful plaudits he had received for his own performance. And he did not care if Chelsea did not exhibit flair and finesse, as long as they won. Michael said, 'People sometimes talk about beautiful football but it is not so simple as that. Both Bayern and Chelsea define themselves by success, nothing else. The pressure of expectation is high and that is always part of playing for these two clubs. It is fantastic if a side is playing beautiful football. But what counts first and foremost is success.

'It was the same with Germany in the World Cup. If you are successful, it automatically means you have played well. But I don't like to talk about playing beautifully. I don't get caught up by that.'

Ballack was buoyant, but after a career of undulating fortunes, he was acutely aware of the potential for a sudden setback to be lying in wait for him. In his next outing for Chelsea, in true, existential fashion he was the author of his own downfall. When a rejuvenated Liverpool visited Stamford Bridge in late September 2006, the first of a televised double header of heavyweight matches (the second of which involved Manchester United hosting Arsenal), Chelsea knew how important it could be to strike an early psychological blow in the quartet's joust for supremacy.

Didier Drogba responded superbly to the challenge with an exquisite pivot and explosive volley on the edge of the penalty box, but Ballack covered himself in shame when he viciously scythed down Mohamed Sissoko and was deservedly sent from the field.

Chelsea showed the courage and resolve of champions to withstand late Liverpool pressure following Ballack's dismissal, but in the end they, and not their disgraced German team-mate, were celebrating after securing a precious 1–0 victory. Afterwards, Ballack stressed that his sending off was the first straight red card of his career but also did the decent thing and apologised to Sissoko for his act of unnecessary villainy. Having seeing the gruesome re-run of the incident, he said, 'It was a bad situation for me, I came in a bit late and I didn't want to injure him. I have just seen him now and I have said sorry.

He added: 'The team worked very hard after this and we went on to win the game. It wasn't easy for them, and I said sorry to them, as it was important for us.'

For once, Jose Mourinho could not defend the actions of his penalised player.

'He arrives late and the ball is not there any more,' he said, in a slightly milder description of Ballack's ill-timed lunge. Naturally, Chelsea did not challenge Ballack's sending off and he was handed a three-game suspension which covered away games for the Blues against Fulham and Reading, with a home encounter against Aston Villa sandwiched in between. At least he escaped the controversy and ill-will created by the fracturing of goalkeeper Petr Cech's skull and Carlo Cudicini's concussion in the fractious win at Reading.

And his enforced period on the sidelines had given him the opportunity to ruminate on his new life, both on and off the pitch. Living in London and the toll it takes on the wallet was, as will be discussed in a future chapter, certainly taking some getting used to for Ballack.

'It really is something new for me. As a family it changed the day we left Germany and I am still living in a hotel,' he commented in an interview with *Welt am Sonntag*. Yet as far as his football was concerned, Ballack said he could not be happier with the passion and pace, frenzy and fury of the English game. He was quoted as saying in one interview: 'I am 30 now and Chelsea could be the last club I will play for. My family and I really want to feel at home here. I like the atmosphere, the speed of the game and there's real competition to win the Premiership.

'English football fans live for football – they identify themselves most with football. For a player, that's great to see. In Germany we follow the English game very closely and now I am here, I am just like the fans. I live for football. In this environment I know I can show my qualities. As a team we are getting better but we need time too. Excellent individuals have to learn how to play well as a team like any other players.'

However, his football in 2006 had not been outstanding and worthy of the world-class tag he been accustomed to wearing, according to *Guardian Unlimited*'s Scott Murray, who denounced the selection of Ballack and many of the other 29 nominees chosen in October of that year for the FIFA World Player of the Year award, which was due to be presented that December. Murray wrote how 'His only meaningful action in the World Cup saw him hoofing a free-kick three miles over the bar at the business end of Germany's semi-final against Italy. By the end of his Lampardesque year, the "best" all-action midfielder in the world was reduced to panicked two-footed lunges on the best all-action midfielder in the world, Momo Sissoko. Shame, shame, shame.'

A rather unfair assessment, one might say, although in his current form, Ballack was doing his best to win over his critics. When he returned after his suspension, he appeared in Chelsea's superb 1–0 win over Barcelona in the Champions League, muscularly marshalling the Blues' midfield, which disrupted the Catalans' penchant for pretty passing and fluid movement. The memorable victory ignited his hopes of finally laying his hands on European football's most coveted prize. In an interview with uefa.com, he said, 'Defeating Barcelona was vital and has given our confidence a real boost, especially as we played such good football. We were highly concentrated and it was a great game to watch. Every season you have about two or three very special matches and this one against Barcelona was one of them. If you win such a crucial clash, the boost is tremendous.'

He went on to say: 'There's still a long way to go. It would be great to get to the Champions League final and win the title with Chelsea. Winning the Champions League is one of my biggest career goals, but for the time being I am focusing on other things. Our starts in the Champions League and Premier League have been okay but we can play much better football and that's what we are aiming for.'

Ballack continued his steady improvement by scoring his first Premiership goal with a header from 10 yards after being set up by Didier Drogba as Chelsea battled to a 2–1 win over

Portsmouth at Stamford Bridge in October. Like fellow goalscorer Andriy Shevchenko, his exuberant celebrations, which involved him running to receive the joyful embraces of the Chelsea fans behind the goal, brought – in many people's eyes – an unjustified penalty of a yellow card.

Yet nothing could take the gloss off a day of delight for Ballack, who received a standing ovation from the Stamford Bridge hordes when he was substituted just before the end of the game. The elated Chelsea player told uefa.com, 'It's always very special to enter a new league and join a new team. Scoring my first Premier League goal and then being cheered by the fans at Stamford Bridge was an incredible experience.'

He then considered what lessons could be learnt from Formula One great and fellow German, Michael Schumacher, who had ended his illustrious motor-racing career the week before. 'That's really hard to say. Both of us are athletes, but our sports are entirely different. Schumacher competes alone, while I am part of a team. If he has a bad day, nobody can help him and he loses. If I have a bad day, ten other team-mates may have a good one and we might win after all. That makes it hard to compare our situations. Regardless, I often ask myself how individual athletes repeatedly manage to motivate themselves one hundred per cent to achieve their goals. This experience can certainly help a team player, because in team sports there are times when you have to take a back seat to help the team and its game plan. In contrast, Michael Schumacher is always focused on his performance and solely dependent on himself.'

Ballack was certainly exhibiting Schumacher's irresistible

combination of instinctive brilliance and stunning consistency in his performances for his new club.

He scored for the second successive match when Chelsea came away with a 2–0 win from Sheffield United's Bramall Lane. Again, his goal was a simple header from midfield cohort Frank Lampard's left-wing cross, showing that, when in his pomp, he is the identikit modern midfielder capable of scoring with either foot and his head too. His combination with Lampard, fodder for much debate in the build-up to the season, was suddenly beginning to click, leaving *The Times*' Matt Hughes enthusing. He said, 'The $64,000 question is no longer whether Frank Lampard and Michael Ballack can play together, but how on earth do you stop them? It is enough to turn Steven Gerrard green with envy.'

Sheffield United manager Neil Warnock drooled, 'If you'd put them in my team and put my two in theirs. Ballack oozes class, took his goal well and was very, very clever.' But his praise was tempered by his disapproval of Ballack's ability to escape the referee's wrath despite persistent fouls. He added, 'Ballack must have committed nine or ten fouls and was in the referee's ear all afternoon but didn't get a yellow card. He might get away with a couple of things you wouldn't if you were Robbie Savage because Savage looks a little bit like a villain, whereas Ballack looks like a top-class model, drinks the best, lives the best and probably is the best.'

The other goalscorer in Chelsea's victory, Frank Lampard, admitted he was relishing developing his relationship with Michael. 'I think we're doing well together,' he said. 'I'm linking well with Michael and am very happy to be playing with him. He's a very intelligent player, a very good player who plays the simple ball, which is not always as easy as it sounds.'

Ballack was getting better by every match, although in the Champions League he was inept in Chelsea's thrilling 2–2 draw in the Nou Camp against Barcelona, twice blazing shots over the bar and doing little else other than play tidy passes. His contributions were insipid and horribly inadequate compared to the exhilarating endeavours of the dynamic powerhouse that is Michael Essien and the inspirational Frank Lampard.

The *Guardian*'s Richard Williams believed Lampard had been stirred to raise his game following Ballack's arrival. He wrote, 'So far, at least, the chief beneficiary of his arrival seems to be Lampard, now seemingly awoken from his long slumber. The two are so similar in style that Jose Mourinho, never mind Lampard, may have had qualms about their ability to fit into the same formation, and that question has yet to receive a definitive answer. But there is no doubt that the Englishman has been stimulated by the need to show himself at least the equal of the German, and on Tuesday he gave an all-round performance worthy of his very best days, crowned with a marvellous goal.'

However, Williams believed Ballack would come to the fore sooner or later, adding, 'One imagines that sooner or later he will turn a match, or at least be seen to be making it flow according to his own graceful, almost stately rhythms.'

Ballack's best was indeed yet to come, according to his former team-mate at Bayer Leverkusen, Dimitar Berbatov, ahead of Chelsea's derby game with Tottenham at White Hart Lane. Berbatov said, 'I don't think people have seen the best of

Michael Ballack yet. I think he will be a very good player who will develop and be even better than he was at Bayer.'

So far, Ballack's brilliance had been displayed against lesser teams in the Premiership, and Tottenham's 2–1 victory in a breathless encounter was a chastening reminder for him and Chelsea that they could not afford to let their standards slip against teams of greater quality if they were to achieve success. He was thoroughly disappointing, blasting a shot over the bar when the goal was at his mercy, as well as being booked for dissent as Chelsea tempers frayed.

Pulverising the season's surprise package Aston Villa 4–0 in the Carling Cup was a temporary antidote to this disappointment and epitomised Chelsea's redoubtability, offering further encouraging signs of Lampard and Ballack's ability to confound the critics and continue to flourish in tandem.

'Suggestions that they would not be able to dovetail in midfield look increasingly wide of the mark,' affirmed the *Guardian*'s Jon Brodkin. Ballack's cross enabled Lampard to head Chelsea in front, the German picked out Lampard for the England international to supply the centre for Shevchenko's goal, and there was further evidence of an understanding as much of Chelsea's passing impressed.'

Chelsea recorded a further 4–0 victory in the league against lowly Watford, before losing 1–0 to Werder in Bremen in the Champions League. Ballack, who limped off in the defeat to the Germans, then made an astonishing admission about how he was struggling to adapt to the strenuous demands of the Premiership. In an interview with the *Frankfurter Allgemeine Zeitung*, he said he had 'reached his limit' after playing only seven Premiership games. Wary of the fact that England does not allow a winter break in the football season unlike Germany, Ballack said he would appreciate being rested 'for the odd game' during the season.

He said, 'I'm not running on reserve just yet, but I have reached my limit in terms of the physical demands.'

However, he insisted that he had no regrets about leaving the comfort zone of football in Germany for the rigours of England. 'I deliberately gave up the nice footballing life that you have in Munich, as I wanted to prove myself and impose myself again,' he continued. 'Everything is quite new: the surroundings, the team, the level of expectation. At Chelsea all the players are of a high quality. The respected and privileged position that I carved for myself in Germany is no longer there. Good performances are crucial. But I'm happy that I took that step.'

For many harshly critical football followers, his insistence that he would improve could not dispel the growing notion that Ballack's bleating was evidence of a footballer so rich that he did not possess the appetite for the fight. The only way the German could defy his critics was to become more battle-hardened and add grit and resilience to his polished make-up.

According to Manchester United's Cristiano Ronaldo, Chelsea had added nothing to their armoury by acquiring Ballack and Andriy Shevchenko. He said, 'I think Chelsea are about the same as they were last year, though, and the transfers of Shevchenko and Ballack haven't changed them too much in terms of their superiority to everybody else. They have to work harder to win games and they just do enough to win.'

Ronaldo was speaking in late November, when Ballack and co travelled to Old Trafford to meet Premiership leaders Manchester United, in what was undoubtedly the most significant fixture of Chelsea's season to date. United were blazing a trail at the top of the table, thanks to some intoxicating attacking football, and were determined to steal a march on the champions by beating their closest rivals and therefore stretching their lead to six points.

For Michael, returning to Manchester evoked happy memories of his goal-scoring exploits for Bayer Leverkusen in the Champions League in 2002, when a 2–2 draw facilitated his side's voyage to the Champions League final.

Frank Lampard had every faith that his under-fire midfield colleague was capable of excelling again, and would, along with fellow Chelsea new boy Andriy Shevchenko, rise to the challenge and prove they were worthy of their world-class reputations. Lampard said, 'I think these big games are the ones when you need your big players to stand up and be counted. Big players thrive on these games and I'm sure those two will. They are world-renowned top players because they perform in big games as well.'

However, Ballack and Shevchenko were singularly failing to raise their game when it mattered most and again both were subdued as United dominated the first-half and deservedly opened the scoring through Louis Saha. Jose Mourinho's midfield diamond formation of Ballack, Lampard and Michael Essien was looking decidedly rough and it was only when the electrifying Arjen Robben was introduced at Old Trafford that Chelsea began to dictate matters.

A thumping header from Ricardo Carvalho, which entered

the net via the head of Louis Saha, brought Chelsea level, to set up a pulsating finale, as play surged from end to end. It was the Premiership at its best: pace, passion, utterly enthralling, although skill was sadly in short supply, most notably from a disorientated Ballack, who consistently conceded possession and looked ponderous when on the ball compared to the assured and classy Michael Carrick, who was awarded the man-of-the-match award for Manchester United.

The *Guardian*'s Kevin McCarra reported, 'Rarely can a player as accomplished as Michael Ballack have waved an apologetic hand as frequently.' He went on to say that Ballack should be 'anguished and embarrassed' by his wretched performance. To soften his blow somewhat, the Scot added, 'The best that can be said about Ballack, however, is that he never hid. He was always looking for the ball, always wanting to be involved. That takes a special man because Ballack had an abysmal game, conceding free-kicks, losing 50-50s, passing the ball to opponents.'

The *Guardian* unsurprisingly gave the lacklustre German a less-than-flattering mark of 5 out of 10 for his efforts, or lack of them, supplemented by the comment: 'His body language was that of someone uninterested as he strolled on the periphery for long periods.'

The harsh reality for Ballack was that, despite the mitigating factors of his acclimatisation to England and the fact that he was understandably fatigued from his World Cup exertions, his endeavours in seminal encounters were not befitting of his status as the world's wealthiest footballer. Alan Hansen, writing in the *Daily Telegraph*, was distinctly unimpressed, chiding Ballack for playing with 'a huge cigar in his mouth'.

He said, 'I had seen more of Ballack playing for Germany than for Bayern Munich but in two World Cups he was in fabulous form, especially when going forward, and Chelsea must have thought they were providing the perfect stage for him. And yet Ballack has scarcely exerted himself in the Premiership. Even if you allow him time to adjust to English football, there is no surge to his play, everything seems very lethargic and there is no urgency to him at all. I have watched him closely during his brief time with Chelsea and I'd have to conclude that if you didn't know he was captain of Germany, you would say he was a very average player.

'Ballack needs to be challenged, privately or publicly by Mourinho, to prove that he can still do it at every level. He needs to be told that Chelsea have paid a lot of money for his services and that they are entitled to something in return.'

For other pundits, Ballack's pallid performances gave credence to the belief that the diamond formation was hindering Chelsea's hopes of conquering England again. It might have been functioning fabulously in Europe, where teams favour a more relaxed and patient build-up, but domestically Chelsea seemed to be sorely missing their marauding wide men Arjen Robben, Joe Cole and Shaun Wright-Phillips, and their ability to stretch teams on the wings.

Since Jose Mourinho was showing no inclination to drop Ballack, the other solution available to him seemed to be to dispense with Andriy Shevchenko, who was being firmly put in the shade by his strike partner Didier Drogba. Introduce Arjen Robben for Andriy Shevchenko and Chelsea's formidable 4-3-3 formation would be restored.

In all the heat of discussion of the merits and drawbacks,

whys and wherefores of Jose Mourinho's tactics, it was easy to forget that Chelsea had blunted Manchester United's euphoria and remained firmly in contention for English football's greatest prize following their draw. A trip to Bolton is a potentially hazardous voyage for the leading lights in English football at any time, and for Arsenal in particular. Chelsea, however, have in recent seasons survived the barrage of balls into the box and the wholehearted commitment of Sam Allardyce's well-drilled men to always come out on top. On the ground where they sealed the title in 2005, they succeeded again, thanks to a spirited display and timely goal from a much-maligned Ballack, who rose above Kevin Davies to head in Frank Lampard's corner. This prompted the following eulogy from Jose Mourinho: 'I am pleased with Ballack, not just because he scored the winning goal. I am pleased with everything. It was crucial in this game to keep the ball, defend well and press high. I paired him with Claude Makelele and Ballack is a team player. His contribution was great.'

Meanwhile, an old friend and latterly, foe, of Ballack, Bayern Munich chairman Karl-Heinz Rummenigge, launched an attack on the financial muscle of Chelsea owner Roman Abramovich and how the Russian was distorting competition in European football. Perhaps still rankled by Chelsea's snaffling of Ballack on a free transfer, in an interview with *Kicker* magazine he urged the European Union to clamp down on Abramovich and the prodigious power of his wallet.

Chelsea chief executive Peter Kenyon hit back by outlining his club's commitment to keeping the core of his side English, although football's many devotees would side with Rummenigge in this thorny debate.

Despite Kenyon's assertion about Chelsea's wish to keep their playing staff English as much as possible and despite Ballack's struggles, the German was still considered one of his 'nine untouchables' by his manager. It was a masterstroke from the wily Portuguese, who was providing a timely confidence boost for Ballack when the questioning of his ability and commitment was at fever pitch as Chelsea prepared for another monumental match, at home to Arsenal in December 2006.

Ballack cheerfully acknowledged his coach's glowing endorsement, commenting, 'Jose is a great coach. If he says that, it must be true. Jose has an idea about football and I agree with him.'

Joking aside, he recognised that he urgently needed to improve. 'Of course, I can play better,' he said. 'But I've only been here four months. It's not easy for players from abroad to fit straight in. There is a certain difficulty integrating into a team. There are not just five or six great players in this side, there are thirteen, fourteen, fifteen world-class players. So it is difficult for the coach to keep everybody happy, but I think you just have to carry on and try to make it through.'

In a wide-ranging interview conducted through an interpreter, Ballack went on to reveal he was finding the English Premiership a complete contrast to the Bundesliga. He added, 'The stress here is put on physical strength. Teams will come out and attack us in a physical way. There are also teams who play football as well, so the style of how we play depends really on the opposition. We have a good mix in the team.'

He also defended Chelsea's often functional playing style, widely perceived to be less aesthetically pleasing than Arsenal's swashbuckling soccer, insisting, 'I certainly don't share the opinion that Arsenal play more attractive football than Chelsea. It was the same when I went from Bayer Leverkusen to Bayern Munich. At Leverkusen we played attractive football but we didn't win anything. You might play more attractively but you might take risks and lose. Success is about winning.'

Ballack also warned his team-mates to take Arsenal for granted at their peril, pointing out that the Gunners were a vibrant young side and the fact that they had reached the Champions final the season before. 'When they come up against the big teams, they show their class,' he said. 'We need to be careful. We can't be satisfied with a draw.'

Even though he required the services of a translator to expound his views, his willingness to meet with the media reflected well on him, showing he was not prepared to hide and bury his head in the sand while hungry hacks circled above him, picking at his wounded flesh. Instead, he was candid, diplomatic and honest about himself and his team, much to his credit.

He could not relax just yet: his performances needed to be ratcheted up several levels before the cynical media men would put down their poison pens. But where better place to start than Stamford Bridge against Chelsea's London rivals Arsenal? Although Ballack was not as ineffective as he had been against Manchester United, he was again put in the shade by his colleague in midfield, Michael Essien, whose trademark energetic performance was embellished by a stunning 35-yard goal.

Ballack had seared a shot from long range wide himself in the first-half, while Essien hit the bar as Chelsea displayed the resilience that is the hallmark of champions to secure a 1–1 draw with Arsenal. This did still not represent the dominant, purposeful performance that ought to be produced regularly by a player of world-class standing and gargantuan salary, however.

Chelsea had now slipped five points behind Manchester United in their pursuit of the Premiership crown, but infinitely more perturbing for Ballack was the fact that in the Blues' next home match, against Newcastle, he was barracked by some sections of the Stamford Bridge crowd.

At least Jose Mourinho was still faithfully sticking by him, unlike Andriy Shevchenko, whose consistent ineffectiveness saw him languishing on the substitutes' bench, as the Chelsea manager opted to revert to the 4-3-3 that had served him so handsomely. Didier Drogba was also confined to the sidelines, but the difference was he was being rested for a hamstring injury and when he did come on, his goal was decisive as Chelsea earned another valuable victory.

The effervescent Ivorian was putting both Shevchenko and Ballack to shame with his startling consistency and match-winning performances that could teach the under-achieving pair a thing or two about the benefits of hard work in adversity. But Jose Mourinho was not yet willing to accept received wisdom and leave Ballack out of his starting 11. He said, after the win over Newcastle: 'The fans don't make the team, I make the team. I don't select players because of the fans, I select them from my analysis. He [Ballack] is still untouchable.'

The only way Ballack could vindicate such admirable, unwavering faith from his manager was to stamp his authority on a game and justify the towering hype and expectation that his arrival had created. He may not have done this in Chelsea's game against Everton, but he did the next best thing – he scored yet again with a delightful free-kick which he curled around the wall into the net via a post and Tim Howard's back.

His goal, although it was officially recorded as an own goal from Howard, equalised Everton's opener from Mikel Arteta, but it was Chelsea's outstanding performers Frank Lampard and Didier Drogba, who covered themselves in glory for the Blues' 3–2 triumph after lashing in two goals of luminous quality. With Manchester United losing at West Ham, Chelsea had marvellously muscled their way back into the title race and were now lying only two points behind their Lancashire rivals. Meanwhile, they had comfortably qualified for the knockout stages of the Champions League after topping Group A, finishing the section with a perfunctory 2–0 defeat of Levski Sofia at Stamford Bridge.

Continued progress in the competition looked promising as Porto were their opponents, prompting Ballack to admit Chelsea had 'a good chance' of securing European football's Holy Grail. He confessed, 'We had a difficult group, but we ended on top, which was very good for us. We beat Bremen and Barcelona at home, and away against them we had one draw, which is okay. We all know that Barcelona is strong – and Werder Bremen is a very good team. It is difficult to say how far we are going to go but our group was not easy and we have a good chance this year.'

Ballack's career at Chelsea had, in the incipient stages of his time in England, been a case of the good (recall his majestic power penalty against Werder Bremen, a sublime free-kick against Everton and a magnificent performance against Charlton), the bad (a dismal showing in Barcelona, an afternoon to forget at Old Trafford when his masterclass in misplaced passing and lethargic performance were more evocative of pub player than world-class footballer) and the ugly (his callous chopping down of Liverpool's Mohamed Sissoko).

His half-term report would read 'must do better', although the likelihood was that the best of Ballack would not be seen until season 2007/08 when he had become accustomed to the frenetic football, fervour and pugnacity of the Premiership. The challenge for the enigmatic midfielder would be to get fitter, hungrier and more productive. Only then would he finally endear himself to the Stamford Bridge faithful and persuade unconvinced English football fans that he was more Jürgen Klinsmann than Karlheinz Riedle in his ability to leave an enduring impression on their fields.

2

East German Wunderkind

Apart from being blessed with sumptuous skill and having achieved worldwide acclaim in the process, football luminaries Diego Maradona, Pelé and Zinedine Zidane all share another important common denominator – they have all come from fairly impoverished backgrounds.

However, this trio of legends never let humble beginnings be a barrier to ultimate footballing excellence, and neither has Michael Ballack. While it may be an over-exaggeration to describe his fairtytale football career as a 'rags to riches' tale, his rise to prominence is a lesson in how a talented youth's passion for the beautiful game and unswerving dedication helped him withstand an underprivileged existence and emerge triumphant.

In just 30, memorable years, he would become the world's highest-paid footballer – against all the odds. So where did it all begin for the German maestro and what shaped his rise to become one of the most recognisable and wealthy Germans on the planet? The contrast between Michael's early life and his modern-day incarnation as a global superstar is certainly stark; he was born on 26 September 1976 in the small East German town of Görlitz near the Polish border – a world away from the glitz and glamour of London's West End. Lying 200 kilometres to the south of Berlin, Görlitz's origins date back to 1071 and the town has a rich architectural heritage which remained undamaged, unlike other German cities during the World War II.

However, aesthetically-pleasing buildings are of no consequence whatsoever to a little baby and, in any case, Michael would leave his birthplace in the spring of 1977 when he moved to a place which was appreciably less easy on the eye – the nearby city of Karl-Marx-Stadt. Now called Chemnitz or 'stony brook' following German reunification in 1989, Karl-Marx-Stadt was, unlike Görlitz, bombed extensively during the war and its modern buildings were unerringly utilitarian and ugly.

Indeed, Michael Ballack, the only child of Stephan, a construction engineer, and Karin, a secretary, spent his early years in an eighth-floor flat in one of 300 austere tower blocks in a dreary suburb in the third-biggest city in the Saxony region. The Ballacks' address in those days resonates with the communist political climate of the time – The Fritz-Heckert Estate, named after a workers' leader, on Salvador Allende Strasse – a street named after the Chilean socialist — in Karl-Marx-Stadt.

While Michael and his family may not quite have been living on the bread line, their life in East Germany was by no means privileged and pampered. They were subject to the harsh constraints of the communist regime, imposed by the German Democratic Republic leader, Erich Honecker, who presided over an era of authoritarian socialism which offered scant rewards and opportunities. Poverty was rife, and unemployment afflicted one in four of the 80,000 population at the time.

Michael Ballack was particularly poorly off, given that he was deprived the luxury of a television or a computer – an unthinkable prospect for a child in Britain growing up during the 1980s. To earn much-needed pocket money, he even resorted to the unenviable task of collecting wastepaper and bottles off the streets every few weeks. Thankfully, what saved him from a world of mind-numbing, miserable drudgery was football, a universal game that offers escape and refuge for anyone, irrespective of wealth or background.

The young Michael soon became passionate about the game, playing it incessantly with other children on the Fritz-Heckert estate every day after school. He and his resourceful friends would use washing lines as goalposts and would incur the wrath of angry householders whose laundry became routinely dirty under the constant bombardment of a muddy football and whose windows were regularly smashed by the over-exuberance of the football-crazy, boisterous youths.

His embryonic football career was certainly being nurtured in the school of hard knocks through misadventure and mischief. He would often mix with rough and ready older children and fights and quarrels would be commonplace, frequently leaving the sensitive Michael in tears. However, as he grew older, and spurred on by his father, he would learn to defend himself and fight back against his combatants. This was proof of Michael's developing ability to deal with everyday difficulties and surmount any obstacle thrown at him. His determination to win would be further exemplified in his determination to win in the swimming pool, where he initially struggled but, through dogged perseverance and constant practice, he eventually mastered the essential strokes.

Although the Fritz-Heckert estate had a number of green spaces where their son could kick a ball around to his heart's content, Mr and Mrs Ballack realised that, now and again, a change of scenery would do wonders for their wunderkind. They would therefore regularly take the boy that they affectionately knew as 'Micha' to the foot of the mountains at weekends. Michael also began to display an innate aptitude for football; for instance, by the age of 6, he was comfortable with both feet and was able to do 50 'keepy-uppies'.

Stephan Ballack, himself a former footballer, can take some of the credit for Michael being able to play with both feet. When he started playing football, Ballack junior was predominantly right-footed, until his father encouraged his son to practise with his left foot. However, his kindergarten teachers had other plans for Michael, insisting that his tall, lithe physique was more suited to the sport of speed-skating. The strong-minded youngster, though, would not be swayed from pursuing his new obsession, becoming a devotee of his local side, Chemnitzer FC and, in particular, their flamboyant midfielder and East German international, Rico Steinmann.

Michael's view of his future career at that time was far from starry or full of ambitious flights of fancy, though. He told German journalist Wolfgang Golz that his aims in football at a young age were parochial rather than grandiose: 'At that age, you can't see beyond the end of your nose. It was all so far away in the future. My role model then was Rico Steinmann from Chemnitz. Perhaps I did dream of playing in the East German first division.'

Thankfully, his parents continued to encourage his interest in football and, when their son was 7, they sent him to train with local side, BSG Motor 'Fritz Heckert' Karl-Marx-Stadt, a communist corporation club. Michael developed his skills under the tutelage of coach Steffen Hänisch, who had played second division football in East Germany and who has hailed Michael as the biggest talent he has ever witnessed.

Hänisch was particularly captivated by Michael's aptitude with either foot and once recalled that his protégé would remain behind after training for two or three hours, relentlessly kicking a ball into an empty net. He was also impressed by his ability to compete comfortably with boys several years older than him.

Such coruscating youthful promise and commendable desire to improve soon rewarded Michael with a place in Hänisch's youth team and also won him celebrity status among his peers on the Fritz-Heckert estate. He came on as a 7-year-old substitute during a 2–1 win over Motor Ascona Karl-Marx-Stadt on 4 October 1983, giving a brief yet tantalising glimpse of his precocious skills.

Before long, the little maestro had served notice of the fact that he had the capabilities to become an influential, goal-scoring midfielder. Indeed, in his third season, he rattled in an astounding 57 goals in only 16 games. It was clear, then, that his talents needed to be tested on a bigger stage, and Michael duly moved to the club he worshipped at the time, FC Karl-Marx-Stadt, when he was 10.

Coaches Jürgen Häuberer and Eberhard Schuster would, with Michael as their star man, usher in a brief yet successful era for FC Karl-Marx-Stadt, who became a formidable force in football in East Germany. Michael and fellow key player Kevin Meinel – born on the same day as each other – formed a potent scoring partnership, netting goals galore in some thumping wins. Naturally, as the net bulged, the trophies followed – first in 1988, when the district indoor championships were secured, and then the Saxony indoor title was won in 1991. Finally, in 1994, Michael, Meinel and their team-mates emerged victorious in the Under-19 Championship of the Federal State (at which time Karl-Marx-Stadt was now called Chemnitz, following the collapse of the Berlin Wall).

However, Michael's young football life would not only involve a steady stream of success, it would also be blighted by misfortune and scarred by tragedy. Indeed, three seminal life lessons during his early years would put iron in his young soul and help to make him mentally the resolute player he is today.

Firstly, in February 1989, the young prodigy was left heartbroken by Karl-Marx-Stadt's 4-2 defeat to Schwerin in the final of the district indoor championships. While standing sobbing by the winners' podium, Michael was approached by his father, who issued the following salutary advice: 'Michael, enjoy this moment. Who knows if you will get to another German final again?' His father's caring counsel would leave a lasting impression on the lad and, when he endured the heartbreak of a succession of second-place finishes with both club and country in the future, he would duly savour the experience first and allow himself only a brief moment of personal misery.

The second episode to leave an indelible imprint on the young footballer during his formative years was the horrendous moment when he watched an incident that ended prematurely the football career of his team-mate and friend, Kevin Meinel, at the tender age of 14.

During one of Karl-Marx-Stadt's indoor matches, Michael – who was playing in goal at the time – watched perplexed as Meinel suddenly and inexplicably sat down on the floor. He was subsequently carried out of the hall and Michael and his team-mates carried on playing, completely oblivious to the true extent of what had happened to Meinel. It would later emerge, once the team was back in Chemnitz, that Meinel had, in fact, suffered a stroke, paralysing the right side of his body and leaving him temporarily without speech.

On learning of his friend's condition, Michael was overcome with emotion and the tears flowed as he wondered how this awful tragedy could happen to one so young who, only weeks earlier, had been charging about the pitch with youthful exuberance. Michael and his parents would later visit Meinel in hospital and watch helplessly as the stricken youngster struggled to speak and move in his hospital bed.

While trying to rationalise how a teenager had been left incapacitated by what appeared to be a freak condition, Stephan and Karin would later wonder whether the intolerable, unyielding pressure of being a football prodigy in East Germany had taken its toll on Meinel. Therefore, in a bid to stave off the threat of a similar fate befalling their son, they urged him to speak to them if he ever felt that life or his football career were becoming too much for him to cope with. Michael was fortunate that he had two such caring and attentive parents who, throughout his life, would forever be on hand to provide unstinting love and support when he needed them most. Meinel, meanwhile, has managed to recover and works as a courier for a parcel company.

Finally, the third bout of bad luck experienced by Michael arrived when he was 16 and suffered career-threatening cartilage damage to his right knee. What started as nagging, persistent pain in his knee resulted in him having an operation to smooth out the cartilage and then led to him hearing the words every footballer dreads: 'You will never play football again.'

A horrified and tearful Michael was faced with the appalling prospect of a life without football, his passion, his drug, his life. Yet his growing maturity and innate optimism would not allow him to sink into a deep depression when confronted with this sickening possibility. He was not prepared to give up on his career without a massive fight. Instead, he embarked on a gruelling rehabilitation programme under the guidance of one of Chemnitzer FC's scouts, Ullus Küttner, who could empathise with his predicament given that he, too, had sustained knee damage during his football career.

However, if Michael had expected sympathy as well as empathy from Küttner, he would be in for a nasty shock; the man who oversaw his recovery was an old-fashioned, Sergeant Major type, who would bark out orders and preach the benefits of blood, sweat and tears on the training pitch and in the swimming pool. It would be tough and torturous, and there would be many times when he must have felt like he had had enough and wanted to throw in the towel.

Yet during the many occasions he was pounding the running track or taking a rib-battering with the medicine ball, he vowed not to give up, as the alternative was an altogether more excruciating proposition – never playing football again. Eventually, a year after it had looked as though he would never kick a ball again, he stepped on to the football pitch again and never looked back.

The injury would have ended the careers of boys with less tough mental states and courage than Michael, who made a full recovery to demonstrate that he possessed an unwavering determination to succeed in his sporting passion, and to overcome whatever life threw in front of him. Perhaps one factor that helped him was his adherence to his mother's favourite motto, 'Don't take everything in life too seriously. It's about enjoyment, not success...' Those words must have inspired him during his rehabilitation and throughout other difficult moments in his life, and they have underpinned his outlook ever since.

Such qualities of resilience, doggedness and hard work were certainly needed in spades during Michael's pressure-cooker-esque education at Chemnitz's local sports college, which the youngster joined at the age of 12. At an institution whose alumni include the ice-skater Katarina Witt and the discus thrower Lars Riedel, he underwent an unforgiving regime which combined stringent tuition and coaching in various sport and educational activities – four hours divided between each discipline – between 7.00am and 6.30pm. Those who underwent such a relentlessly rigorous routine either burnt out or, like Michael, emerged with an impeccable range of sporting prowess. His two-footedness was honed to perfection during non-stop, competitive drills. As such, to this day, it is hard to say for sure which is the German's weaker foot.

This disciplined, regimental educational system had its detractors, but there's no doubting the success of its students when you look at the list of luminaries to have emerged from its machine-like depths. Football skills were afforded elevated status within the system, and most of Germany's better footballers of the last twenty years have come from the former German Democratic Republic – the ginger-haired midfielder and sweeper, Matthias Sammer, being a prime example. It truly was a survival of the fittest, testifying to East Germany's relentless pursuit of sporting success in the communist era.

Sadly, the former GDR's association with sport will be forever sullied by the revelations that many athletes during the 1970s and 1980s were alleged to have taken illegal, performance-enhancing drugs. It was beyond doubt, however, that Michael's athletic prowess was entirely natural and owed nothing to artificial enhancement, as he has never had a positive drugs test result.

Meanwhile, while excelling on the football pitch, Michael was also flourishing in the school classroom, achieving a good *Abitur*, (the equivalent of A-levels) in 1995. He particularly enjoyed German, History, Russian, Geography and Maths, and professed a dislike for Physics and Chemistry. Who said most footballers are intellectually challenged? These days, his former teachers recall with affection his cheeky charm, confidence, sense of mischief and optimistic outlook on life.

In view of his academic excellence, the prodigious youth was therefore faced with a slight dilemma when school ended – should he proceed to college and study engineering, or would he better off attempting to fulfill his ambition of becoming a professional footballer? Ultimately, it would be no contest; the irresistibleness of the beautiful game proved more compelling than the appeal of academia. Indeed, Michael's former head teacher, Stefan Kamprad, has admitted that while his pupil was an excellent student and could easily have prospered in further education, it had always been clear that his heart lay with football.

In 1995, at the age of 19, Michael was awarded his first professional contract for his hometown heroes, Chemnitzer FC, where his burgeoning talent really blossomed. Despite the fact that Chemnitzer FC suffered relegation to the multi-tiered, regional third division of the Bundesliga in his first season, his eye-catching performances in central midfield drew comparisons with none other than the German legend, Franz Beckenbauer. Michael's coach at the time, Reinhard Hafner, explained the comparison on account of the teenager's tendency to swagger around the football pitch, head held high, like Beckenbauer in his glory days. It would not be the last time in his career that such a flattering similarity was made.

He was soon forging a significant impression for his new club, making his début for the team known as the 'Sky Blues' on 4 August 1995, in a 2–1 to VfB Leipzig. Incidentally, Chemnitzer FC's equaliser was scored by Silvio Meissner, today a player with VfB Stuttgart. Following the club's relegation, Hafner was replaced as Chemnitzer FC's manager by Christoph Franke in May 1996, the culmination of a season which had seen Michael make 15 appearances for the Sky Blues.

Franke had coached Michael in his formative years at the club and, under his guidance, the midfielder notched 10 goals in 34 appearances for the club in the 1996/97 season. The first of these was netted on 1 October 1996, when Chemnitzer FC defeated Dynamo Dresden 1–0 in a cup tie. Sadly, he was not able to steer Chemnitzer FC to promotion, but he did succeed in helping his team to the 1997 Saxon Cup (Sachsenpokal), which was achieved by the convincing margin of 3–0 against the Dresden Sports Club. His personal progression would be accelerated when he attracted admiring glances from a number of suitors from the former West and became a German Under-21 international.

By now, life had changed beyond recognition in the East following German reunification in 1990. East German footballers had been afforded a new-found freedom after the seismic events of 1989, when the Berlin Wall was torn down, allowing them to jump on the bandwagon to the West, where fame and fortune was promised. Michael says he watched the Wall collapsing on television, and then distanced himself from the host of new trends which pervaded Chemnitz. He has recalled that a local disco in the city would become a melting pot of diverse influences; he confesses that he was distinctly unimpressed by both right-wing radicals and left-wing leeches, who purported to be politically-minded through their dress sense and their taste in music, masquerading as young rebels.

While many of his peers chased spurious dreams and binged on beer and women – he admits he abhorred the former and had only brief, unfulfilling liaisons with the latter – Michael shunned shallow and superficial groups, and was utterly steadfast in his pursuit of one aim, and one aim only. Football and football alone filled his thoughts and he, too, was beginning to attract the attention of the big footballing guns in the West. High-profile Bundesliga clubs such as Werder Bremen, Hamburg, 1860 Munich, Bayer Leverkusen and Kaiserslautern all expressed an interest in securing the signature of one of Germany's most-sought-after young talents.

Werder Bremen, his favourite club at the time, were first to make a concrete offer. Their then coach Dixie Dörner and general manager Willi Lemke met Michael and his father, and attempted to woo him with the promise of riches, even if he could not be guaranteed a regular place in the Bremen team. The mere mention of money would be enough to snare many a young player, but not Michael. The thought of stacks of bank notes did not interest him in the slightest; he was motivated solely by playing football on a consistent basis and believed his talents and Under-21 international pedigree demanded this. He therefore snubbed Bremen's offer, after mulling it over first with his father. Those who latterly have criticised him for his 'greed' and 'money obsession' would do well to remember that this was an option for Michael from a young age, but one which both he and his father rejected.

However, he was still faced with one of the biggest decisions of his young life to date – should he cross the mighty Rubicon and enter the promised land of the West in search of footballing greatness, or stay put in Chemnitz with his friends and family and revel in the hero status he had cultivated? Michael admits he changed his mind several times at this juncture, but he eventually succumbed to the lure of self-advancement and achievement on a world stage in a challenging new environment.

FC Kaiserslautern, managed by Otto Rehhagel, the man who would mastermind Greece's astonishing success in the 2004 European Championship, finally succeeded in persuading him to begin his footballing odyssey in the West. It would be a journey which would see the young footballer experience a gamut of emotions, including joy, despair and frustration, as his career and personal profile gradually took off, elevating him to the superstar status he now enjoys.

He was well-equipped for the latest stage in his life; he had heeded the lessons of the past, which would prepare him for anything, and was looking to the future with relish. And, just like his upbringing, it is a future that makes compelling reading.

3

Frustration on the Western Front

The late 1990s were a golden era for FC Kaiserslautern as they became the first German club to win the Bundesliga in 1998 after being promoted the year before. *Die Roten Teufel* (the Red Devils) continued to confound all perceived wisdom when they reached the quarter-finals of the Champions League in the 1998/99 season. Any player participating in their amazing success that season must recall those heady days with a great deal of satisfaction, a feeling surely echoed in the hearts and minds of the FC Kaiserslautern faithful.

One might be forgiven for assuming that the young Michael Ballack must look back on his time at Kaiserslautern with enormous pride. In fact, he has mixed feelings about his two-year stay at his first Bundesliga club, whose followers would arguably not name him as one of their all-time greats, given the brevity of his time there. Of course, he has a great deal to feel satisfied about, particularly being part of a championship-winning team in his first season. On the other hand, what started out in 1997 as an ocean of opportunity for the 20-year-old player swiftly turned into a frustrating and fallow period in his football career.

While FC Kaiserslautern enjoyed a golden period of long-awaited success, Michael was left to chew the bitter pill of isolation, becoming a marginal figure at odds with his coach, Otto Rehhagel, who had lost faith in him. It was certainly a character-building experience, a steep learning curve for the young East German who had entered a brave, new Western world which was both unforgiving and intensely demanding. However, rather than endearing him to FC Kaiserslautern's faithful for eternity, his brief stint at the Fritz-Walter-Stadion will merely be remembered as a workmanlike stepping stone to bigger and better things. Yet he can derive a number of positives from his big move, apart from his Championship medal; he found love and forged lifelong friendships which helped sustain him during the desolate, demoralising days when he was left to languish on the sidelines.

So why did Ballack choose FC Kaiserslautern over established German heavyweights such as Werder Bremen and SV Hamburg, which would have been the logical choices for most emerging young footballers in Germany? Firstly, FC Kaiserslautern, based in the 'city in the woods' in the midst of the Palatinate Forest, one of Germany's largest forest areas, had just won promotion to the Bundesliga and therefore were viewed by Michael as a club 'on the up', charged with exciting potential. Secondly, he wanted somewhere he could learn his apprenticeship in

German football without the all-consuming, burdening expectation which surrounds leading clubs such as Bayern Munich. Rather than having to excel immediately, Michael could bide his time in an up-and-coming side with modest ambitions. He was joining a club with experience and class running through its core; he could learn much from established Bundesliga servants such as crafty winger Andreas Buck, Andreas Brehme – the man whose penalty won the 1990 World Cup for Germany – and doughty midfield cum-full back Martin Wagner.

Furthermore, he was following in the footsteps of other East German-born players who had played for FC Kaiserslautern in the 1990s – Mario Kern, Dirk Anders and Rainer Ernst. He would also be playing in front of fanatical fans who live and breathe football in Kaiserslautern and who turn the Fritz-Walter-Stadion into a bubbling cauldron of fervour and excitement on big-match days. Then there was the mouthwatering proposition of playing under one of Germany's legendary coaches, Otto Rehhagel – known in his homeland as King Otto, for his magisterial managerial career – which had seen him lift two Bundesliga trophies, the European Cup Winners' Cup with Werder Bremen and briefly take control of Bayern Munich.

Rehhagel had been alerted to Ballack's potential by his sporting director, former German international defender Hans-Peter Briegel. However, he has always insisted that he was already acutely aware of Michael's abilities as a footballer and had therefore added him to an impressive list of other celebrated German players he has unearthed, like Rudi Völler, Karl-Heinz Riedle, Marco Bode and Dieter Eilts.

He went about wooing Michael's parents and speaking personally with the youngster himself in a bid to persuade him to move to the Rhineland-Palatinate.

The eccentric Rehhagel could be viewed as being a slightly more extravagant German version of Brian Clough or Jose Mourinho, a renowned authoritarian famed for his outspokenness and colourful rants, and a self-confessed opera buff who likes to quote Goethe during press conferences. Doom-mongers could therefore have predicted that Michael, an introverted East German, would clash with his gregarious and larger-than-life gaffer, who ruled with an iron fist on and off the pitch in a strict manner which has been described as his 'Ottocracy'.

One of his earliest instructions to Michael was for the youngster to find himself a partner, introducing him to his current girlfriend, Simone Lambe, in the Café am Markt in Kaiserslautern café. Kaiserslautern, with a population of only about 100,000, also attracted Michael, given its similarity to his hometown of Chemnitz. It was not an overcrowded, impersonal city, more of a homely, large town – perfect for a diffident, young East German who had never left home before. His quiet, unassuming nature and humility soon endeared him to his new team-mates, however.

Striker Olaf Marschall, for instance, recalls in Michael's authorised biography *Sein Weg* that the midfielder astonished his wife by using the formal version of the German words for 'you' – '*Sie*' – like a nervous pupil addressing his teacher.

'Some players come to a new club and ask, "Where's my Porsche?"' Marschall comments. 'When they have their first setbacks, they can't understand the world any more. Michael was not that type.' The flip side of that, though, is that had Michael been a more forceful and materialistic character, then he might have made his way into Kaiserslautern's first team earlier than he did.

Otto Rehhagel would only use the youngster sparingly in his first season, first throwing him into the first-team fray in Kaiserslautern's seventh match of the 1997/98 season, away to Karlsruher SC. Even then, Michael only played four minutes of his side's 4–2 win. He was regularly forced to operate as a spectator from the subs' bench as FC Kaiserslautern sensationally soared to the top of the league, magnificently building on their shock 1–0 win at Bayern Munich in the opening game of the season.

But Rehhagel preferred a more mature, experienced spine to his team than anything Michael could offer at the time, and was openly critical of the youngster's 'softness' and inconsistency. 'He has much to learn,' he said of his protégé during one interview. It was a thoroughly miserable experience for the youngster, who soon became lonely and homesick. He spoke to his parents daily and, whenever possible, would drive home to see them for support, while Stephan and Karin Ballack repaid the compliment by making regular trips to see their son. At his lowest ebb, Michael even contemplated returning to Chemnitz, but was encouraged by his father to persevere.

After being the home-town hero in Chemnitz and enjoying a regimented existence at college, it would take some time for the Bundesliga new boy to adjust to his new environment. Thankfully, he could also draw comfort from the friendships he had developed away from football, not only with his new girlfriend, Simone, but also Toni and Maria Vicino and their son Giuseppe, owners of the Italian restaurant Isola Bella in nearby Otterbach.

Toni and Maria have served a whole host of legendary footballers over the years, including Rudi Völler, Uwe Seeler and Youri Djorkaeff, but none made the indelible impression that Michael Ballack did when he first set foot in Isola Bella. Toni remembers that Michael stood out, he was noticeably different, and that his good looks and curly black hair made him look like a footballing equivalent of Pete Sampras. They would take him under their wing and would become almost a second family for Michael.

Michael made the Isola Bella his second home, dining there at lunchtimes and in the evening – a welcome sanctuary for him from the pressures of new-found fame, and new-found frustration, in Kaiserslautern. Rather than sit alone in his flat in Otterbach, bought for him by FC Kaiserslautern, instead he chose to spend most of his free time with Toni and Maria, who'd cook for him and look after him until Toni had finished in the kitchen, and then they'd go out into the city and have a drink. Michael recalls sometimes sitting in the restaurant until 4.00am, eating spaghetti and talking... but only when he wasn't training or playing the next day.

Back on the football pitch, he continued to be confined to sporadic, substitute appearances and reserve team football, only making his début on 28 March 1998. In that game, he was given the not-inconsiderable task of marking the Brazilian playmaker Emerson when FC Kaiserslautern took on Bayer Leverkusen. He did a reasonable job, but was powerless to prevent his side slipping to a 3–0 defeat.

In total, he made 16 appearances for his new team in the 1997/98 season, the last of which was in a 1–1 draw against SV Hamburg on 9 May 1998. FC Kaiserslautern pipped Bayern Munich to the title by two points, a sensational achievement in their first season back in the top flight. But Michael had been unable to break into a powerful Kaiserslautern midfield, which usually featured right-wing raiders Andreas Buck and Ratinho, Martin Wagner on the left wing and the classy Swiss Ciriaco Sforza in the centre.

He was, for the most part, a mere spectator as Olaf Marschall scored goals with stunning regularity and the rock-solid Michael Schjönberg and Mirsolav Kadlec expertly marshalled the defence of the *Roten Teufel*. Yet he had still shown fleeting glimpses of talent and potential – particularly in the dénouement to the title race – which would blossom fully in years to come. Indeed, despite his role as an 'understudy' in the proceedings, Michael's début season in the Bundesliga was not an unmitigated disaster by any means. He secured his first medal and earned a mark of 2.94 from German football magazine *Kicker*, an above-average score for what had been a season of severe frustration for the player.

He still cherishes the memory of the unforgettable day when it seemed that the whole of Kaiserslautern spilled on to the streets to celebrate the club's wonderful title triumph, too. Players danced and jigged arm-in-arm with supporters in carnival scenes which may never be repeated – it has made an indelible mark on his memory. Not surprisingly, two of his favourite venues in the town were among the ports of calls for the raucous celebrations – Café am Markt and the Isola Bella, where he joyously hugged Toni and his family.

Once this unfettered euphoria had subsided, he was faced with the challenge of pushing for a regular first-team spot – and the even greater task of currying favour with his seemingly hard-to-please manager. He and the German champions were also entering the promised land of the Champions League and would have to raise their game in the Bundesliga as they would be *the* team to beat. Emulating the phenomenal and unheralded success of the previous season would be hard enough; surpassing it would be virtually impossible. Accordingly, Otto Rehhagel strengthened his squad for the significant tests ahead, adding Manchester City's Uwe Rösler to his strike force, goalkeeper Uwe Gospodarek from VfL Bochum and Egyptian defenders Hany Ramzy and Ibrahim Samir, as well as Janos Hrutka from Ferencváros Budapest.

Rehhagel also made Michael a regular first-teamer for the champions, who made a reasonable start to the 1998/99 campaign – although they suffered 4–0 defeats to VFB Stuttgart and Bayern Munich in September and October.

October also saw him score his first goal for Kaiserslautern, when he fired in a direct free-kick to level the scores at 2–2 against Hansa Rostock. His goalscoring contribution duly earned him the honour of a place in *Kicker*'s team of the week, alongside fellow midfielders Stefan Beinlich and Zé Roberto of Bayer Leverkusen. The champions went on to win the game 3–2 and continued a rich vein of form throughout the autumn and winter.

Meanwhile, their progress in the Champions League was equally outstanding, as they stormed through Group F – their opponents were Benfica, PSV Eindhoven and HJK Helsinki – winning four of their six matches and losing only one.

However, in the quarter-finals, they were no match for an irresistible Bayern Munich, who won 2–0 at home and 4–0 away to cruise into the semi-finals. They would eventually go on to endure heartbreak in the 1999 final against Manchester United, who won the match 2–1 with United's two goals being scored in the final three minutes of injury time. It was a harsh lesson for Michael, who appeared six times in the competition, on which he would make a far stronger impression in years to come.

Back in the league, the midfielder was enjoying his regular outings for *Die Roten Teufel* and would end up scoring 4 times in 30 appearances while operating in a defensive midfield holding role, earning rave reviews from the German press in so doing. He helped FC Kaiserslautern to a commendable fifth-place finish in the process. However, he was never quite able to win a place in the heart of the man who mattered most – Otto Rehhagel. It was widely acknowledged in the football fraternity that Rehhagel's blue-eyed boy was the livewire midfielder-cum-forward, Marco Reich, who in 2006 was playing in the English Championship with Derby County. Reich was signed up on a six-year contract, and many German pundits believe that his hunger and ambition diminished once he had been given this comfortable, long-term security.

Rehhagel wanted Michael to commit himself to a similar long-term deal and offered him a four-year extension to his three-year contract, due to expire in 2000.

Yet Michael rejected the offer, given that he did not feel entirely supported and trusted by his coach. It was the beginning of the end of a fraught relationship between the stern manager and his stubborn, headstrong player. Michael resigned himself to leaving for pastures new. He was also uneasy that his then adviser, Wolfgang Vöge, was a good friend of Rehhagel and his wife Beate. Therefore he severed his ties with Vöge and hooked up with Dr Michael Becker, who represented his friend and FC Kaiserslautern team-mate, Olaf Marschall.

After scoring in his side's 1–1 draw against Hertha Berlin in March 1999, Michael seemed to be sending out a 'come and get me' plea to other clubs when he expressed the view that he would soon be excelling with the German national team.

For some observers, including his enraged club coach, his pronouncement was borne of arrogance, however. Rehhagel, then, seemed to want to puncture the ego of his star and bring him down a peg or two when, as documented in Michael's authorised biography, he lambasted him at half-time in the game against SC Freiburg for, in his eyes, allowing the opposition to score too easily. He accused Michael of 'blindness' and said he was tempted to call the then German national coach Erich Ribbeck and implore him to withdraw his midfielder from the squad.

To complete the young player's humiliation, Rehhagel then promptly substituted Michael, who fled the stadium in disgust. He would never forgive Rehhagel for subjecting him to such a vitriolic display of anger in front of a stunned dressing room. Now he was even more determined to continue his career elsewhere. However, Kaiserslautern did not want to relinquish their prodigy too easily when Bayer Leverkusen displayed interest in Michael. Their general manager, Rainer Calmund, and sporting director, Rudi Völler, would not be deterred and, after a persistent and persuasive pursuit, they finally got their man for £2.5 million. It would prove to be money well spent as Michael would become a Leverkusen legend for both the right and the wrong reasons.

4

The Conductor of a Bittersweet Bayer Symphony

Michael Ballack could have been forgiven for being slightly unsure of himself when he moved to Bayer Leverkusen. It would have been perfectly understandable if his confidence had been ever so slightly dented when he felt compelled to leave FC Kaiserslautern due to his fractious relationship with Otto Rehhagel. There was the added pressure for him of adapting to a new environment, new team-mates and a new coach in Christoph Daum.

However, his opening gambit on arriving at his new club underscored his immense inner confidence and proved he was neither a shrinking violet fazed by his latest challenge, nor was he still bearing the scars of his previous club. He chose the number 13 shirt. Not only was he undaunted by the connotations of ill fortune that this number carries – perhaps unwisely given some of the negative experiences he would endure – but he was also unconcerned by the fact that it was indelibly linked in Leverkusen folklore with the mighty Rudi Völler. Furthermore, the hallowed jersey had not been worn by anyone else at Bayer Leverkusen for three years. The audacious Michael even went so far as to admit that he chose the number 13 to 'provoke a little'. Quite a statement of intent from the callow new boy. Now all he had to do was wear the shirt with the same distinction as Völler – quite a task, to say the least.

So what had happened to the timid young East German who had been left out in the cold at Kaiserslautern? On the face of it, a remarkable metamorphosis had taken place, resulting in Michael becoming a nerveless man of steel, cocksure and sure-footed, and determined to hit the ground running at his new club. Such a perception was a little far from the truth, however. While he was capable of bold deeds, having come with something of a reputation as a skilful player, he was still considered too introverted to make a major impact on the Leverkusen team and needed to be prised out of his shell. Accordingly, Bayer coach Christoph Daum knew that he had to challenge Michael and set him targets if he were to maximise the obvious and abundant gifts that his midfielder possessed.

Leaving Michael on the bench and chastising him in public – tactics employed by Otto Rehhagel at Kaiserslautern – would not work. Neither would pats on the back and a softly, softly approach, so Daum realised he had to be uncompromising and demanding in his dealings with Michael, bellowing out the constant refrain of 'more... more... more!' He felt Michael was too nonchalant on the pitch and was desperate to see more fire and aggression from him. He wanted to see his combative side on the pitch at times, telling his man to be more robust in his challenges, something with which Michael initially struggled, given that he viewed it as an open invitation simply to commit more bruising fouls more often.

The Bayer coach would therefore often pull Michael quietly aside and implore him to exert himself more and would challenge his charge to respond if he remained tight-lipped. Daum wanted him to be more ruthless as a leader and to criticise his side when he had to, something that was unnatural to Michael, given the emphasis on team spirit he had experienced in East Germany. Severity needed to be counterbalanced with sensitivity, too, however.

Daum was also quick to praise his man to give him the confidence boosts he needed. For example, in an interview with *Kicker* magazine, he enthused, 'He is a cross between (Franz) Beckenbauer and (Johan) Cruyff, with a dash of Uwe Seeler, who'd never give up, too. In terms of running style, Michael resembles Franz, but he's stronger in the air. And he's more robust than Cruyff.' He also realised that Michael's abundant abilities were wasted in the deep-lying position he was accustomed to occupying in the midfield and therefore pushed him further forward up the pitch and urged him to take more risks. It was a tactical masterstroke from Daum, which would pay off handsomely, as Michael would be a revelation in his new position, displaying a prowess for scoring vital goals with both feet and his head, too.

After fearing that his development could have been stymied under Otto Rehhagel, Michael would come of age during his time under Daum's tutelage, whom he would refer to as 'the manager who taught me the most'.

On the face of it, the move to Bayer Leverkusen – founded by a pharmaceutical company in 1904 – was not a significant step forward for him. The town was not much bigger than Kaiserslautern and the club was of a comparable standard as well. Yet the significant difference between the two clubs was that, at Kaiserslautern, Michael battled constantly – and ultimately vainly – for acceptance, while at Bayer he was loved and cherished immediately. Bayer general manager, Rainer Calmund, would bestow on him the flattering soubriquet 'the Little Kaiser', or 'little emperor', in recognition of his similarity to German legend Franz Beckenbauer, who was known as *'Der Kaiser'*, both in a playing sense – his elegant, upright running style – and his curly black hair.

It was Calmund, a long-time admirer of the East German, who instigated Bayer's move for Michael while he was at Kaiserslautern. He sent Bayer sporting director Rudi Völler and his assistant Andreas Rettig to Frankfurt to meet the midfielder with a clear instruction – 'Bring me Michael!' However, it had not turned out to be a smooth transaction; despite his reservations about Michael's capabilities, Kaiserslautern coach Otto Rehhagel was not prepared to let go of his asset lightly. Finally, Völler's persuasive tongue, coupled with his rapport with Rehhagel – the pair had been together at Werder Bremen – and a transfer fee of £2.5 million proved too much for Kaiserslautern to resist.

For Bayer the gain would turn out to be at the expense of a considerable loss for Kaiserslautern, as Daum's managerial magic and the unreserved appreciation of the Bayer hierarchy would witness the making of a maestro. In a midfield comprising the Brazilians Emerson and Zé Roberto, along with Stefan Beinlich, once of Aston Villa, Michael would emerge as one of the most potent attacking midfielders in Germany and then in Europe.

However, the path of true genius would not run smoothly; the pitfalls and hurdles were very much in evidence as he gradually built his reputation and developed into one of the all-time Leverkusen greats.

Firstly, he missed nearly three months of the 1999/00 season with a hamstring tear. He returned to action in late November to galvanise Leverkusen's concerted championship challenge and scored his first goal for his new club in February 2000, in a 4–1 defeat away to Bayern Munich. He also made an impression in Europe, scoring in both legs of Bayer's third-round tie against Udinese, which the Italians won on away goals. Unfortunately, injury had prevented him taking any part of their Champions League participation prior to this.

Often, participation in European competition proves an unwelcome distraction for clubs battling for a league championship – witness Liverpool's 2004/05 campaign, in which they won the Champions League, but missed out on an automatic league place for the following season's campaign and had to pre-qualify. Once this was no longer a factor, Bayer and Michael went on a barnstorming charge towards the Bundesliga title.

Michael was outstanding as he dictated play superbly and scored once in Bayer's scintillating 9–1 mauling of SSV Ulm 1846 away in March. A further six wins and a draw meant that Bayer only needed to secure a point from their final match – away to SpVgg Unterhaching, a club based south of Munich – on the final day of the season. This was an eminently achievable prospect for Bayer, it seemed, given the magnificent form they were in, although injuries to strikers Paulo Rink and Oliver Neuville meant that Michael had to play as a striker. Still, the championship trophy was theirs for the taking and the commemorative T-shirts were neatly pressed and ironed, ready to be worn at the final whistle by the champions-elect.

However, football has a tendency to throw up a few surprises, no matter how much of a favourite a team might be on paper. Fate loves nothing better than ripping the form book to shreds and favouring the underdogs. A fired-up SpVgg Unterhaching, spurred on by the promise of barrels of sausages from Bayern Munich, who needed Bayer to lose if they were to win the Bundesliga, were intent on spoiling Michael's big day. They played with verve and gusto belying their mid-table mediocrity, while Bayer were nervous and unfocused, feelings that intensified as the stadium's big screen flashed up regular, and hugely deflating, updates from Bayern's game against Werder Bremen.

Bayern raced into a three-goal lead within 20 minutes and, a minute later, Michael endured one of his worst moments in football when he scored a calamitous own goal past his goalkeeper, Adam Matysek. The tone was set for one of those horrible games where everything seemed to conspire against Bayer and, on 72 minutes, Markus Oberleitner scored a second for their opponents to set the seal on a miserable day. A championship title which had seemed destined for Leverkusen had been thrown away on the last day on goal difference to Bayern Munich, who had triumphed 3–1 against Werder Bremen.

Michael who cried copiously on the pitch at the final whistle was then rendered dumbstruck as Bayer's players sat dejectedly in the dressing room afterwards while some of his team-mates and Christoph Daum wept openly and others kicked out in rage and frustration at anything that wasn't nailed down. There were many unspoken questions and criticisms that remained firmly within the minds of several players in that dressing room that afternoon, and neither did anyone dare to share any analysis of the heartbreaking game in which they'd all just played a part.

The recriminations and the whys and wherefores of what had just befallen Bayer's dejected players were simply unspeakable. How could a team that had scored in every match of the season fail when it mattered most? How could their best player catastrophically put the ball in his own net? It was unbelievable, and it should never have happened, but sadly and inexplicably, it had.

Thankfully, Michael has a relaxed outlook on life which sustains him during difficult moments. Many players might have been irrevocably damaged after committing what was tantamount to professional suicide, while their clubs would implode and slump into a terminal decline. Yet he is blessed with innate resolve and set about helping his distraught team-mates out of their depression, enabling them to look forward to new challenges, instead of focusing on what might have been. With his mother's motto in mind, and trying not to take life too seriously, he managed to find ways of shedding the disappointment and humiliation of loss. In general, he always tries to put the bad times behind him as quickly as possible, often using an escape to the golf course as a way of unwinding. While many players would allow themselves to plummet into a pit of misery and despair, Michael's carefree approach to football meant that he would soldier on stoically, head held high, and bravely look forward to the next challenge. Onwards and upwards, and there's always next season.

Michael and Bayer's torment was also partly assuaged by the groundswell of sympathy their plight attracted from many corners of Germany and abroad. The Leverkusen club was deluged with emails, letters and faxes with messages of support, although the club was also the subject of a wounding jibe from Bayern Munich sporting director, Uli Hoeness, who said, 'Bayer will never win anything. When they play decisive games, they put their nappies on.'

Luckily, Michael immediately had the 2000 European Championships with Germany to take his mind off his Bundesliga nightmare. Sadly, this would prove to be no antidote to his torment, as Germany suffered a shock exit in the first round and he only saw limited action in the tournament. At least when he returned to Bayer, he would be entrusted with more responsibility in the team, given that Leverkusen's popular Brazilan midfielder, Emerson, had moved to AS Roma.

However, just when he thought his luck would improve, he was dealt another grievous blow when Bayer coach, Christoph Daum, tested positive for cocaine and was eventually forced to leave his post. The sorry saga ended a messy tug-of-war for Daum's services between Bayer and the German national team. Daum had wanted to succeed Erich Ribbeck as Germany coach after Euro 2000, but Leverkusen refused to release him from his contract. He eventually resigned from his Leverkusen post, before being sacked by Germany in November 2000.

In December 2000, Bayer adviser Rudi Völler would step into the breach as national coach, while former Germany coach Berti Vogts replaced Daum – who had fled to Florida in disgrace – at Leverkusen. It was a confusing and unedifying state of affairs that naturally left Michael and his fellow Bayer players shocked and bewildered. They insist they had been completely unaware of Daum's narcotic addiction and were devastated at the revelation.

The diminutive Vogts, initially at least, continued Daum's good work and led Bayer to the top of the table before the winter hiatus in Germany. In Europe, meanwhile, Michael scored two goals in Bayer's Champions League campaign, which once again saw them finish third and drop into the UEFA Cup after being paired with Spartak Moscow, Real Madrid and Sporting Lisbon. They were also unable to overcome AEK Athens in the UEFA Cup, losing 6–4 on aggregate in the third round.

The season was beginning to bear a depressing resemblance to the previous campaign, given that Bayer had made storming progress in the league, but had been unconvincing in Europe. For Michael and his team-mates, the omens pointed to another 'so near, yet so far' outcome and this time they also had a robust coach to deal with. After Bayer resumed league action in February 2001, they began to falter and Vogts made Michael the scapegoat, levelling well-worn criticisms at him, such as 'too casual' and 'doesn't try hard enough' in a number of high-profile attacks in the media. Indeed, if the action were transported to the classroom, one can imagine surly schoolmaster Vogts writing 'must try harder' on his errant pupil's report card. For his part, Michael was rebellious, lambasting Vogts after being substituted in one match.

Support for Michael would arrive from a rarely-heard source – from his girlfriend, Simone, who intervened when Michael's promised day off, after Bayer's game against Freiburg had been rained off, was cancelled at short notice. Michael had wanted to visit his parents, who were celebrating their wedding anniversary, and his anger at not being allowed to travel to Chemnitz was voiced not by him but, amazingly, by his furious partner.

A seething Simone stormed into the BayArena and angrily confronted the bewildered Bayer officials. Rainer Calmund, Bayer's then managing director, recalls her astonishing behaviour, saying that she was spitting bullets at anyone who moved. She was said to have been looking forward to spending time together as a family, not just Michael, her and their son Louis, but with Michael's parents too. To his credit, however, Michael reluctantly adhered to his club's decision.

Thankfully for him, Berti Vogts would not last much longer as manager and was sacked in April 2001 for a series of disappointing results and for failing to win an automatic place in the Champions League group stages, much to the relief of Michael and his fellow disaffected players. He later commented that although Berti Vogts had great knowledge of the game, he found working with him difficult.

Michael would go on to finish the season with 7 goals from 27 league games, as Bayer finished in fourth place in the Bundesliga. It was a creditable return from a season of considerable unrest for him and Bayer, who were still undoubtedly haunted by the nightmare of their dramatic, final-day collapse the year before.

A new manager, the chain-smoking Klaus Toppmöller, whose curly mop of greying hair made him look like a bygone Dr Who, was recruited by Bayer in May 2001. Toppmöller was a surprising choice for some Bayer supporters, given that he had previously coached second division FC Saarbrücken and VfL Bochum. However, his appointment was an inspired choice as he would go on to engineer a stunning reversal in fortunes for both Michael and his club.

The charismatic new Bayer chief urged his side to throw caution to the wind and instigated a wonderful attacking approach which, although it would leave central defenders Jens Nowotny and Lucio horribly exposed at times, would yield goals galore and produce some explosive performances. A master tactician, Toppmöller would blend Brazilian flair with German industry, and would also borrow speeches from Sir Winston Churchill to inspire his team during team talks, which he would conclude by telling his players, 'Never, never, never give up.' Bayer would respond by becoming an indomitable force, infused with an unbreakable team spirit.

Michael, meanwhile, would be the figurehead of a mesmerising midfield quartet comprising Yildiray Bastürk, Zé Roberto and Bernd Schneider, with the rampaging blond warhorse Carsten Ramelow adding further steel to the spine of Bayer's 2001/02 team.

Like Daum before him, Toppmöller gave Michael licence to roam all over the pitch, and encouraged him to continue his habit of making late and timely incursions into the penalty box from midfield. An empowered Michael was in his element, and would enjoy his greatest club season to date, conducting the Bayer orchestra with grace, skill and class. No wonder Bayer physiotherapist Dieter Trzolek nicknamed him 'Herbert' after the legendary German conductor Herbet von Karajan.

While Bayer had struggled to cope with Europe's premier clubs in the two seasons Michael had been there, their third successive attempt to survive in the intoxicating realms of the Champions League against the cream of the continent would be surprising, successful and stirring. First, though, they had to qualify for the group stages and pitted their wits against Red Star Belgrade in the third qualifying round.

After earning a hard-fought 0–0 draw in Belgrade, Bayer surged into the group stages, winning the home leg 3–0. Barcelona, Lyon and Fenerbahçe now lay in wait in Group F and, on paper, Bayer and their French and Turkish counterparts knew they would be battling it out for second place behind the might of the Catalan club. Bayer started brightly, beating Lyon 1–0 in France, and followed this up with a marvellous 2–1 win over group favourites Barcelona at home. They maintained their 100 per cent record in the group by prevailing over Fenerbahçe 2–1 at home, with Michael scoring a second-half winner.

Michael and Bayer then succumbed 2–1 to Barcelona in the Nou Camp, before earning a superb 2-1 win away against Fenerbahçe. Three points in their final group game against Lyon could have propelled them to top spot in the group, but a 4–2 loss to the flamboyant French pushed them into second place, two points behind Barcelona. Nevertheless, Bayer had qualified for the second phase and their remarkable helter-skelter Champions League journey meandered onwards. Would it all end in dead-end disappointment or take Bayer and Michael on a path towards further unchartered territory and exhilarating success?

The unpredictability of football is central to its allure. What was certain was that the Champions League would, as a conveyor belt of quality European teams, provide Bayer with another set of formidable encounters. Now intent on halting Bayer's progress in the competition were Juventus, Arsenal and Deportivo La Coruña. Any notion Bayer had that they would now deal comfortably with anything Europe's most prestigious competition could throw at them was brutally shattered when they suffered a 4–0 trouncing in Turin against Juventus in the Group D opener.

After being jolted out of their European reverie, Bayer responded magnificently by putting Deportivo La Coruña to the sword 3–0 at home. Michael scored the third goal to cap a stylish victory which reinforced the BayArena as an intimidating fortress for opposing teams.

However, just when it seemed that Bayer and Michael were an enduring marriage made in heaven, in December 2001 came the announcement that Leverkusen's legend in the making would be severing his ties with his club and was heading to Bayern Munich the following year. It was a canny pre-emptive move from Michael, who had also been coveted by Real Madrid, given that it was a fair bet that Bayer would not be able to consolidate or even surpass their glorious brilliance of the 2001/02 season. While small provincial clubs like Bayer can every so often enjoy fleeting success, Bayern Munich are primed for perennial pursuits of trophies and a player of Michael's quality needed to be a part of this culture of consistent glory.

He and his adviser Dr Michael Becker also felt it was prudent for him to remain in Germany throughout the build-up to the 2006 World Cup Finals, being staged on German soil, to capitalise on the advertising exposure he was expected to enjoy in the run-up to the tournament. And what's more, Michael and Simone's first son Louis was only a few months old, and they didn't feel it was the right time for a big move.

Michael said of his £9 million transfer, the biggest ever between two German clubs, 'I have decided to take advantage of an exit clause in my contract with Bayer Leverkusen and will join Bayern Munich at the start of the next season. This was not an easy decision. The main reason is the sporting perspective. Bayern Munich is in every regard the top club in Europe.

'I had two more lucrative offers from abroad. This is a move for Germany.'

It was also claimed that when Leverkusen agreed an astronomical transfer fee for Michael with Real Madrid, he turned it down and said it was more important 'what you earn yourself'. For his critics, this was indeed evidence of his immense greed and an over-inflated ego – accusations which would return to dog him in the future. Michael could quite easily have been distracted and unsettled by his impending transfer but, to his credit, he did not allow his performances for Bayer to suffer. Indeed, he ratcheted up his performance level even further to support his team's bid for a remarkable treble – the Bundesliga, the German Cup and the Champions League.

Back in the Champions League, a hard-fought 1–1 draw at

A youthful and somewhat
nervous Michael Ballack prior
to an international game.
© Empics

Above: Michael Ballack of Bayer Leverkusen battling with Real Madrid's Flávio Conceição. It was at Bayer Leverkusen that Ballack made his big breakthrough – over his three seasons there, he scored 27 goals in the league, and a further nine in Europe.

© Empics

Below: Ballack, playing for Bayern Munich, competing with his now teammate Frank Lampard.

© Empics

Above: Michael Ballack collides with three South Korean players. He was subsequently booked for a later challenge.

© *Empics*

Below: Ballack overcome with joy as he scores the winning goal and secures Germany a place in the World Cup Final for the seventh time.

© *Empics*

Michael Ballack with his partner Simone Lambe at Oktoberfest, the famous beer festival in Munich, October 2004.

Above: Once again in traditional Bavarian dress, this time at a restaurant with his Bayern Munich teammates Niko and Robert Kovač.

© *Empics*

Below: Ballack scores a penalty, his second goal in the German Cup Final against Kaiserslautern, May 2003 – just one of the many highlights of Ballack's illustrious career in Germany.

© *Empics*

Ballack proudly lifts a huge glass of Bavarian beer as if it were the Championship trophy. Following their victory at VfL Wolfsburg, Bayern Munich were crowned the German premier league champions for the eighteenth time, despite having four games still to play. April 2003.

Above: Michael Ballack is handed the trophy as he celebrates with his Bayern Munich teammates after they win the German first division champion's title, May 2005. Bayern Munich achieved their fifth domestic double in the 2004-05 season. © *Empics*

Below: Ballack and his Bayern Munich teammate, Oliver Kahn, brandish the trophies of the German Soccer Cup and the German Soccer Championship, after once again achieving the double, May 2006. © *Cleva*

Michael Ballack and girlfriend Simone arriving at the Bambi Awards show in Munich.
The Bambi Awards are annual television and media prizes that are given to recognise
individuals who have achieved something outstanding for their country. In 2005
Michael Ballack was honoured for his outstanding athletic achievement.

home against Arsenal provided further reason for optimism for Michael and his team-mates, although Bayer's perils on the road continued when they were routed 4–1 at Highbury. Their fluctuating fortunes continued, though, when they humbled Juventus 3–1 at home.

To maintain their pursuit of the Champions League, Bayer would have to buck the trend of failing on the road and achieve a favourable result away to Deportivo in their final group game. Mercifully, Michael and his team were buoyed by the fact that the Spanish outfit had already qualified for the knock-out stages and fielded a weakened side.

Bayer coach Klaus Toppmöller selected a three-man attack with Carsten Ramelow as the midfield battering ram, Thomas Brdaric roaming forward on the left, Zé Roberto on the right, and Michael tasked with attacking from his central midfield role at every available opportunity. It worked wonders as Michael gave the visitors a deserved lead on 34 minutes when he headed home from a fine cross by Croatian international Thomas Brdaric. Bayer's non-stop pressing game and commitment to attack yielded further goals from Bernd Schneider and Oliver Neuville, with Diego Tristan grabbing a consolation for Deportivo. The surprise package of the Champions League had survived against all odds again and swept onwards to the next phase of the competition, which carries the potential for more drama, controversy and potential glory or despair given that it is played over two legs.

After ousting one English giant in the second phase, Bayer Leverkusen had the chance to get the better of another when they were drawn against Liverpool in the quarter-finals. Irritating inconsistency abroad again proved to be their undoing in the first leg at Anfield, which Liverpool won 1–0. However, roared on by a capacity 22,500 in the BayArena – the scene of some blistering performances by Michael and his team-mates thus far – Bayer were highly capable of keeping an impossible dream alive. Yet they had to be extremely wary of the counter-attacking game favoured by a strong Liverpool side, which boasted the twin striking threats of Emile Heskey and Michael Owen, who had both run riot in England's 5–1 thrashing of Germany the previous September.

In the opening quarter of a nerve-shredding encounter, though, Bayer bossed the game through a majestic Michael, who was operating in a deep midfield role. Time and time again, he was the architect of Bayer's best moves, loping around languidly, before suddenly bursting forward and lashing the ball past Jerzy Dudek into the net with a vicious left-foot strike from 25 yards.

The Bayer fans were ecstatic and began to taunt English fans with raucous chants of *'You only sing when you're winning...'* and *'Football's coming home...'*

Their goading turned to groaning, however, when Liverpool snatched an equaliser as half-time loomed. Abel Xavier's downward header caused confusion between Diego Placente and Bayer goalkeeper Jörg Butt, who pushed the ball into his own net. Complete embarrassment for Bayer, but pure joy for Liverpool.

The second-half was even more compelling and surpassed the heart-stopping drama of the first 45 minutes. A pulsating, thrill-a-minute match saw chances missed for either side, but it was Michael who would brilliantly seize the initiative for Bayer again when he leapt above Xavier just after the hour mark to power in a header from Oliver Neuville's precision cross. This was vintage Michael, the midfielder's ninth goal in 26 European matches, and arguably his most important of the season. Dimitar Berbatov added a third on 68 minutes, to reward incessant German pressure, but then Jari Litmanen finished with cool aplomb to haul Liverpool back into contention.

With just six minutes remaining, the Brazilian forward Lucio lolloped forward and lashed the ball past Dudek to complete a breathtaking and brilliant night for Michael and Bayer. It was undoubtedly his most impressive display on the European stage, confirming that he unerringly raises his game for the grandest of occasions and against the highest calibre of opposition. Who could doubt their Champions League credentials now after they had dismissed Liverpool with such panache?

The semi-finals presented Bayer with their third, and arguably most threatening, English opponent of the Champions League – Manchester United. Michael was to pit his wits against one of Europe's most accomplished and fearsome midfielders in the form of Roy Keane. They would also be facing a Red Devils' side who had extra incentive to secure a final berth, given that the Final would be played at Hampden Park in Glasgow, birthplace of their manager, Sir Alex Ferguson. However, Ferguson's opposite number, Klaus Toppmöller, insisted that his side did not care a jot about sentiment.

'I know Sir Alex desperately wants to go back to Scotland for the final. But after our victory over Barcelona in the first group stage, another Glaswegian, the referee Hugh Dallas, said to me, "I'll see you at Hampden." I've clung on to that ever since. Maybe it's our destiny.'

Toppmöller knew that his men faced an even bigger task than those offered by Arsenal and Liverpool, given that Manchester United combined the creativity of the former with the organisation and defensive solidity of the latter. Michael would have to be on his mettle again if Bayer were to emerge victorious, although United were arguably finalists-elect, and favourites to go through. On paper, Bayer were certainly the also-rans in the semi-final stage of European football's showcase event, never having won a German championship, let alone the Champions League, while the other three clubs had won the Holy Grail a staggering 11 times between them.

Thankfully, raw statistics do not determine the outcome of football matches – courage, spirit, skill and luck do. Michael and Bayer had certainly demonstrated all these elements during their memorable Champions League run and therefore headed to Old Trafford, the self-styled Theatre of Dreams, confident of gaining a crucial advantage in their two-leg route to the Final. They were boosted by the absences of David Beckham, who had broken his foot, and Roy Keane, who was sidelined due to a hamstring injury and only played for the final 8 minutes. And without the tigerish Keane to track him in midfield, Michael was again immense as Bayer obtained a gutsy 2–2 draw in Manchester. He scored a deserved equaliser on 62 minutes, ghosting into the box in trademark fashion to ram home Bernd Schneider's cross to crown a bravura display.

Although United went ahead through Ruud van Nistelrooy's penalty, battling Bayer were not to be denied and goal-poacher supreme Oliver Neuville netted a precious equaliser with 15 minutes left. Bayer were now tantalisingly within touching distance of the Champions League final and, with their renowned strength at home, were favourites to get there. Naturally, the German media were thrilled and saluted their team's magnificent achievement.

'BRAVO!' bellowed the headline in *Kicker* magazine, adding, 'Bayer can now dream of the final.' And, in front of 30,000 frenzied supporters, Bayer completed their miraculous ascent to the European summit by earning a tense 1–1 draw with United in the BayArena. They had gone behind to Roy Keane's fabulous strike in the first-half, but Oliver Neuville brought them level seconds before half-time. Bayer would then repel the relentless waves of United attacks, with Michael a virtual brick wall in midfield, who embodied his team's gritty defensive dictum of 'Thou shalt not pass', despite the discomfort of a badly bruised foot which nearly prevented him from playing. When the final whistle sounded, the BayArena exploded with joy as the ecstatic home fans belted out rapturous choruses of *'Football's coming home...'* to celebrate their club's magnificent achievement in reaching its first-ever Champions League Final.

Rainer Calmund later offered his thoughts about Michael, the Bayer conductor's, towering performance, 'This was for me the emergence of Michael as a leader. I knew then that he could do what nobody else could. He could play the violin as well as the drums.' Klaus Toppmöller was similarly in awe of his central performer, praising his ability to withstand injury and turn in a display of such laudable character. He said, 'In the morning, he could hardly walk, but on the pitch there he was, showing everybody the way. It's in situations like this that you recognise a great player.'

A weary but ecstatic Michael lay down in the dressing room

afterwards, unable to digest the enormity of his club's achievement. While his flesh had been weak, his heart had still been willing and his tenacious spirit had willed him to complete the full 90 minutes in inspirational fashion.

Meanwhile, Bayer coach Klaus Toppmöller prepared to party in style, describing his team's accomplishment as 'a time for cigarettes and drinking'. A small-town club had gate-crashed the big boys' party and Michael was determined to earn a slice of the cake. And if you had asked him which opponent he would have chosen to confront in the final, the legendary Real Madrid – conquerors of Barcelona in the semi-finals – would quite possibly have been his ideal choice.

Bayer's sensational season had been set up for a grandstand finish, as they were still chasing a historic treble of German championship, Cup and the Champions League. No German club, not even the mighty Bayern Munich, had achieved this incredible feat, while Bayer had not won a trophy since lifting the German Cup in 1993.

However, in mid-April, Bayer began to lose momentum and stumbled as the finishing line approached and their dreams of an unprecedented triple triumph faded dramatically. Werder Bremen struck the first, fateful blow to Bayer's pursuit of the Bundelisga when they won 2–1 at the BayArena in late April. It was undoubtedly their worst performance of the season and it had happened at the worst possible time.

Old wounds, inflicted on the final day of the previous season, were brutally re-opened and, suddenly, the unwanted tag of serial chokers was ready to be applied to blundering Bayer. They were now only two points ahead of Borussia Dortmund and maintaining this lead and winning the

Bundesliga was the top priority for Klaus Toppmöller to give departing players like Michael and Zé Roberto the perfect send-off. He said, 'Winning the title would mean everything to this club. We are conscious that players like Michael Ballack, who has already achieved wonderful things this season, will be leaving and they will be missed.'

However, football does not always countenance fairytale endings as Michael and Bayer knew only too well. In their next league game, they succumbed to a 1–0 defeat away to FC Nürnberg and, despite a 2–1 victory over Hertha Berlin in their final league game, achieved through two goals by Michael, they were pipped to the title by Borussia Dortmund by just one point.

Once again Michael and co had, quite remarkably and agonisingly, lost the title on the final day of the season after surrendering a five-point lead. It was the fourth time they had finished Bundesliga runners-up in six seasons. If that was distressing enough, they would endure further heartache when they were the victims of Schalke, who won 4–2 in the German Cup Final, in an ill-tempered game in which their conquerors' coach, Huub Stevens, was sent to the stands. Michael was beginning to wonder if he was forever destined to be a runner-up, while Bayer were developing a gut-wrenching habit of falling at the final hurdle, which saw them being renamed 'Neverkusen' by the media and their rivals.

He would also dwell on the thorny question of whether his side would shake off this tag and prove they could actually embrace a major trophy and not just flirt with success. In addition, he was left questioning whether Bayer's threadbare, bruised and battered squad would be able to lift themselves from their utter dejection and rise again for one, final challenge. There was certainly no bigger stage than a European final for Bayer to end their perennial bridesmaid's role, while Michael was determined to bow out of Leverkusen by securing an elusive winner's medal in his final match.

Klaus Toppmöller was certainly putting on a brave face to the media in the build-up to Bayer's biggest game in their history. 'We just want to show the world we have excellent players and an excellent team. We just want to do our best to have a special victory to end our season after the two chances we have missed in Germany. Real might be favourites, but I don't want to build them up too much, or make them out to be stronger than they are.'

In all fairness, Toppmöller didn't need to be fearful of building up Real's status as the pre-eminent club in Europe – The team's quality spoke for itself. Zinedine Zidane, Luis Figo, Raul, Roberto Carlos et al were modern-day maestros, a multi-million dollar assembly of dazzling skill, resilience and experience, who were entirely capable of emulating the feats of Madrid heroes of the past such as Alfredo Di Stefano and Ferenc Puskás. Bayer, meanwhile, would need to muster all the legendary grit and resolve they could, while Michael would need to perform at the top of his game, or higher, if they were to deprive Real of their ninth European Cup. They were already shorn of the services of stalwart defender Jens Nowotny, who had torn his right cruciate knee ligament against Manchester United, and the wily Brazilian Zé Roberto, who was suspended for the final.

Unfortunately for Bayer, they did not hit this particular ground running, with several of the German players looking every inch the condemned men the media predicted they would be as their defensive uncertainty allowed Raul an easy chance after only 15 minutes, which the Spaniard gratefully seized to put Real 1–0 up. However, brave Bayer would not be cowed and nearly equalised five minutes later when a free-kick from Bernd Schneider on the left swung into the goalmouth and Lucio powered in a header, which Cesar in the Real goal did well to hold. The Germans' determined onslaught continued, with Michael, Schneider and Bastürk enjoying the better of the midfield exchanges, forcing their illustrious opponents on to the back foot.

Yet their combined efforts were outshone by a flash of genius from Zinedine Zidane, who unleashed a spectacular left-foot volley from Roberto Carlos' cross past Jörg Butt. Michael Ballack could only look on in awe and envy at the Frenchman's *coup de grâce* which proved that he had much to do if he had any aspirations of usurping Zidane as the world's best midfielder.

Many clubs would now have conceded defeat and resigned themselves to the fact that Real's advantage was unassailable. But Bayer's success throughout the 2001/02 season had been underpinned by the never-say-die ethos of their coach and it would be exercised again in a courageous second-half display when they doggedly refused to bow down to their natural superiors. They launched wave after wave of attacks upon the Spaniards' goal and finally broke through on the hour through Lucio's header.

Real saw out the game barely clinging on to their slender winning margin, an unlikely situation given Zidane's sumptuous strike and their early dominance. The men from

Madrid had substitute goalkeeper Iker Casillas to thank for three outstanding saves to thwart Bayer's best attempts. However, for all the credit they won in competing commendably against Real's star-studded side, the brutal reality was that Bayer had ended up as plucky losers once again. Klaus Toppmöller would also reveal that Michael Ballack, who had been below par and somewhat subdued throughout the match, had had to have pain-killing injections on his injured foot to allow him to take part. He would also pay generous tribute to the men who had enjoyed a thrilling and, ultimately, fruitless season, which would live long in the memory.

'Sometimes football is cruel,' said Toppmöller, who would be named German Coach of the Year in 2002 for transforming Bayer from European nobodies into a force to be reckoned with on the continent. 'We have come second again. But if we had said at the start of the season we would be runners-up in the Champions League this season, people would have said we were mad.

'My players can be tremendously proud of what they have achieved. You are not always rewarded for all of the sweat and commitment you put in. We don't have players such as those of Manchester United, Barcelona, Bayern Munich or Juventus, but we defeated a lot of famous teams this season. We played so hard tonight, it hurt. The absence of Zé Roberto and Jens Nowotny was too much for us in the end, but we have played to our upper limits for most of the season.

'Losing the Bundesliga was the hardest for me to take because we had led it for so long, but what we have done overall this season is almost impossible to believe.'

Toppmöller also lamented the imminent departure of his best player. 'It does not make me happy that Michael is leaving. In fact, it hurts. When you see what we've done this year, we should be a team who attract players, but we are losing them.' Michael said he understood his coach's frustration, commenting, 'I know how much it upsets him. Under his guidance, I've learnt a lot.'

While he was initially downcast at another failure to add to a burgeoning list of second places, he could draw great satisfaction from his goalscoring exploits during the 2001/02 season – 17 goals in the league, 6 in the German Cup and 6 in the Champions League. Ballack had experienced the best of times and the worst of times at Bayer; he may have been once, twice, three times a loser, but he had also thundered out a seismic message to the world of his arrival as a footballer of great ability and commendable character. After starting the season as a relative unknown in households outside Germany, he had ended the campaign as one of the most accomplished midfielders on the planet, on a par with the likes of Roy Keane, Luis Figo and Rivaldo. His endeavours won national and worldwide acclaim and saw him win Germany's Footballer of the Year award, as well as being voted into the uefa.com users' Team of 2002.

'I'm incredibly happy about this,' said Michael, of his Footballer of the Year award, which saw him beat Oliver Kahn and Miroslav Klose. 'This is also an award for Bayer Leverkusen. After all, soccer is a team sport.'

German coach Rudi Völler added, 'The award is highly deserved. Over the entire year, he performed the best.'

Michael's team-mate, Zé Roberto, was also an ardent

admirer of the man he was due to join at Bayern Munich. He said, 'Michael is a player who can achieve fame like Beckenbauer or Klinsmann. I think he will be at their level.'

Like many who have risen to greatness, and have achieved international acclaim, Michael Ballack also had to endure the rough with the smooth. Along with the plaudits, there have always been detractors who were keen to point out his perceived faults. No doubt, they said, Michael had definitely played his part in Bayer's almost-great season, but they were also quick to highlight his 'supreme self-confidence', which was often interpreted as arrogance. This resulted in him being ranked as the third most disliked player by Bundesliga players in a sports magazine.

After such a tumultuous season, which left him and his unfortunate team-mates empty-handed, many players would regard themselves as eternal runners-up, and would allow the carping and mocking to affect their ability to play at the highest level. But Ballack has, and always will, 'meet with triumph and disaster and treat those two impostors as just the same', as Rudyard Kipling once wrote. And he'll look forward to the next opportunity, not dwell on the one just missed.

And the bittersweet symphony that Michael Ballack had conducted at Bayer Leverkusen was set to continue at Bayern Munich.

5

League Dreams...
and European Nightmares

While Michael Ballack's career had, by 2002, endured wildly contrasting fortunes of extraordinary highs and desperate lows, what had stayed constant was his steady progression up the ranks from his professional début in 1995.

His impressively burgeoning football career had carried him from the regional leagues of the Bundesliga into Germany's top league, which he won in his first season with FC Kaiserslautern. It would also take him to within touching distance of the European Champions League trophy, a competition he would grace with distinction, becoming in the process Germany's Player of the Year and a name familiar to football devotees around the world.

After repeating his superb club form with his national team by helping them to reach an implausible World Cup Final, it was a logical step for Michael to further his career with the best club in Germany – Bayern Munich. He was guaranteeing himself the chance to play alongside the best players, and therefore infinitely increasing his chances of securing silverware. Furthermore, he was ensuring that he would maximise his advertising exposure in the build-up to the 2006 World Cup in Germany by plying his trade in his home country.

While it was undoubtedly a shrewd choice from Ballack and his advisers, it would be a quantum leap for the 26-year-old, offering increased responsibilities, demands and an entirely new level of pressure, akin to moving from Aston Villa or Bolton to Manchester United, for example. While FC Kaiserslautern and Bayer Leverkusen, his previous two teams, are relatively workmanlike, unfashionable outfits, Bayern Munich is *the* team in Germany, a veritable titan of the football world.

At his former clubs, trophies were an unexpected bonus; victories and cups are demanded at the four-times European champions. Expectations on Ballack's broad shoulders would intensify to almost intolerable, stratospheric levels, with scrutiny of results and performances at Bayern infinitely more acute than at his provincial clubs.

What's more, within such a climate, there were sure to be a high proportion of inflated egos and prima donnas ready to destabilise the status quo. Indeed, for this very reason, Bayern Munich are known to their detractors as FC Hollywood; many of their players are renowned for their narcissism and flagrant disregard for rules and regulations. It remained to be seen whether new recruit Michael Ballack would play a starring role or be swallowed up at Germany's most glamorous sporting institution.

At least the Bayern coach, Ottmar Hitzfeld, had the utmost faith in his new recruit; signing Ballack for £9 million along with Germany's other mercurial midfield dynamo, Sebastian Deisler, represented a major coup, given that leading world football institutions such as Real Madrid and Barcelona had expressed their interest in the much-sought-after Bayer man. Along with fellow new recruit Zé Roberto, who had left Bayer Leverkusen with Ballack, Bayern would now be tantamount to unstoppable, according to Hitzfeld. 'We are delighted that he has decided to come to Bayern Munich,' said the man who steered Bayern to the 2001 Champions League. 'It's the right decision. With the addition of Ballack and Sebastian Deisler, it will be tough for anyone to beat us.'

Moving to Bayern for a record-breaking transfer deal in Germany worth 100M marks (around £30M) – the Munich club paid a £9M fee for Ballack, handed him a £9M signing-on fee and were reported to be paying him over £10M over the course of a four-year contract – was pressure enough for him. When your new manager makes such bold public pronouncements, you simply have to deliver. There was also the added burden of having to replace your new club's former captain, Stefan Effenberg, who had moved to Vfl Wolfsburg, the driving force behind Bayern's Champions League win a year earlier. The outspoken Effenberg had been a commanding presence at Bayern, brilliantly orchestrating their play and calling his team-mates to order on the field. He was also a flamboyant character off the pitch, always stirring up controversy with colourful comment or sensational, provocative soundbites. The brash and flash playmaker had no qualms about criticising his team-mates or coach and had become an *enfant terrible* who was loved and loathed by his peers in equal measure.

Given that Ballack was ostensibly a direct replacement for Effenberg – both are central midfielders – it was inevitable that comparisons between the two players would be routinely evoked. Yet Michael Ballack is no Stefan Effenberg; for many observers in Germany, he lacked the alpha-male authority of the blond and belligerent former Bayern stalwart and is appreciably more reserved than his counterpart. Try telling that to myopic sections of the German media or the Bayern faithful.

If Bayern were winning and Ballack played well, he would be universally hailed as Effenberg's heir apparent. However, if his team lost and he underperformed in the process, there would be cries of howling indignation that Ballack was a wholly inadequate replacement for the much lauded ex-captain. It was a no-win situation for him, but one that throughout his time at Bayern, particularly in his opening season, would present itself with depressing regularity, one of the curses of being a high-profile footballer.

On arriving at Bayern after his heroics with Bayer Leverkusen and rousing displays for his national team, Michael Ballack was confidence personified; he felt he was well-equipped to escape the all-pervading presence of Effenberg – at least as far as playing football was concerned. He said, 'I wasn't worried about establishing myself here, because I know what I can do.'

His confidence would prove to be well founded, but after the severe mental and physical toll the previous season's exploits with Germany and Bayer had taken on him, it was inevitable that he would not make an instant impression. As it transpired, Michael's and Bayern's season turned out to be a tale of both scintillating success domestically and perplexing, dismal failure in Europe.

Indeed, Ottmar Hitzfeld's prediction that his side would be a formidable force was certainly borne out in their imperious dominance in the Bundesliga. Ballack scored his first goal for his new club in the 6–2 dismantling of Arminia Bielefeld in August 2002 and from then on, there was only ever going to be one winner of a completely one-sided German championship race.

Europe was an altogether different story for Bayern, however. Indeed, Hitzfeld's supreme optimism smacked of arrogance in the context of their dreadful performances in the Champions League. Although their qualification for the group stages was achieved without difficulty via a 6–1 aggregate rout of Partizan Belgrade, they were then pitched into a highly-competitive Group G featuring AC Milan, Deportivo La Coruña and Lens.

With such a strong squad and a high-quality player in Michael Ballack, who had ignited the Champions League the previous season for Bayer Leverkusen, Bayern should have been among the contenders for a top-two finish and a place in the next stage. However, home defeats to Deportivo and AC Milan by margins of 3–2 and 2–1 respectively, and a 1–1 draw away to Lens, left them struggling even to finish in third place and qualify for the UEFA Cup.

After slumping to a 2–1 defeat in Milan, Bayern had to win away to Deportivo to remain in Europe in late October, then beat Lens at home, while hoping other results went their way.

Naturally, given the size of his price tag and his reputation in Germany, Michael Ballack would be singled out for much of the condemnation of his side's spectacular failure on the continent. His critics believed that his exertions the previous year with Bayer Leverkusen and during the World Cup had left him jaded and below par, a shadow of his former self. 'Everything just passed him by,' said *Frankfurter Allgemeine*, after Michael was virtually anonymous during Bayern's defeat in Milan.

He confirmed that overwhelming fatigue had contributed to his unconvincing European form, telling the website of sport magazine *Kicker*, 'Physically I'm in a bit of a hole... I'm a bit tired. It's nothing to do with a lack of desire, it's because I've lost weight. And the winter break is not going to help a lot. The cause is this crazy schedule without a break. It's even worse this season. The Bundesliga ends on May 24 and on June 11 we have European Championship qualifying matches. I'm getting really fed up with it.' And of course Michael would soon be in line for a few more disturbed nights, as Simone was expecting second son Emilio that coming September.

Bayern goalkeeper Oliver Kahn, however, believed that there was another culprit undermining the Munich club's European campaign – coach Ottmar Hitzfeld. Kahn attacked his coach's adventurous approach, which he believed was leaving Bayern exposed defensively. He also suggested that Bayern were plagued by bad luck, although this claim was not given much credence by the German media.

While the more reserved English footballers would not dream of articulating their thoughts in public, German footballers think nothing of speaking their mind about their coach, something Ballack himself would do later in the season.

Hitzfeld's response was surprisingly mild given the severity of Kahn's sentiments. He observed dryly, 'He's a goalkeeper. He always wants to keep a clean sheet. He would like us to defend with nine men. But we brought some new players in ahead of the new season and it will take time before things settle down. I'm not as pessimistic as Kahn.'

Whatever the reasons for Bayern's miserable fortunes in Europe, the sad reality was that the Munich club tumbled out of the Champions League after losing 2–1 in Spain to Deportivo and drawing 3–3 at home to Lens. It was an ignominious and embarrassing exit for Bayern, who had been convinced that they would comfortably negotiate the group stage of the Champions League, having reached the competition's quarter finals for the previous six consecutive years, and having won the trophy in 2001. Bayern's disgruntled fans were also voting with their feet to show their dissatisfaction at their club's turgid tumble from grace – only 22,000 turned out to witness their final group game against Lens.

Suddenly, Ottmar Hitzfeld's forecast of his side becoming an invincible football machine and Bayern chief executive Karl-Heinz Rummenigge's assertion that the German giants had their best-ever side appeared ludicrous. To add further insult to injury, the under-achieving Germans supplied plenty more ammunition for their critics through the unsavoury antics of their players during the 2002/03 season. Defenders Bixente Lizarazu and Niko Kovač clashed in training, while Oliver Kahn – habitually the rock on which Bayern could always depend – was disintegrating into a wayward liability, making the headlines for all the wrong reasons through sloppy performances in goal and wild behaviour off the pitch. If he was not sniping at his manager, Kahn's 'extra-curricular activities' would see him become a paparazzi favourite and on one occasion he was seen partying at 5.30am in a Munich nightclub while recovering from a knee injury. Towards the end of the season he would further disgrace himself after announcing a trial separation with his wife after admitting to an affair with a 21-year-old barmaid.

In contrast to his under-fire team-mate, Michael Ballack was attracting positive press when, at the end of 2002, he was given due recognition for his efforts with both Bayer Leverkusen and Germany when he came fifth in the European Footballer of the Year award, won by Real Madrid's Brazilian superstar Ronaldo. He also finished seventh behind the Brazilian maestro in the FIFA World Player of the Year award, which is voted for by coaches of footballing nations across the world. Those who selected Michael as the best of the bunch were Luxembourg's Allan Simonsen, manager of the Seychelles; Dominique Bathenay, Michael's former coach at Bayer Leverkusen and then Scotland supremo Berti Vogts; Spain's Iñaki Saez Ruiz; and Syria's Milosav Radenovic.

Back at Bayern, in February 2003, Michael was making headlines himself for all the wrong reasons. Like Oliver Kahn and fellow team-mate Claudio Pizarro a month earlier, he felt it was time to give his views on his coach's tactics. In an interview with *Kicker*, he expressed his displeasure at Ottmar Hitzfeld's deployment of him in a defensive midfield role in the Bayern team. He said, 'If you take on a player such as me and you know that he is dangerous in front of goal, shouldn't you be playing him accordingly?' He also suggested that

Bayern should sacrifice a defender to maximise their attacking potential.

While it may be an accepted norm in Germany that players vent their spleen about their manager and team, it comes at a cost – especially when the target of your ire is a renowned disciplinarian such as Ottmar Hitzfeld. Accordingly, Ballack was slapped with a £10,000 fine, £3,500 more than his team-mate Pizarro had been asked to pay given that Hitzfeld deemed his comments to be more offensive. Hitzfeld said, 'We cannot allow a player to demand a position or a playing system just to benefit himself. I won't tolerate that in the future. Accordingly, Michael Ballack has paid a fine that is clearly higher than that of Claudio Pizarro.'

Hitzfeld's pay-as-you-misbehave policy had been instigated regularly throughout his tenure, with Lothar Matthäus, Bixente Lizarazu, Mehmet Scholl, Giovane Elber and Thomas Helmer all incurring fines for stepping out of line. In the autumn of 1999, controversial midfielder Mario Basler was actually shown the door by the uncompromising Hitzfeld after one transgression on a night out too many.

Hitzfeld's disciplinary tactics certainly polarised opinion in Germany. Stefan Effenberg, no stranger to controversy himself, was unsurprisingly opposed to his former coach's methods, saying, 'Some players will get stomach ulcers over it, but others will go to work on their golf and wait for another contract with another club.' However, other observers felt that Hitzfeld's penchant for discipline had made Bayern into a more competitive force, and that the former maths teacher's tactics and man-management skills were considered in some quarters to be among the best in Germany. Daimler-Chrysler chief Jürgen Schrempp once suggested that Hitzfeld was an excellent role model for German business leaders.

Despite Hitzfeld's ruling with an iron fist, Michael Ballack and his team-mates' indiscretions and outbursts added fuel to a growing anti-Bayern sentiment in Germany, particularly among the media, akin to the loathing that Manchester United and Chelsea have attracted in England in some quarters. The hatred poured out on the German supremos was crystallised in Torsten Geiling and Niclas Müller's book *Pull the Lederhosen off Bayern*, complete with a list of 'the best defeats in the history of the club', while the tabloid newspaper *Bild* ridiculed Bayern by dressing its players in tutus and called them 'FC Unsympathisch'.

Bayern were also suffering financially, mainly due to the millions in lost revenue from their fleeting participation in the Champions League. In the spring of 2003, president Franz Beckenbauer said that money at the club was so tight that they could only afford to splash out £5 million on defenders Tobias Rau from Wolfsburg and Martin Demichelis from River Plate following their £20 million outlay on Michael Ballack, Zé Roberto and Sebastian Deisler the previous year. He said, 'Everyone must tighten their belts. The transfer market will not take place in the summer. Even we can't afford anyone following our purchases over the past year. We'll be happy if we are able to break even this year. Our revenue has been hit by being knocked out of the Champions League earlier than normal and because of declining television revenue.'

Faced with a mounting and seemingly never-ending series of problems, many clubs would have self-destructed. But often, the absence of European commitments helps a team focus its energies on league duties and Bayern flourished in the 2002/03 campaign. Indeed, Michael admitted to *Kicker*, 'This Champions League just wasn't our competition. We didn't play well but we weren't so bad, sometimes just two or three per cent was missing. But perhaps this elimination won't be a bad thing for the team as a whole. We can start afresh and set new targets.'

Indeed, Bayern simply went from strength to strength in the league as they opened up a sizeable gap at the top of the Bundelisga after their European exit. Their season was kick-started by a 2–1 defeat of nearest challengers Borussia Dortmund in November 2002, to leave them five points clear at the top of the table. They would then go on to lose only three games – 1–0 at home to Werder Bremen, 1–0 away to Borussia Dortmund in April, and 1–0 away to Schalke on the final day of the season – and therefore won the league by 16 points from nearest challengers Borussia Dortmund.

After shrugging off his early-season weariness, and eventually flourishing despite his misgivings about Ottmar Hitzfeld's tactics, Michael was instrumental in Bayern's triumph, contributing 10 goals. Among several stellar performances during the campaign were his two goals at Energie Cottbus, which proved the perfect response to doubters after he had incurred a fine for his outspoken discontent over his manager's tactics.

He even could afford to miss seven weeks of the season after tearing ligaments in his left ankle in March, something that didn't hamper Bayern's championship challenge at all, which had for most of the season seemed destined to end in success.

His side became champions for the 18th time with four games remaining of the season after a 2–0 win at Wolfsburg, thanks to goals from Giovane Elber and Claudio Pizarro.

Ballack was influential in the momentous victory, threading a perfect through ball for Elber to slot home Bayern's opener. He said afterwards, 'We had a good time out there today. Although we have not done well in the Champions League, we have proven we are a good team with good individual players by being so dominant in the league... I'm just glad to have won something after last season when I got nothing.'

An elated Ottmar Hitzfeld enthused, 'It was superb that Ballack was on the pitch and his class spoke for itself. He was the decisive man and he put us back on course for success.' Meanwhile, Bayern chairman Karl-Heinz Rummenigge was compelled to make an even loftier pronouncement about the accomplishment of his team. 'It's the best team we've ever had.'

For Ballack and Bayern the crowning glory was the German Cup Final against Kaiserslautern, which saw the Munich club secure their fourth domestic double.

Against his former club, Ballack was outstanding, scoring twice in Bayern's 3–1 triumph and setting up a third for Claudio Pizarro. His first goal was a header from a free-kick by England midfielder Owen Hargreaves on 3 minutes, and he doubled the advantage from a penalty 7 minutes later after Hargreaves had been brought down in the box. He then set up Peru striker Claudio Pizarro, who flicked the ball over Kaiserslautern goalkeeper Tim Wiese to put Bayern 3–0 up five minutes into the second half.

'Last year I lost the final, but this time I've got the trophy,' said a delighted and relieved Michael. 'It was important for all the team to win today. The early goals were the foundation stones for our victory.' In a separate interview with Sat 1 television after the match, he added, 'It has been even sweeter to win trophies this season after losing so much last year. It was great that we scored three goals but the main thing was to win.' He was then rewarded by having a glass of beer poured over his head by a jubilant team-mate.

While the start of the season had been troublesome and traumatic, the end of the campaign was sheer, unadulterated bliss for Michael who, for once, would be weeping with joy rather than wallowing in self-pity and consoling team-mates at finishing empty-handed. For now, he would savour the sweetness of success – two club trophies now supplemented his Bundesliga win with Kaiserslautern, and he could also add a second successive German Footballer of the Year award. He had more than justified Bayern's sizeable investment and had metaphorically stuck two fingers up at those who had questioned his abilities by plundering 10 goals from his deep-lying midfield role. He magnanimously paid tribute to his former club when he spoke of his delight about the award. 'I am absolutely delighted... this also is an award for the team of Bayer Leverkusen, where I played last season. Football is a team sport.'

The task for Ballack and Bayern in 2003/04 would be both to emulate their pre-eminence in Germany and significantly improve their performances in Europe. The addition of Dutch striker Roy Makaay from Deportivo La Coruña for £12 million signalled Bayern's intent to do just that, although this was tempered by the loss of the charismatic Brazilian striker

Giovane Elber to Lyon. Ironically, Lyon would be Bayern's opponents in Group A of the Champions League, alongside Celtic and Anderlecht.

Michael's team began their Champions League challenge with an undeserved 2–1 home win over Celtic and drew 1–1 with both Anderlecht and Lyon. A 1–0 loss in Lyon, courtesy of Giovane Elber, and a 0–0 draw with Celtic in Glasgow left Ballack's men perilously close to Champions League elimination for the second successive year. This time, their European results mirrored their lacklustre German form – in the autumn of 2003, they lay 6 points behind VfB Stuttgart in the Bundesliga and struggled to dispose of Second Division Nuremberg on penalties in the German Cup.

The alarming slump of the German champions prompted a harsh rebuke from their bombastic bear of a goalkeeper, Oliver Kahn, who angrily questioned the desire of his team-mates. Perhaps Kahn had a point. Maybe the FC Hollywood all-stars, inured to success at home, did not have the requisite appetite to compete at a higher level? Certainly, there was a growing feeling in Germany that Ottmar Hitzfeld's men were bereft of team spirit and were more a fragmented team of talented individuals than a cohesive winning machine. Their ambition, courage and team spirit would all, therefore be under intense scrutiny in the final Champions League group games near the end of 2003.

Celtic, Anderlecht and Lyon all had 7 points in Group A, with Bayern just a point behind. Thankfully, Bayern had home advantage in their favour, with Anderlecht the visitors to the Olympic Stadium, while Celtic travelled to Lyon. Roared on by their own supporters, Bayern succeeded in edging out the

Belgians 1–0, thanks to a 42nd-minute penalty from Roy Makaay, while Oliver Kahn preserved their vital win with some crucial saves.

The narrow, tense victory was enough to ensure that Bayern progressed to the next round in second place behind Lyon, who had overcome Celtic 3–2. On the positive side, Michael and Bayern were fêted for their ability to win when it mattered most, reviving memories of their recent successes in the Champions League when they ground out unattractive victories through attrition and courage despite lacklustre performances. For example, when they made the semi-finals in 2002, they simply had to beat Rangers in their final group game, and they did – through a penalty and the heroics of Oliver Kahn, who made a string of superb saves. In 1999, when they reached the fateful final only to lose to two late sucker punches from Manchester United, they only secured one point from two games and then they had to beat Barcelona home and away – which they did.

Yet this time, Bayern's flaws and fallibility made it unlikely that these past successes were to be repeated. One perceived deficiency was that old chestnut – a lack of a leader. Unsurprisingly, it was Michael who was singled out by some commentators as not having the necessary charisma and assertiveness to inspire his men in the most trying of circumstances. However, Uli Hesse-Lichtenberger from ESPN Soccernet proffered another reason for Bayern's demise; he believed Ballack and his fellow ex-Bayer Leverkusen team-mate, Zé Roberto, were victims of Hitzfeld's tactics. He wrote, 'Zé Roberto plays like a man who doesn't have a clear understanding of what's going on and what he's supposed to do. And you could say the same goes for Ballack. At Leverkusen, the two played in a 4-3-3, with Zé Roberto on the left wing and Ballack as one of the two central midfielders behind Yildiray Bastürk, who played in the hole and fed the three forwards. That was ideal for Ballack because he is a great ball-winner... as soon as he had got the ball to Bastürk, there were acres of space in front of him to run into. But Bayern initially used a rigid 4-4-2. If Ballack was assigned a defensive role within the middle four, he'd win the ball, find no one in the hole and would have to carry the ball upfield himself. If he was given an offensive role, he wouldn't have any space to roam because there were only Makaay and Pizarro in front of him, trying to draw defenders out of position.

'That may be why, a few weeks ago, Bayern switched from 4-4-2 to 4-3-3, yet it's still not working properly. At Celtic, Ballack was the central offensive midfielder, but he seemed to be looking for a Bastürk-like team-mate to feed or use as a wall-player. Hitzfeld then created this position at Bremen and against Anderlecht, using three strikers plus Pizarro in the hole. But the Peruvian is basically a target man himself.'

Tactical concerns aside, it was certainly not all doom and gloom for Michael as a New Year heralded fresh and exciting challenges for the Bayern man. No lesser side than the peerless Real Madrid, a team of unsurpassed footballing talent, were Bayern's opponents in the last 16 of the Champions League. There was therefore no excuse for Bayern not to be motivated and desperate for success in this élite meeting of two of Europe's greatest clubs. Quite simply, if the grand old German club had any pretensions of re-establishing themselves as a dominant force in European football, these were the types of games they had to win.

In an interesting sub-plot, Ballack was also intent on avenging his defeat to the Spanish stars in the 2002 Champions League Final when he was at Bayer Leverkusen. It was also the perfect opportunity for him to dispel the developing notion that he was no longer capable of matching Europe's finest footballers, including the incomparable Zinedine Zidane, the man who made Madrid tick.

Reassuringly, Michael – who recovered from bronchitis to play in the game of this and many other seasons – was not lacking in confidence, despite both his own and his team's wretched European displays. He told the UEFA website, 'Of course we can beat Madrid. I think we can beat every team, even though Madrid are a huge name. They have some great players in the side and they are the favourites in every game, but they can lose.

'Madrid have so many good players in their ranks like Beckham, Figo, Ronaldo, Raul – they are all world-class players and Zidane is also one of them. I have never played directly against him. We play different positions and I do not think we will meet too often on the pitch.'

His Real rival in midfield, Zinedine Zidane, was more pithy but just as optimistic about a favourable outcome for the men from Madrid as Michael had been about his own team's prospects. He said, 'We will win the game. We are always really motivated when we play a team such as Bayern and that is why we are not worried.'

Although Real were firm favourites to emerge triumphant, Bayern could draw comfort from a superior head-to-head record in recent clashes. It was the fourth time in five seasons that the two European powerhouses had met, and Bayern had won six times to Real's three.

In the first leg, an important victory, built on patience and controlled discipline, seemed to have been assured for Bayern after Roy Makaay scored with a header on 75 minutes. However, 8 minutes later, Oliver Kahn committed a horrendous error when he fumbled Roberto Carlos's 30-yard free-kick and allowed the ball to squirm underneath his body. It was a grievous blow to Bayern's hopes of progressing, although their despair was partially assuaged by the realisation that they had rediscovered a semblance of their old form.

It was Real who eventually prevailed, though, in the battle of the big guns by winning 1–0 in the second leg in Madrid and it was goalscorer Zinedine Zidane, who upstaged Michael in the midfield skirmishes. Immediately, there was an outpouring of criticism for Bayern's underperforming talisman, with the president of the Munich club, Franz Beckenbauer, accusing Michael of 'going through the motions' in an insipid display in the Bernebeu. Beckenbauer said, 'He [Michael Ballack] plays without enthusiasm and does not change his rhythm at all, it's always the same tempo. The domestic title is out of our reach for some time... all that matters now is to come second and gain automatic access to the UEFA Champions League.

'I think we have to analyse our current problems – What's Ballack's problem? Do the other players accept him? Is he physically not fit? And how can coach Ottmar Hitzfeld motivate his squad the way it should be?'

In an interview with *Bild*, Michael hit back by saying, 'The fact is, I was poor in Madrid but you cannot put too much emphasis on one game. I am a player that can take criticism but that was a bit too much.' He also rose to the defence of his beleaguered coach, Ottmar Hitzfeld. 'Everyone needs support at difficult times and I have had that from Mr Hitzfeld. He is the one of the few people in the club who backs me 100 per cent. That is important. Just like Oliver Kahn, I think he is the best manager for Bayern.'

While losing to Real Madrid was no disgrace, exiting the German Cup to second division Alemannia Aachen was shameful for a club of Bayern's pedigree. If major English clubs feel aggrieved at times about rough treatment by their country's tabloids, they can take comfort from the headline in *Bild* which illustrates the intense dislike Bayern often generate in the German press: 'BAYERN HA, HA, HA! The whole of Germany is laughing itself sick about you'.

There was further joy and exultation in many parts of Germany when Bayern failed to retain the Bundesliga, finishing 6 points behind champions Werder Bremen, who clinched the title with a 3–1 win in Munich. Ottmar Hitzfeld paid the ultimate price for Bayern's trophyless season and left the club by mutual consent in May 2004.

For Michael Ballack, meanwhile, his second season at Germany's premier club was one of intense frustration and unfulfilment. He was beginning to sincerely resent the unrelenting and often invidious pressure foisted on players at Germany's biggest club. During Bayern's troubled 2003/04 season, he was quoted as saying, 'As soon as two games are lost, it's instantly a crisis. And if, as a player, you no longer deliver a performance, you are dropped like a hot potato.'

Ballack also had his run-ins with Bayern officials, including a dispute in the autumn of 2003 with Karl-Heinz Rummenigge. The latter had urged him to miss Germany's crucial Euro 2004 qualifier with Iceland due to a sore ankle, although Michael angrily disagreed. In the red corner, Rummenigge had said, 'We're [Bayern] always the ones who suffer. We won't create problems and we'll give him up, but it would be better if Michael didn't play and rested his ankle.' While in the blue corner, Michael retorted, 'I was just agitated. It's the most important game we're playing this year. I certainly won't be sitting at home.' In the end, it was Michael who won this battle of wills and represented his country with distinction in their 3–0 win over Iceland, scoring the opening goal.

He would also reveal disgust and disaffection with life at Bayern and the personal criticism he was enduring in an interview with Ludger Schulze of the *Süddeutsche Zeitung* newspaper. When asked whether the rumours were true that he was a 'difficult' player, he replied, 'It must be a compliment because the club seems to revel in difficult characters. I think I have just stood up for myself on occasions and reckon that shows that I have certain strengths. If individuals for whom I have respect make comments – people like Karl-Heinz Rummenigge, Uli Hoeness, Ottmar Hitzfeld or Franz Beckenbauer, for instance – I often just add my view. Maybe that is seen as "difficult". But in reality I am a simple soul.'

Despite his misgivings about certain aspects of life in Munich, including the crippling weight of expectation and merciless media bashing he would often endure, he was insistent that he would fulfil his four-year contract with Bayern. 'Your every move is monitored, but I deliberately sought this challenge. If I had wanted a peaceful life, I could have stayed at Leverkusen. It would be naïve in the extreme to arrive in Munich and imagine that nothing was going to happen, but it is difficult at times.'

Indeed, having already experienced desperate troughs in his career with both Bayer Leverkusen and Germany, the ever-optimistic Michael realised that, when everything was put into perspective, life was not all that bad. By his own admission he had still scored seven league goals despite an 'average' season and, in March 2004, arguably the world's best-ever exponent of the beautiful game, Pelé, named Michael in his list of 125 of the greatest living footballers to mark the 100th anniversary of FIFA. He joined nine other Germans in the list – Franz Beckenbauer, Gerd Müller, Jürgen Klinsmann, Karl-Heinz Rummenigge, Lothar Matthäus, Oliver Kahn, Paul Breitner, Sepp Maier and Uwe Seeler.

Michael was fully aware that, in his third season, he would need to be a great deal more consistent and dominant in his form if he was to avoid further criticism and prove he was worthy of such lofty accolades. He was fortunate that he was offered the reassuring support of one of the most vocal and influential players at Bayern, Oliver Kahn, who said, 'Bayern should never sell Ballack. Even if he plays a game or two below par, they must convince him that the club's future is based on him.'

Michael was given a further vote of confidence from the new coach at Bayern, Felix Magath, who arrived from Vfb Sttutgart. The former German midfielder immediately won favour by stating that the young German would be the only automatic starter in Bayern's midfield. He was also encouraged by the arrival of his former Bayer team-mate, the Brazilian defender Lucio, while midfielder Torsten Frings was another astute addition by Magath to Bayern's squad.

In the Champions League, Bayern were paired with Juventus, Ajax and Maccabi Haifa of Israel and, on paper, qualification looked perfectly achievable. However, in view of Bayern's indifferent European displays in recent years, hypothetical results could not be relied upon – the much-maligned men from Munich needed to go out and prove their continental class through impressive wins and improved performances.

A 1–0 win in Tel Aviv was an encouraging start, and then a resounding 4–0 victory over Ajax in Munich confirmed Bayern were back in business as far as Europe was concerned. However, 1–0 defeats home and away to Juventus served as a chastening reminder that Bayern had not yet regained their place among Europe's élite, but at least they were disposing of sides they were expected to beat – like Maccabi Haifa, who were thrashed 5–1 at the Olympic Stadium – unlike in recent seasons. 'This was fantastic! This was just incredible!' screamed *Bild* following Bayern's superb showing.

Michael's first Champions League goal of the season arrived in Bayern's final group game, a 2–2 draw with Ajax in Amsterdam when he deftly headed in Zé Roberto's cross. After emerging with a creditable, hard-fought draw from the encounter – Bayern's 300th game in Europe – the Munich side became the first German club to avoid defeat against Ajax in Amsterdam.

Bayern therefore eased into the second stage behind Juventus and would now play the artists of Arsène Wenger's Arsenal, who had been installed as second favourites behind Chelsea for Europe's Holy Grail in the last 16. And it was a triumphant return to the irrepressible Bayern of old in the first leg as the Munich outfit, deprived of an injured Michael, swept aside Arsenal 3–1 at the Olympic Stadium.

He recovered for the second leg, although Bayern were without top scorer Roy Makaay. Felix Magath was in buoyant mood, though, and preferred to focus on the positive element of his talisman's return rather than the potentially debilitating absence of his key striker. He said, 'We will be even stronger because Ballack is a fantastic player who gives us so much more power.'

Michael duly fared well in his personal midfield duel with Patrick Vieira and, despite Bayern losing 1–0, he was now left contemplating the increasingly tangible prospect of European glory. The *Daily Telegraph's* Henry Winter wrote, 'Two-footed and multi-faceted, Ballack was supreme, running midfield with his smooth passing and relentless hounding of anyone in a red shirt. He even threatened to score after seven minutes, but was denied by a flying block from Patrick Vieira. He then thumped a shot wide. A cynical streak stained Ballack's stylish approach, notably when he blatantly body-checked Henry, who was elegantly speeding past him.'

Although Michael was currently hitting the right notes on the pitch, and attracting a number of deserved plaudits, the public perception of the player among the fans was mixed – they delighted in his inspiring performances for Germany, and those he occasionally turned in for Bayern, but the element of unpredictability was still there, lurking beneath the surface. Fans never really knew which Michael Ballack would turn up, and were frustrated that the greatness he clearly had within him was not always on display. Hopefully, experience and maturity would enable that greatness to come more fully to the fore, and be evident on a more consistent basis.

Having dispatched Arsenal, neither Michael nor Bayern could rest on their laurels – there were still many difficult hurdles to surmount in this most demanding of football tournaments. Firstly, the quarter-finals presented them with another excellent English club to overcome – Chelsea. After excelling against Arsenal, Ballack was undaunted by the prospect of tackling the favourites for the Champions League. He was quoted as saying before the match, 'We like playing English sides because they come at you and we are perfectly suited to hit them on the break. Look at the Arsenal game. They had a lot of possession, but couldn't hurt us and it was a great success for us in the end. The reaction to the draw from the players in our dressing room was positive and that is a good sign for me. We were pleased to face another English side and, after beating Arsenal, why not Chelsea?

'You look at what happened with Barcelona and it is hard to back against them. Chelsea deserve to be favourites to win this competition, but if we beat them, then the tag may be placed on us. The bar is always set very high at Bayern and our aim is to be the European Champions this season. I wasn't here when Bayern won the Champions League in 2001 and I'd give anything for a repeat. I'm confident because this club is built around winning the Champions League. As we proved in the two Arsenal games, we have the desire, the mental toughness and the big-game players, guys who deliver when it really matters. I wouldn't write us off and nor should anyone else. We can give anyone problems.'

However, Chelsea were an altogether different proposition to Arsenal; they were formidable in all departments, uncompromising and assured and, above all, they were instilled with an insatiable desire to win by their serial winner coach, Jose Mourinho. Chelsea's strength and quality told as they overpowered Bayern 4–2 in the first leg at Stamford Bridge, thanks to an inspirational display from Frank Lampard, who scored two fine goals. The margin of victory would have been greater if Michael had not coolly converted a late penalty, which Bayern were awarded after he tumbled in the box following a challenge from Chelsea defender Ricardo Carvalho. It was a debatable decision and one which incited furious protests of diving from incensed Chelsea players and officials.

Chelsea captain John Terry added his voice to the criticism, saying, 'There's taking the piss and then there's doing what Ballack did. I've seen the incident a number of times on TV and it definitely wasn't a penalty. Ballack was diving all night and he wasn't the only one. The ref should have been on to Ballack but he wasn't listening and that goal took the shine off our great night.' Striker Eidur Gudjohnsen added, 'The authorities have been pointing their fingers at people who dive and trick the referee, and they want it out of the game. Unfortunately, it happened in this game, although I think it was just that one incident.'

Yet the man at the centre of the furore, Michael Ballack, protested his innocence, insisting, 'I wanted to reach the ball but was pulled back. I believe you can whistle for that. That goal was the chance for us to get back into this tie.' He was supported in his claims by Bayern defender Lucio, who told the *Sun*, 'I respect John Terry so much as a player because he has proved to be a great leader for Chelsea, but he was wrong to call Michael Ballack a diving cheat. Michael is not the sort of player who dives – it's as simple as that – and he didn't at Stamford Bridge. Some German players dive a lot but, in Michael's case, John Terry's accusations were unfair. Ballack is a fighter and one of the most competitive men I know.'

Bayern and England midfielder Owen Hargreaves balanced up the two rival camps' carping when he said, 'If you are fouled or you get shoved in the box and the referee gives it, then it's a penalty. The referee has given it and it's his responsibility, his job to judge the situation.'

Ultimately, though, it was UEFA who had the deciding vote and cleared Michael of diving, or the 'art of simulation' to give it its correct term. So, would the ill-will between the two teams now die down? Not quite, for while Chelsea supremo Jose Mourinho had to watch the second leg from a hotel room as he was serving a two-match touchline ban, a fired-up Ballack added further fuel to an already combustible encounter by saying, 'We have shown many times that we can easily score two goals at home against anyone. We can do it again against Chelsea.'

Then, as the Bayern and Chelsea players gathered in the tunnel prior to the second-leg kick-off, he and Oliver Kahn were involved in an unseemly contretemps with John Terry. It is alleged that both Kahn and Michael deliberately barged into Terry and the burly goalkeeper barked out menacingly, 'After! After!' as a clear warning about his post-match plans for retribution. An unflustered Terry was reported as replying, 'Okay, I'll see you in here after.' Thankfully, no after-match 'gathering' ever materialised and the focus was switched back to football matters. It is interesting to note, however, that Ballack ironically cited his bust-up with Terry and the Englishman's 'fighting spirit' as a key factor in his eventual decision to move to Chelsea.

After all the posturing and macho swaggering, it was inevitable that the football would not quite live up to the fire and brimstone of the pre-match exchanges. It certainly came close, though, as Bayern staged a thrilling comeback almost to complete the improbable defeat of the English champions.

Didier Drogba had put Chelsea 2–1 ahead on the night after 80 minutes, seemingly to seal Bayern's fate, but two goals from the valiant home side in stoppage time nearly achieved a miracle for Michael and his brave team-mates. In between, he had had a header kicked off the line by Eidur Gudjohnsen as Bayern pressed with renewed dynamism and resolve. As he had been against Arsenal in the previous round, Bayern's midfield dynamo was an inspirational driving force throughout, despite suffering a badly bruised thigh, but his efforts could not reap due dividends.

Chelsea now progressed to a semi-final meeting with eventual Champions League winners Liverpool, who went on to beat AC Milan in one of the most thrilling finals in living memory. Ballack and Bayern were left licking their wounds. A dispirited Michael commented, 'We tried to attack but Chelsea were just a bit better and more fortunate with the two deflected goals,' while his crestfallen coach, Felix Magath, added, 'It's very disappointing. We didn't have any good luck early on and then we got hit with bad luck. It's very unfortunate.'

While the Germans could justifiably have indulged in mutual back-slapping at their heroic efforts and bemoaned the absence of luck on a night of near misses, Oliver Kahn offered a brutally honest assessment of his team's failings. 'Instead of patting each other on the back and saying how well we played, we need to analyse what went wrong. We had so many chances but still got knocked out. We have to analyse why. I think at this level you can't afford to squander too many goal chances.'

On a personal level, Michael Ballack can consider himself unfortunate that he was part of another disappointing Bayern failure in Europe's premier competition. While his performances may not have lived up to the unforgettable flight of fancy he enjoyed with Bayer Leverkusen, he was still considered one of the Champions League's most accomplished performers of 2004/05. *Champions*, the official UEFA magazine of the Champions League, voted him one of the ten most valuable players – the only German player to achieve this distinction – of the campaign.

As so often was the case with Bayern since Michael had arrived, while Europe was an unhappy hunting ground, the Bundesliga was still able to offer enormous riches. In both the League and the Cup, it was a dogged Schalke outfit who provided Bayern with their stiffest test and proved their mettle by defeating their glamorous rivals twice in the Bundesliga. Indeed, Bayern only shook off their plucky rivals three days before the end of the season when they beat Kaiserslautern 4–0, with Ballack netting the opener with a low shot from Roy Makaay's deft back-heel flick, while Schalke could only draw 3–3 with Bayer Leverkusen.

It was Bayern's 19th championship win and it was a bittersweet moment for Michael as the title had been clinched on his old stomping ground, where he had won the Bundesliga in 1998. He soon shrugged off any feeling of sympathy for his former club-mates to join in the Bayern celebrations which included spraying Bavarian beer across the pitch, however.

Sadly, his partying in a Munich disco later in the evening saw him become the subject of unwanted newspaper attention. He intervened in a brawl between Bayern officials and other revellers at the disco, which naturally resulted in sensationalist tabloid headlines.

Michael also made the news for more positive reasons during the 2004/05 season. Berlin-based official Lutz-Michael Fröhlich was awarded the Fair Play trophy from the German Sportswriters' Association after owning up admirably to his own mistake in wrongly booking Michael in November 2005. During the Bundesliga game between Bayern and Hannover, Fröhlich showed Michael a second yellow card for a foul committed by Bastian Schweinsteiger. Following furious protests from Bayern players, Fröhlich consulted his linesman, changed his decision and apologised to Michael for his error.

There were further reasons for Michael to feel satisfied with life, as Bayern were proving to be unstoppable in the German Cup; they reached the Final of the competition with a 2–0 win at Arminia Bielefeld. Ballack put his side ahead after only 3 minutes, bulleting a header beyond Bielefeld's goalkeeper

Mathias Hain from Bastian Schweinsteiger's corner. Roy Makaay then dispatched a late penalty to confirm Bayern's place in the Final in Berlin's Olympic Stadium. And on a personal level, in March 2005 Michael proudly announced the birth of his third son Jordi.

In front of a crowd of 74,349, Bayern's final showdown with Schalke would be more one-sided than their title battle had been, although the scoreline did not reflect their dominance. Felix Magath's men were determined to secure another double and exerted relentless pressure in the first half, carving out a succession of goal-scoring opportunities.

Schalke's Sven Vermant clearly handled the ball to block Ballack's goal-bound effort and then Lucio had a goal wrongly ruled out for offside. Bayern would not be deterred, however, and took the lead 3 minutes before half-time when Michael's cross found Zé Roberto, whose shot hit a post and fell to Roy Makaay, who scored with cool aplomb. Schalke, though, responded immediately when Lincoln converted a debatable penalty after referee Florian Meyer adjudged Ailton to have been brought down by Willy Sagnol.

A less eventful second half spawned fewer chances for either side, but Bayern were always the more likely to prevail and, when the inevitable second goal arrived after 76 minutes, Michael was unsurprisingly involved in the build-up. He played in Roy Makaay, who teed up substitute Hasan Salihamidžič to tap home from close range and from an offside position. 'I think it's been a great fight, which we have won deservedly,' he remarked after Bayern's 12th cup triumph and fifth domestic double.

The 2004/05 campaign also marked the end of an era for

Bayern when they played their final game at the Olympiastadion, which had been built for the 1972 Olympic Games and which is famous for its instantly recognisable 'cobweb' canopy. Their final home game against Nuremberg was naturally an emotionally-charged affair and they could not have wished for a more stirring farewell at their historic bastion of football, which had hosted 578 Bundesliga matches over 33 years of football.

Michael scored the second goal after 24 minutes as Bayern cantered to a 5–0 half-time lead. Nuremberg responded superbly in the second half and scored three goals of their own, although Bayern added another goal to run out 6–3 winners. It was Bayern's 421st win in the Olympic Stadium, which also witnessed the presentation of the Bundesliga trophy by league president Werner Hackmann to goalkeeper and captain Oliver Kahn.

In addition to the valedictory victory for Bayern's spiritual home, the champions and the supporters present also bade a fond farewell to some faithful servants who were heading to pastures new – Vahid Hashemian, Alexander Zickler, Thomas Linke, Robert Kovač and Sammy Kuffour.

Speaking on his official website, Michael said of the celebrations at the end of the season, which culminated in an open-bus convoy to the Marienplatz in downtown Munich, 'Everything was perfect on that day... the weather was nice, the ground sold out and the match a gigantic football party with lots of goals. I have played at the Olympic Stadium for three years, and there is a bit of wistfulness about having to say goodbye. The stronger feeling, however, is happy anticipation with regards to the new stadium. The atmosphere at the Allianz Arena will be fantastic – for the players, but especially for the fans.'

The end of the season was joy unconfined for Ballack as he picked up yet another accolade, the German Player of the Year award conducted by *Kicker* magazine. He collected 516 votes from German journalists with FC Cologne striker and international team-mate Lukas Podolski his nearest rival with 103 votes. It was the third time in four years that he had been named Germany's greatest footballer.

6

Breaking New Ground

Everything looked bright and immensely promising for Michael Ballack and Bayern as a new home strip and new stadium, the 66,000-seater, three-tiered Allianz Arena, heralded the 2005/06 season. Felix Magath believed the Allianz Arena would become as feared a fortress as the Olympic Stadium had been for Bayern's opponents. He commented, 'I'm sure the new stadium will prove its value to us, particularly in Europe. With an atmosphere like this, UEFA referees will find it difficult to make calls against us.'

While Bayern basked in the glory of their swish surroundings and revelled in a record annual turnover of 204.7 million euros, Michael Ballack was beginning to have itchy feet and was becoming increasingly disgruntled by his steadily deteriorating relations with his employers. The impending end of his contract and the strain of performing under unremitting pressure, while facing jibes and diatribes from both the Bayern hierarchy and the media, had made him seriously consider his options. He could therefore easily have gone through the motions in what proved to be his final season for Bayern, but his pride and class would guarantee that his high standards would not slip. Whatever the future held for him, he wanted to exit with his head held high and with more winner's medals to display proudly.

Once again, domination of the Bundesliga was almost a foregone conclusion, but conquering Europe remained frustratingly elusive. Along with Juventus, Bayern were expected to qualify from Group A of the Champions League, which contained Club Brugge and Rapid Vienna. On his official website Michael said he was confident that they would succeed: 'At long last, we know the teams we will face in the Champions League – Juventus, Bruges and Rapid Vienna are our opponents – not an easy group, but no mission impossible either. I'm certain that we should go through if we deliver what we're capable of. In any case, I'm looking forward to the matches, especially the game against Juventus, as we've got something to make up for. It remains to be seen whether we'll be stronger in Europe this year on account of the new ground.'

He was absent for Bayern's first game away to Rapid Vienna, although the Germans still achieved a valuable victory, thanks to a goal from the Peruvian Paolo Guerrero.

Ballack returned for Bayern's home encounter with a defensively-minded Club Brugge – their 50th encounter in the Champions League – which again ended in a 1–0 win for the hosts. It was a promising start, but Bayern's Champions League credentials would only be truly revealed in back-to-back encounters with Juventus. In what was rapidly becoming an intimidating arena for opposing teams, the Allianz Arena witnessed one of Bayern's most rousing Champions League performances of recent years as the Germans earned a 2–1 win over Italy's Old Lady. Zlatan Ibrahimovic's last-minute consolation for Juventus was the first goal Bayern had conceded at their new home.

That scoreline, though, was reversed when the two clubs met in Turin and Michael and his team-mates were heartbroken when they succumbed to David Trezeguet's winning goal five minutes from time.

Qualification to the knockout stages for Bayern was assured in convincing style when the Germans crushed Rapid Vienna 4–0 at home, although Michael missed the game due to a thigh injury. Now it was just a case of whether Bayern would finish in top spot or second behind Juventus. Eventually, it was the Italians who emerged as group winners after beating Rapid in Vienna, while Bayern had to settle for a 1–1 draw away to Club Brugge.

At least by finishing second, Bayern avoided playing group winners Chelsea and Real Madrid, but they were still presented with the considerable hurdle of AC Milan. *Bild* had heaped the pressure on Michael prior to the match with the Italians by saying, 'Ballack last played a really strong Champions League match in the 2001/02 season for Bayer Leverkusen. At Bayern Munich, he has yet to put in a truly noteworthy performance.'

Cometh the hour, cometh the man, as Michael Ballack answered his critics in magnificent style with a spectacular goal and a marvellous all-round display as Bayern drew 1–1 with Milan in the first leg in Germany. Months, and even years, of pent-up frustration at being persistently pilloried for his lacklustre European form evaporated when Ballack, who wore the captain's armband for the night due to the injury of Oliver Kahn, unleashed a 25-yard volley past the despairing dive of Dida in the Milan goal.

Ballack's wild celebrations reflected the significance of the goal and his exuberant pounding of his chest and badge-kissing illustrated his commitment to a club he was due to leave at the end of the season. He refused to speak to reporters at the end of the match, but others were more than happy to wax lyrical about Bayern's prodigal son and his stunning contribution, his first goal in the 2005/06 Champions League.

'It's not surprising to us that he played well,' said Bayern coach Felix Magath. 'There's no pressure on him. This was the sort of match he excels in. He's played well in recent weeks and scored many important goals.'

'It was a beautiful goal from Michael,' said Germany coach Jürgen Klinsmann, who was in Munich to watch his captain.

Bayern had dominated their Italian opponents and Michael Rensing, standing in for the injured Oliver Kahn in goal, hardly had a save to make. A debatable penalty, earned when it was adjudged that Valerien Ismael handled the ball in the box, was slotted home by Andriy Shevchenko to earn the visitors a precious away goal and thus the crucial advantage in an exhilarating clash. The stage was now set for two of Europe's most stylish midfielders – Kaká of Milan and Michael Ballack – to go head-to-head in the San Siro, with the winner of the pair's personal duel likely to influence significantly the outcome of the finely-balanced tie.

Kaká enthused of his older German rival in *Kicker* magazine, 'I like Ballack very much and I would happily play alongside him. He is a clever player who has excellent technique and would fit in very well at Milan. I'll invite him to come for a coffee with me in Milan. Perhaps he will like it and decide to stay.'

Milan coach Carlo Ancelotti was similarly wary of Ballack's threat. He said, 'We have to try and stop him getting into dangerous positions and using his qualities, particularly his ability to get on the end of balls coming from deep.' Ancelotti's wish was granted and Ballack and Bayern's dreams of Champions League glory were shattered when Milan routed the Germans 4–1 in the San Siro.

While Europe had been fallow territory for Bayern, Michael knew he had every chance of securing the consolation of yet more success on home soil. Ankle and thigh injuries interrupted the early part of Bayern's season, although the league was again proving to be a formality for Munich's finest.

Although Bayern had three straight 1–0 wins without their captain, with him the champions thrashed their first four Bundesliga opponents by a combined score of 13–3. However, many football followers in Germany were becoming increasingly disillusioned with Bayern's predictable dominance of their domestic league, which was becoming akin to a processional march. In a desperate bid to revive interest in the Bundesliga, a German brewery even offered 10,000 litres of free beer to the fans of whichever team succeeded in beating Bayern.

In late September, it was the supporters of Hamburg who enjoyed the intoxicating rewards of a rare victory by their club over the champions-elect. An inspired Hamburg beat Ballack's men 2–0, ending their 15-match winning run in the process, and also closed to within one point of their Munich rivals.

As the speculation over his future intensified as autumn approached, Ballack could have been forgiven for being distracted and disinterested in Bayern's routine rule of the Bundesliga. Paradoxically, he appeared even more motivated, scoring crucial goals in October such as the winner in Bayern's 2–1 victory over FC Cologne. Bayern coach Felix Magath confirmed Ballack's contract talks had worked in his team's favour. 'We're profiting from the negotiations,' he said. 'As long as he keeps scoring the important goals, I don't get so nervous that he hasn't signed with us.'

As 2005 ended, Bayern still harboured hopes of retaining their most influential footballer. Karl-Heinz Rummenigge said, 'If he chooses to stay with us, we would all be happy.' He added that sections of the Bayern support who had turned against Michael could soon be won over, yet deep down Rummenigge always had his reservations about Michael's commitment to the cause. He went on record as saying that he found Michael to be overly introverted, distrustful and uncommunicative, hurtful comments indeed, especially in view of the fact that Michael and Rummenigge and their families regularly dined out together.

Bayern sporting director Uli Hoeness also questioned Michael's attachment as it appeared more and more likely that he would sever his ties with the Munich club and try his luck abroad. At the club's Christmas function he told Ballack, 'I find it very sad, Michael, that in the two years you've been here [it was actually three at the time] you haven't grown into part of the club.'

Michael Ballack and Uli Hoeness had never completely seen eye to eye; the former could never satisfy the latter, a dyed-in-the-wool Munich man, and lifelong fan of the club of his commitment to Bayern. Perhaps such differences of opinion did not ultimately sway his decision to leave Bayern, but they certainly did not persuade Michael to prolong his association with the club, and particularly one that seemed to appreciate his talents and workrate less and less. As relations became more and more strained he confessed in an interview that he had never enjoyed the camaraderie and team spirit there that he had experienced at his previous clubs. Despite some fantastic performances on the pitch for Bayern, it seemed that he had never been fully embraced as 'one of the lads' in the dressing room... or perhaps more significantly, he had never really integrated himself with his Bayern team-mates in the way that he had done for previous clubs.

While he was feeling the wrath of his employers at Bayern, his dignity and amazing resilience were the subject of a flattering eulogy from ESPN Soccernet reporter Uli Hesse-Lichtenberger. He wrote an article called *Ballack: The Definition of Unperturbed*, in which he lauded Michael's extraordinary ability to perform brilliantly in spite of unstinting criticism and speculation about his future. He said, 'Ballack himself is not only unperturbed, he is getting better by the hour. How often have you heard a player excuse a dip in form by saying he's mentally unstable because the contract situation is getting to him? Here we have a player who appears to be gaining confidence and strength the more muddled things become. He must know that two bad games in a row or a missed penalty will let the press hounds loose and rapidly darken the mood in the stands. But Ballack simply rises above the defence and coolly heads the ball home to level the score. Amazing.'

Michael was certainly more than worthy of such plaudits as he was simply on fire when Bayern resumed Bundesliga action after the German winter break. Time and time again he was the man who made the difference for his club with a number of decisive goals and some masterful midfield play. The other impressive factor about the four goals he scored in three weeks at the start of 2006 was their variety – a free-kick, a header, a left-foot effort and a right-foot shot, exemplifying huge versatility. Perhaps his most memorable goal was the winner against his former side, Bayer Leverkusen, when he trapped a long cross with his chest, swivelled around and hit the ball home with his left foot. Unsurprisingly, it was voted the Bundesliga's Goal of the Month.

ESPN's Hesse-Lichtenberger said, 'You could say that all this is amazing in itself, which it probably is, although it's not what I find so stunning at this point in time. Ballack has been doing these things all along. After all, every single one of the seven goals he scored during the first half of the season, six in the league and one in the Cup, was a go-ahead goal for his team. I repeat – every single one! You would think Bayern have enough lethal strikers to lead the way in moments of crisis, but it seems their one-man cavalry is really called Ballack.'

It was not all plain sailing for Bayern and their imperious midfielder, though; they had to guard against complacency if they wanted to maintain their stranglehold on the Bundesliga. In April, their seemingly unassailable lead at the top of the Bundesliga ahead of Hamburg was trimmed to four points when they crashed to a 3–0 defeat at third-placed Werder Bremen.

Michael described the situation as 'dangerous', warning, 'Nothing's gone wrong so far, but we know we're not in great form at the moment. We have to keep our cool, but we mustn't be over-confident. Our difference is slowly melting away, so we need to perform for the remainder of the season, and then we'll basically be safe and dry.'

Bayern successfully achieved the first leg of their double quest when they retained the German Cup in late April against lowly Eintracht Frankfurt, who lay 36 points behind the champions in the table. Despite the enormous chasm between the two teams, an obdurate Frankfurt side caused Bayern plenty of problems and only a Claudio Pizarro header separated the two sides at the end of the 90 minutes.

Even in victory, Michael Ballack was akin to a condemned man after Franz Beckenbauer lambasted an 'average' performance by Michael and accused him of 'saving his strength' for his future employers, Chelsea. By now, such remarks were water off a duck's back, although what hurt him more was the increasing instances of booing he was suffering from the Bayern faithful.

Bayern secured the championship – their 20th – with one game remaining when they drew 1–1 at Kaiserslautern. In turn, they became the first German club to win the double in successive seasons.

Sadly, Michael, unlike Bayern's other history-makers, would

not receive the unreserved appreciation of his home crowd; in his final game, a chorus of jeers accompanied his every touch. Despite the off-putting cacophany around him, Ballack was on target in a thrilling 3–3 draw with Borussia Dortmund. And after being further barracked by supporters during a post-match celebration, he joked that his treatment indicated how important he had been to Bayern. He commented, 'I want to stress that it is not, and never has been, about money. I am not 23 or 24, have a great contract at Bayern and my family and I are comfortable in Munich. I just want a new challenge and the time is right.'

Bayern coach Felix Magath was philosophical about Ballack's impending departure, saying, 'He deserves to have a fair send-off and it is his right to say he wants to play somewhere else. Ballack will be missed, although we will move on.'

At least Michael could reflect with satisfaction on a tremendous season for himself and his club. In winning the double, he had scored 14 goals and been Bayern's outstanding performer. He polled 63 votes from German sports journalists to finish third in the Player of the Year award, which was won by Werder Bremen's Brazilian striker Ailton. In four seasons at Bayern, Ballack had won three Bundesliga and German Cup doubles and scored 47 goals in 135 matches. Between 1998 and 2005, he had notched up 61 goals in his domestic league.

Despite this admirable set of statistics and awards, though, question marks will forever remain over his failure to replicate his domestic form on the European stage and many Bayern supporters never truly took him to their hearts, interpreting his languid demeanour as a sign that he was not completely committed to the Munich club. For his part, Ballack will, no doubt, admit that he was never comfortable with the baggage life at Bayern brings – the unyielding criticism, the jealousy, the hype and the hyperbole. It was therefore the right time for him to continue his football career elsewhere.

They say that you only realise how much a person is missed when they are gone and this certainly was the case when Bayern struggled without their playmaker. During the 2006/07 season, Bayern defender Willy Sagnol admitted, 'We have lost four important players with the departures of Ballack, Zé Roberto, Jens Jeremies and Bixente Lizarazu. We're missing a bit of experience. Of course things were better when he [Ballack] was here. He was a great player, and always capable of scoring.'

Bayern president Franz Beckenbauer agreed that the club was still reeling from the loss of Michael. He told *Kicker*, 'I have said all along that I consider Ballack's leaving to be very painful. Many people said if you look at his stats, they weren't that great. But he was the team's captain out there on the pitch... everything revolved around him, he stabilised the others. You didn't see that during our first games. We have been missing him.'

Meanwhile, in November 2006, Bayern coach Felix Magath was missing his former player for reasons other than his prodigious football ability – because of his haircut. He believed that those with long hair at Bayern, including Claudio Pizarro, Daniel van Buyten, Hasan Salihamidžič and Martin Demichelis, should get rid of their locks and copy Ballack's close-cropped hairstyle. Magath said, 'Ballack's haircut shows authority, commitment, belief and aggressiveness. It's a sign that the player wants to do more for his club than just play football. I would like to see them [his long-haired players] visit a barber, but I won't force them – they should take the step.'

Finally, when it was far too late, Michael Ballack had received the acknowledgement he'd craved during his time at Bayern – at last, Magath had conceded that Michael had been a cut above the rest.

7

Transfer Saga

As the shy, short-sighted East German kid kicked a ball around with carefree abandon under the shadow of his looming tower block, he couldn't possibly have ever dreamed of reaching the pinnacle of world football, and one day counting himself among the élite in terms of talent and remuneration. Earning legendary status in Germany and then, in 2006, becoming the highest paid footballer in the world, would have seemed fanciful notions to Michael Ballack in the early 1980s. It is a stunning footballing fable that any fiction writer would dearly love to have dreamed up.

While Michael's wondrous, dream-like ascent to worldwide acclaim has bestowed on him huge riches and honours galore, the fame and fortune have come at a price. Indeed, when he decided he was ready for a new football challenge in 2006 and was courted by the wealthiest club in the world, Chelsea, it was inevitable that he would face a welter of accusations of greed and disloyalty.

In a protracted and messy transfer saga, the like of which has been all-too common in football since the pay scales have shot off the charts, one could have predicted the bitterness and resentment his Bayern Munich employers would feel as Michael's future ended inexorably in a move to London.

Many critics in Germany and abroad cast him in the role of the all-too familiar shallow, money-grabbing footballer, who leapt opportunistically on the Abramovich all-conquering football bandwagon, powered by massive wealth and driven by a bevy of stellar footballers. However, Michael has strenuously denied such criticism, insisting that he moved to improve his own career prospects and to attempt to add an entirely new set of winner's medals to his already impressive CV. The race for his signature was one of the most frenzied and discussed transfers in European football in the 21st century. For several years some of the most celebrated clubs in Europe would vie to recruit the German midfield maestro, although it was not until 2004 that concrete offers were made to Bayern Munich, whom he had joined in 2002 after rebuffing approaches from leading clubs in Spain and Italy.

By now, Ballack was an established performer in Germany, both for club and country; he had performed with distinction – although not to the level he would have liked – in Europe's biggest club competition, the Champions League, displaying an innate eye for goal and an awesome passing ability. He had also excelled for a mediocre Germany side in the 2004 European Championships and inspired his country to the World Cup Final in 2002.

Although the Brazilian legend Pelé had opined that Michael

was 'mediocre' and not a true world star, Europe's finest were convinced of his credentials and would start to knock with anticipation on Bayern Munich's door. Michael's goal-scoring achievements also confirmed that he was, in American parlance, 'the real deal'; he had outscored some of his most illustrious contemporaries in Europe between 1998 and 2005, accumulating 61 goals in league football, as opposed to the 54 goals netted by Ronaldinho, while Luis Figo had notched 52, Zinedine Zidane, 46, and David Beckham, 45. His numerous suitors sensed an opportunity to test Bayern Munich's resolve with a speculative offer after the German club had failed to land a trophy in the 2003/04 season.

Spanish giants Barcelona were the first club to express interest in Michael after Bayern president Franz Beckenbauer agreed that the midfielder could leave if all parties were happy. Sandro Rosell, the Catalan side's vice-president told Spanish newspaper *Mundo Deportivo*: 'Bayern will find it hard to take a decision but we're optimistic. Michael is for them as Ronaldinho is for us, and we know it's not easy to give up a player like him.' Rosell went on to reveal that a deciding factor in any potential deal was whether Bayern could acquire the midfielder Deco from the then European champions, Porto. He said, 'It could be one of the keys. Bayern want to be able to cover Michael's position before letting him go.'

However, despite Beckenbauer giving Barcelona hope that they may be in luck, Bayern's chief executive, Karl-Heinz Rummenigge, promptly slammed the door shut by tersely informing the Spanish outfit's president Joan Laporta that Michael would remain their player and would see out his contract, which was set to expire in 2006. Rarely, though, do transfer scrambles for highly-sought-after players founder at the first hurdle. The chase for Michael was about to intensify and rumble on for a long, long time.

In 2005, the quest for Michael's signature began to gather momentum given that a year later his contract with Bayern Munich was due to expire. Interested parties knew that Bayern were vulnerable to an offer because Michael could leave for free. However, the man at the centre of the transfer interest believed it was beneficial for him to spend World Cup year in Germany, the host country of the 2006 finals, before assessing his options for the future.

In February 2005, he announced to *SportBild*, 'I do not think that it will come to me deciding directly after the 2006 World Cup whether I want to stay or go. I will either choose a new challenge or say, "I feel good here and would like to extend my contract."'

In July, he offered even more optimism to his employers that he might be prepared to remain in Bavaria. He said, 'Bayern have big aims... we want to defend the league championship as well as the German Cup and go far in the Champions League. And I want to be part of that. I'm in the good situation that I can choose... It's a very important decision for the club and for me, and that's why it should be carefully considered. It could take a few days, a few weeks or perhaps a few months. But the possibility that I'll extend is high. I feel good here.'

Meanwhile, Bayern's sporting director, Uli Hoeness, warned that his club would not to be held to ransom, should Michael seek a transfer abroad. 'We insist on sporting success being tied to financial prudence,' Hoeness said. 'The point may come when we have to say no. When people start talking about 10 million-plus I just don't understand the world any more. Surely no one believes Michael earns more than 4 million or thereabouts? And we're supposed to be considering more than doubling that?'

Indeed, despite his assurances to the contrary, Michael not only started to contemplate the prospect of earning more money but, more importantly, the realisation dawned on him that Bayern may not offer him the best chance of Champions League success. In recent seasons, Bayern had been the nearly-men Europe's premier competition and, in 2006, the club would have nine players out of contract – including established team members Oliver Kahn, Brazilian international Zé Roberto, full-backs Willy Sagnol and Bixente Lizarazu. Michael was hardly likely to be enamoured by the thought of playing for a team that was entering a period of increased uncertainty.

He was therefore already eyeing foreign horizons with considerable enthusiasm, and openly mulling over the prospect of a new challenge abroad to the *Frankfurter Allgemeine Sonntagszeitun*. 'There is hardly anyone who played abroad that would advise against making this step. They say it helps your development. That would be very interesting for me.' He was also aware that if he did embark upon a foreign odyssey, he would have the not inconsiderable task of re-establishing German football's deteriorating reputation abroad.

In the new millennium, few top-tier Germans, if any, had succeeded in foreign football environments, although Michael could draw comfort from a golden Germanic past when a trail of Teutonic heroes left their imprints on foreign football fields.

'It's been a long time since someone with the quality seal "Made in Germany" has been so sought after as Michael,' noted the *Frankfurter Allgemeine Zeitung*.

While he would be wracked with indecision over the ensuing months, he was relaxed in the knowledge that whether he stayed at Bayern or moved abroad, his situation was a 'win-win' one. 'I've always made the right decisions so far,' he added. 'I'm now playing at a top European club and still have the chance to play abroad.'

After previously refusing to pay big bucks to retain him, Uli Hoeness bullishly suggested that his club could satisfy Michael's every need and offered his midfield lynchpin a four-year contract extension worth a reported 36 million euros – the highest ever for a Bundesliga player. Hoeness told *Bild*, 'He is part of an intact team with a lot of potential. He gets the respect that he feels he deserves and, as far as the financial side of things are concerned, he certainly won't end up on the streets if he's here.' Bayern coach Felix Magath added, 'He's the focal point of the team, the man who dictates the rhythm. I believe he appreciates what he's got here.'

Yet Bayern's defiance did not deter Manchester United from bounding into the bidding fray in the summer of 2005 when the Red Devils attempted to test Bayern's resolve with an £8 million bid – a substantial carrot, given that Michael would be able to leave for free the following year.

Indeed, in August 2005, it seemed that Sir Alex Ferguson had got his man, according to the *Guardian*'s Daniel Taylor: 'Manchester United have put in place a deal that will see Michael Ballack add his considerable presence to the

Premiership and replace Roy Keane as the leader of their midfield – but not until the start of the 2006/07 season. Michael wants to leave Bayern Munich after one final season in the Bundesliga and the preliminary details of a free transfer have been provisionally agreed for him to sign a pre-contract agreement at Old Trafford next January.'

But Michael's agent, Dr Michael Becker, rubbished rumours that his client had sealed a move to the north-west of England, saying, 'There's no pre-contract, no gentleman's agreement. Michael Ballack is facing the most important decision of his career. Why would he prematurely sign in England if we haven't even spoken with the Italians and Spanish? The only people we're talking to at the moment are Bayern.' As Becker confirmed, Michael preferred to play the waiting game as he carefully pondered what was set to be a career-defining move.

Meanwhile, Manchester United's struggles both in England and in Europe threatened to undermine their bid to recruit the midfielder. Why would Michael head for Manchester if they were an inferior bet to win the Champions League than Bayern Munich who, unlike United, had started the 2005/06 season strongly at home and abroad? That was certainly the belief of Bayern chief executive Karl-Heinz Rummenigge, who was reported to have said that Michael should 'laugh' at the offer from Old Trafford, insisting Bayern were a bigger club than the faltering English side. 'I cannot imagine that he [Michael] would go to Manchester United,' Rummenigge told television channel Première. 'What do Manchester United have that Bayern Munich don't? If you take a quick look at the English table, then it seems it is nothing. If I was a player, I would not go to Manchester United under any circumstances.'

He and other Bayern officials then held four-hour showdown talks with the ambivalent midfielder in a desperate bid to persuade him to commit his future to the German giants. Michael's mind would not be made up that easily, however, as he admitted afterwards, 'I want another four to six weeks. I'm still very undecided and it's difficult when there is such a good chance of staying here. Bayern are a team very close to my heart.'

But Bayern officials were not keen on being kept in limbo and subsequently withdrew their contract offer. He now faced the first of many accusations of avarice – which he angrily denied – as it was suggested that the midfielder was holding out for a bigger salary and a much sweeter signing-on fee at Chelsea. He retorted angrily, 'It's absolutely shameless to say that. The accusation is baseless. I am just trying to leave all my options open. I like the city of Munich and Bayern are great, but there are one or two other clubs that can compete with them and it would be a great challenge to play abroad. It's been a long time since an outfield player from Germany played at a top European club.'

However, Michael Ballack was making Hamlet look decisive as he further postponed a resolution on his future until January, in accordance with FIFA rules.

And he was certainly not giving anything away about his intentions when he told a news conference, 'Foreign clubs can speak to me as of January. It would be a dream for me to play abroad but I can just as easily see myself staying at Bayern. This is my last contract. I just want time to be certain about where I want to end my career and which road I'm taking in life. My heart is with Bayern Munich. That's the reason I didn't say goodbye long ago.'

Sensing a chance to pounce, Manchester United were now, more than ever, determined to succeed in their attempts to bolster their midfield with the much sought-after German. In November, reports emanated from Old Trafford that the Reds were poised to make Michael the highest-paid player in Premiership history with an annual salary in excess of £6 million. The lavish package would have thrust him above Rio Ferdinand, then United's highest earner on £5.5 million a year, and the £5 million of Chelsea's biggest expense, Frank Lampard.

The revelations negated the widely-held view that United's American owner Malcolm Glazer was not prepared to enter into a bidding war with other heavyweight teams in the world of football. Sceptics within the media had scoffed at Glazer's paltry outlay since he'd taken control at Old Trafford and suggested that the American tycoon was unwilling to offer such a hefty salary over five years for a player nearing the twilight period of his career. United's dogged pursuit of their man, though, illustrate just how highly they viewed Michael as a possible replacement for the departed Roy Keane; someone who would add significant international class to a midfield that was looking increasingly lightweight. While players such as Wayne Rooney and Cristiano Ronaldo were bulging with potential, their relative youthfulness needed to be offset with experience and maturity, which Michael possessed in abundance. Sir Alex Ferguson was even reported to have arranged for Michael to spend a day at Old Trafford

– a tried and tested wooing process which, more often than not, brought the desired results.

According to the *Daily Telegraph*'s Mihir Bose, Franz Beckenbauer had resigned himself to losing Michael to Manchester United and suggested that the midfielder's motivations for leaving were financial. Bose quoted Beckenbauer as saying, 'We have offered him a four-year contract, a very good one. He is already the highest-paid player in Germany, but he won't sign. We don't have a Berlusconi or a Roman Abramovich at Bayern, but we are a wealthy club. The problem in Germany is the tax rate. It is more than 50 per cent, while the tax rate in Britain is much lower. Nobody in Germany talks of '*netto*' [as they do in Italy or Spain, calculating how much they get net of tax] and this puts us at a disadvantage.

'Under British tax laws, if Michael moves to Manchester United he can put all that he has so far earned in a tax-free shelter. He will only be taxed for what he earns in this country, and even then part of his income, such as bonuses and fees for his image rights, could be paid to an offshore account, as happens with many other foreign stars playing for Premiership clubs.'

Yet just when he seemed to be Manchester-bound, Sir Alex Ferguson astonishingly ruled out any potential move by declaring that he had decided that Michael was an unnecessary luxury. He said, 'We've given Michael Ballack a lot of consideration for the last few months. We knew his contract was up at Bayern Munich next summer so we spoke to his people and we've had a lot of discussions since. But the priority has always been to find someone who could replace

Roy Keane and Michael plays a different role. We need to look at other players now… players we actually need. He's a terrific player, a fabulous player, but he plays in the same area where we already have Wayne Rooney and Paul Scholes, so we've decided to rule it out.'

It seemed a strange statement in light of the hitherto persistent pursuit by United. Ferguson's assertion that United had discarded Michael from their transfer targets because they had Paul Scholes was severely undermined by the ex-England man's declining fortunes in recent seasons. What was certain now was that another high-profile transfer target had slipped through the Glaswegian's grasp, following his failure to sign a litany of luminous world footballers such as Ronaldinho, Arjen Robben and Alan Shearer.

So, with United out of the equation, a trio of leading European clubs – Chelsea, Real Madrid and Inter Milan – were left to battle it out for the signature of one of the hottest properties in European football. Real Madrid, for instance, were not officially showing their hand, but registering their interest in Bayern's maestro by proxy – through two of their stars. As detailed on Michael's official website, Ronaldo and Zinedine Zidane queued up to laud the German. Ronaldo told *Bild am Sonntag*, 'One day, Michael will knock Zidane off the throne. I consider him capable of becoming one of the truly greats at Real.'

Zidane was next to join the Michael appreciation society, enthusing in *Bild*, 'If there's someone who's got the qualities to play for Real, it's Michael Ballack.'

In 2002 Michael had spurned Real's advances in favour of a move to Munich but this time, if he were to depart the

Allianz Arena, Madrid was recommended by Franz Beckenbauer as the ideal place for him to further his career. 'I'd probably say yes to Real Madrid,' Beckenbauer told magazine *Sport-Bild*. 'They stand above all others in terms of legend. They're the ambition of every player and it was the same when I was playing.'

Meanwhile, an ex-Real Madrid favourite, Luis Figo, was wheeled out by his current club Inter Milan to flatter Michael and encourage him to test himself in another country – preferably Italy. He was quoted in *Bild am Sonntag* as saying, 'He's very talented and on the way to the very top. From my own experience, I can give him the advice to not stand in his own way, to have no fear and dare the move abroad.'

But Franz Beckenbauer reckoned Italy would not satisfy Michael's needs. He mischievously remarked, 'I do not know if Michael would have fun in the Italian league. They often have crowds as low as 7, 8 or 9,000. That's equivalent to the regional league attendances in Germany. In the Bundesliga, we have average crowds of 40,000.'

Inter Milan, however, remained in contention for Michael and could lay claim to having had three successful Germans – Jürgen Klinsmann, Lothar Matthäus and Andreas Brehme – on their books in the 1990s. Unsurprisingly, Inter owner Massimo Moratti soon admitted, 'He is a player who interests us very much. The situation is under control.' Moratti had, in fact, already expressed his admiration for Michael, in October 2002, only a matter of months after he had joined Bayern. He said at the time, 'Yes, it is true that I have an interest in Michael. I like him so much because he's, at the same time, a very good midfielder but also able in attacking situations. And it's true I would like to see him with Inter, but not in the close future. But I know that it's a very difficult negotiation because he's practically just arrived at Bayern and they usually know how to bind themselves to the big talents. Anyway, it's a dream, if you want, that could be realised not tomorrow, but in the future.'

In the spring of 2006, Moratti was alleged to have instructed Inter's vice-president Rinaldo Ghelfi and technical director Marco Branca to discuss terms with Michael's agent Michael Becker, with a four-year contract worth £3 million a season on offer. However, Moratti subsequently refuted the reports, pointing out that Inter could not match Michael's wage demands. He revealed, 'I have read things in recent days that are not true. From what I understand, it appears Michael's requirements are exorbitant and, therefore, we are not interested. This is the end of the Michael affair.'

Michael's agent Michael Becker also ruled out a switch to Milan by insisting that his client did not feel Inter could help him achieve his ultimate goal. 'Michael will continue his career with a side that will win the Champions League,' he said. 'He definitely will not go to Inter Milan. He would only move to a club where he has a better chance of winning the Champions League than at Bayern. Inter are currently third in Serie A, whereas Bayern are top in the German league.'

Becker and Ballack also batted aside rumours that suggested they had agreed a deal with another Italian side, Juventus, in January 2006. Becker said, 'We have neither had any discussions with Juventus nor signed a contract. His next contract is the most important of his career. It's not just about the financial side. The sporting aspect is very important, too.

In fact, the sporting side is the most important thing in Michael's eyes and that's why nothing has been decided yet.'

Meanwhile, Michael was continuing to stay true to form and said he would not be rushed into making a decision – although Bayern had given him a deadline of March to decide whether or not he would stay with the German champions. Given that Bayern were unlikely to match salaries on offer elsewhere, though, the European bookmakers Gamebookers.com stepped in with a last-ditch rescue offer for the German club in February 2006. The firm offered to cover the difference in wages between the money allegedly offered by Chelsea and Bayern Munich's bid in order to keep him in Germany. The unprecedented deal would have seen the company pick up the difference per week in wages to Michael, and would have made Gamebookers a key sponsor of Bayern Munich. The deal offered to Munich and Michael was similar to the revolutionary deal Gamebookers had signed at that time with Greek basketball club Aris. The company bought Vladimir Petrovic for Aris in November 2005, and pays the player's wages for the club.

John O'Malia, the chairman of Gamebookers said, 'We figured, why buy the front of a shirt when you can buy a player? Michael is the finest player of his generation in Germany, and if Bayern lose his services it would be a great loss to both Bayern and to the Bundesliga. If Bayern accept our offer, it will be the beginning of a fantastic new partnership with Munich, and to keep Michael in Germany, especially with the 2006 World Cup Finals coming up, would represent a superb achievement for sport in Germany and for Gamebookers. Furthermore, Gamebookers betters love the great football played by Bayern Munich, and we are committed to ensuring that the quality of football at Bayern and in the Bundesliga doesn't suffer at the hands of other European clubs with fatter wallets. It's our way of giving back something to the beautiful game, as well as to our punters.'

A worthy and ambitious suggestion and one that may have curried favour with Bayern and Michael, had money been the sole consideration for the midfielder.

But it seemed that no amount of cash could persuade him to stay put when the considerable enticement of an exciting challenge abroad was dangled in front of him.

Realistically, only two clubs were now left in the tussle to sign him – Real Madrid and Chelsea – both of whom were sponsored by Adidas, with whom the German had just renewed a personal contract. Michael Becker duly agreed that it was safe to assume that Ballack would play for an Adidas-equipped club. Yet the uncertainty surrounding the fortunes of the nine-times European champions Real Madrid following the sacking of coach Wanderley Luxemburgo and the resignation of president Florentino Pérez within a matter of months meant Chelsea were the more favourable of the two options. Becker confessed, 'There has been a change in the whole set-up at Real and we don't know where we stand – it's very confusing. Nothing has been signed, but there will be ongoing contact with Chelsea. There is strong interest from both sides. The trend is in this direction [to move to Chelsea]. Michael had initially been very keen on Real Madrid, but the leadership changes there in the last few months mean we don't know what's happening.'

Ballack himself confessed that his heart lay in England in an interview with the *Daily Express* in early 2006. He said, 'For me, it is the Premiership rather than La Liga. I am a very physical player and, in England, the pace is fast and the tackles are hard. If you look at the players that have become legends in England, like Patrick Vieira and Roy Keane, I see a lot of myself in players like that.'

It was now only a matter of when he made the switch to West London and dotted the I's and crossed the T's. The wheels were in motion and a seemingly interminable transfer saga was reaching a welcome dénouement as Chelsea manager Jose Mourinho confirmed his interest in the Bayern man. Mourinho had long admired Michael Ballack, even nominating him as a potential recruit when Chelsea's chief executive Peter Kenyon had mooted signing David Beckham in 2005. Now he was prepared publicly and determinedly to articulate his desire to add him to a squad already bulging with top-quality talent. 'I want him,' Mourinho told *Bild*. 'He has said he needs time before making a decision. I respect that. Now it's up to him. For me, he's one of the best players in the world. He's very intelligent, tactically very strong and he scores a lot of goals. For me, in Europe there's only Frank Lampard who plays at that level. The two would form a dream pair.'

Mourinho's admission prompted Uli Hoeness to reluctantly accept defeat in the long-running struggle to retain Michael. He said, 'The thing with Michael is over. We are busy planning for life after Michael.'

It is understood Ballack visited London on two separate occasions in January 2006, during which time he and his agent, Michael Becker, met Stamford Bridge officials as well as the coach. In the end, the irresistible marriage of money and ambition offered by Chelsea was too tempting for him to refuse. He would not have been human if he had not been swayed by the staggering weekly salary of somewhere near £130,000, a generous three-year contract and a significant signing-on fee. And given that Chelsea had agreed to switch kit suppliers to Adidas, his sponsors, Michael could expect to earn a whopping £30 million in advertising revenue and salary over four years, too.

But Michael vigorously argued that what attracted him to Chelsea more than money was that he was joining a formidable squad that was perfectly capable of helping him to fulfil one of his greatest ambitions in football – winning the Champions League. Apart from the World Cup, it was the one outstanding piece of silverware he craved above all else, having already won four Bundesliga titles and three German FA Cups in a glittering career. He had already appeared in a Champions League final for Bayer Leverkusen, but they were an unfashionable outfit – Chelsea had a more realistic chance of securing European football's Holy Grail. To be considered great, and to create a lasting legacy, he was compelled to prove himself abroad. Realistically, it was his final chance to move before age was considered a barrier by Europe's élite.

Michael said, 'I can earn well in any league, including Germany. That's not the main reason for my move. The challenge is to come and play in England. It has always been my dream to be playing abroad from the age of 22. If I had wanted to be a local hero, I would have had to stay in Chemnitz. It was just a question of where and when. In the early days, I thought of playing in the sun but the Premier League is one of the strongest in the world.'

In an interview with the German magazine *Spiegel*, he touched on many of the same sentiments. 'I want to win the Champions League. Money isn't everything. If this was about another regular in the team, nobody would be making an issue of it. A few months back, for example, Willy Sagnol [Bayern Munich's French defender] said quite openly in his contract negotiations, "Willy doesn't want more money, Willy wants *lots* more money." Nobody batted an eyelid.'

Spiegel also challenged him on his perceived 'prevaricating' over the transfer and asked him when he had actually made up his mind. Michael replied, 'The deal was finalised at the beginning of April. There was no dithering. Football is a fast-moving business. I didn't need to know in the autumn where I would be playing the following year. It's my life and my sporting future. It is my risk, and mine alone, to be out of contract... I could get injured at any time in a match or in training.'

He also disclosed in various interviews that he had turned down Manchester United as he believed that Chelsea were a superior side. The German added, 'Manchester United came in quite early for me but I saw the possibility of Chelsea being much greater. They are the stronger team. I analysed Chelsea's aims over the coming years and that attracted me. They have won the title for the last two years. This proves what a super team they are when you consider the competition there is in England. You have Liverpool, who won the Champions League last year, and Arsenal are in the final this week. It shows the strength of the Chelsea team.'

Michael admitted that the indelible experience of having played for Bayern against Chelsea in the 2005 Champions League had also fuelled his decision to come to Stamford

Bridge. 'What I remember most was the atmosphere and playing so close to the fans. It produces a great atmosphere and that's something I want to experience. Maybe I will finish my career at Chelsea,' he said. 'I have a three-year contract and so everything leads to that.'

He could certainly point to impeccable decision-making in his career, having made progress at every club he had joined. London, and its cosmopolitan culture into which Michael expected to integrate well, also appealed to the midfielder, he confessed. He yearned to be afforded some privacy in his newly-adopted country in stark contrast to his goldfish bowl existence in Germany, where his every move and utterance were scrutinised and questioned to often unbearable levels.

Bayern, meanwhile, were trying to maintain a brave face after failing to persuade Michael to remain in the Bundesliga, despite sustained pleading. But their officials were understandably seething that they had joined the ever-proliferating list of clubs whom Chelsea and billionaire owner Roman Abramovich had plundered for their assets. What compounded matters was the fact that Michael had left on a Bosman for free, with the club receiving no transfer fee and unable to prevent his departure, leaving Bayern with a massive void to fill with no recompense with which to do so.

Like an obdurate female who persistently resisted the lure of a persuasive male, they had finally, and reluctantly, succumbed to his wiles. The obvious way to register their disgust at being scorned was to castigate their prodigal son – a Bayern backlash was the obvious result. For instance, Bayern general manager Uli Hoeness launched a stinging attack on the departing star, claiming his decision to leave

Germany was motivated solely by money – despite Michael's insistence to the contrary. He said, 'It was always clear that Michael did not want to learn a new language or new culture but a new currency. It was obviously only about money. I have absolutely no animosity towards Michael but he should have been honest and said he was leaving because he wanted to earn more money.'

Bayern coach Felix Magath was also bitterly disappointed that his approaches to Michael had fallen on deaf ears. 'He had a unique position in the team that he will struggle to build up elsewhere,' said Magath. 'We said it would not be easy to move with three young children far from Lake Starnberg [Michael's former home] to a foreign city in a foreign country, and I never really imagined that Michael would go through with it.'He did, however, admit that his loss would be significant for the team. 'We need to look for a leading figure outside the club. When Michael leaves, we will lose a personality who takes responsibility. We do depend a lot on him but that does not mean we will have problems once he's gone. This is a great opportunity to take a new orientation.'

What wounded Michael more than the criticism from his former bosses, which he felt was unfounded, were the boos which cascaded down from the stands of the Allianz Arena during his final match for Bayern at home to Borussia Dortmund. He was understandably upset that some of the legions who had adored him had reacted so spitefully to the feelings whipped up about his transfer. Michael and other players who were leaving Bayern were in the midst of being presented with flowers, although along with the bouquets came brickbats galore. Uli Hoeness appealed to the crowd to stop their jeers. Michael said of his unsympathetic treatment, 'I always tried hard to do my job and that should be honoured. I want a new challenge now. I've got to accept some jeering. It shows I was an important player but it does hurt. I was not able to make a decision sooner and couldn't force a decision just because Bayern managers demanded one. There are a lot of others at Bayern who don't know whether they have a future at Bayern Munich or not. I've had a great time here and felt good with a great team that won a lot of titles.'

His true feelings at his demonisation were exposed more rawly during a frank interview with Germany's *Spiegel* magazine. When asked if he were bitter about the circumstances surrounding his departure, he replied, 'No, bitter is not the word. But leaving Bayer Leverkusen four years ago was an emotional experience, tears were shed on both sides. The lasting images I have of Bayern Munich are of the happy time with my family at Starnberger Lake, where we lived, amongst friends. From a sporting point of view, it wasn't such a bad period either. Maybe they should have made more of an effort when I arrived. But it may also be that I was reserved myself. When I played for Chemnitz, we would go out in a big gang after the match, 15 of us. At FC Kaiserslautern, there were seven of us. In Leverkusen, there were still at least three. At Bayern, it was tough going. Put it like this – it is a massive club, but one with its own laws.'

Sadly, despite his protestations to the contrary, the belief that Michael had moved to swell his own bank account pervaded Germany as a whole, and throughout the affair, *Spiegel* magazine were delighted to print Michael Ballack jokes. The jibes directed at Michael, though, were not emanating solely from Germany – pundits in England were taking pot-shots as well. The *Guardian*'s '*The Fiver*' column sardonically questioned the reasons behind his switch to the bright lights of London. 'The moment it heard about Chelsea's unveiling of Michael Ballack, *The Fiver* hot-footed it down to Stamford Bridge quicker than a German free agent offered a £2 million signing-on fee and £130,000 a week. Not because it was surprised, nor even because it cared, particularly, but because the prospect of seeing a man trying to justify swapping deification in Germany for a spot in Chelsea's crowded midfield merry-go-round without using the words "money", "big bags of" and "did I mention money?" was just too good to miss.

'"I am very happy to be here," Michael grinned. Having worked out his salary for the next three years and melted his calculator's "0" button in the process, *The Fiver* didn't need to ask why, but Michael spun us all a little story anyway. "They are very friendly people and London is a nice city, I have good impressions. Robert Huth told me good things about this country," he said, clearly unaware that his compatriot had spent more time filing his payslips and collecting medals than he had playing actual football.

'And just when we thought we'd heard enough Michael for one day, Chelsea chief exec, Slippery Pete Kenyon, popped up to explain why he thought the Germany captain had plumped for west London. "I think what we offered him at Chelsea in terms of our sporting ambitions swung it," he slimed unconvincingly, shading the pound signs in his new player's eyes from the paparazzi. And as that's the one time you'll see the words "Chelsea" and "sporting" in the same sentence, we suggest you put today's *Fiver* in your special "For Keeps" mail folder. Just like you do with every other day's *Fiver*, no doubt.'

Steve Tucker of the *Western Mail* offered an even more damning assessment of Michael's decision to join the richest club in the world. He wrote, 'It has been a week in which money has reared its ugly head in sport again, but then doesn't it always? My attention was drawn to the fact that German striker Michael Ballack will be earning £130,000 a week at Chelsea.

'Blimey, can you imagine the size of the envelope that will come in when he picks it up from the boss's office on a Thursday afternoon? Personally, I think nobody should earn £130,000 a week. I don't care if your week goes something like: Monday – found cure for cancer; Wednesday – worked out what the hell is going on in *Lost*; Friday – managed to watch Vernon Kay for five minutes without thinking homicidal thoughts...'

Tucker went on to say, 'Boy, it must be great to sit in your giant, golden house eating money, knowing most of it comes off the back of some poor chick in Indonesia stitching footballs for £2 a week. Michael gets that every time he kicks a ball. I suppose we'll have to accept that these obscene pay packets for people merely playing sports are a fact of life but, to be frank, I find the whole thing a right load of Michaels.'

When he was not being accused of being a reprehensible mercenary, he and Chelsea were the targets for the altogether less hurtful, although equally predictable snipes from the master of the mind-games, Sir Alex Ferguson. Perhaps still smarting from Michael's rejection, he poured scorn on

Chelsea's recruitment of the 29-year-old, and of Andriy Shevchenko, 30, on huge salaries – and talked up his decision to give youth a chance. 'I am producing a team that will last years,' said Ferguson sniffily. 'When you have an old team, maybe all the challenges have gone for them. But the youngsters have a hunger to achieve.'

Michael was not the only one on the receiving end of caustic comments from cynical sections of the media – Chelsea and their billionaire owner, Roman Abramovich, were also viewed as culpable in the whole affair. After making a swashbuckling, knight-in-silver-like entrance to English football in 2003, Abramovich had reinvigorated both Chelsea and the Premiership, which many believed had become stale due to a mundane and predictable two-horse race between Manchester United and Arsenal. Splashing out his roubles with carefree abandon first helped to wipe out Chelsea's debt and armed the then coach Claudio Ranieri with the tools with which to achieve Premiership glory. Ranieri failed gallantly to meet Abramovich's demands – admittedly, he was given only one season and a disparate team of international superstars to do it – and was summarily dismissed; in his stead came the flamboyant Jose Mourinho, a serial winner with Porto.

Back-to-back titles followed, along with the expensive acquisitions of Michael Ballack and then Andriy Shevchenko, as Abramovich's endless pot of money seemed set to cement Chelsea's dominance in England. But was this Russian monopoly on the crème de la crème of football talent healthy for the game? *ITV Sport*'s Ben Sanders thought not.

'His [Abramovich's] unlimited finances have created an

imbalance in the Premiership – at a time when most clubs have either gone through, or are undergoing, a recession, his side are the opposite. Quite simply, no club can match Chelsea's spending power and that makes it hard for teams to match the Blues on the pitch.

The *Daily Telegraph*'s Sue Mott was also sceptical about Chelsea's readiness to splash out cash at a whim on a galaxy of stars. Mott was not only uneasy that Michael – whose salary was the equal of a small African nation's Gross Domestic Product – would be joined by Andriy Shevchenko for £35 million at Chelsea that summer, but she was also somewhat perturbed by the West London club's decision to spend more than £15 million on untried Norwegian teenager John Obi Mikel. She wrote, 'Chelsea are beginning to look like a Christmas hamper packed by a Parisian truffle purveyor. Over-stuffed with riches... not a tower, but a team of Babel. The anticipated arrival of Andrei Shevchenko, the Ukrainian goal machine from AC Milan, at huge cost and on gargantuan wages [a rumour in 2004 put Roman Abramovich's offer at £85 million plus a salary of £225,000 a week], makes Stamford Bridge more star-studded than the pavement in Tinseltown.'

Mott went on to recall that the 1970s New York Cosmos had lavished similar gargantuan sums on top players, such as Pelé and Franz Beckenbauer, before imploding spectacularly as players' egos caused warring factions. She wondered whether Chelsea's spending could, in the 21st century, create a similar climate of destabilising greed, jealousy and 'overkill.' 'Good luck to Abramovich in a way,' she added. 'He has the adventurous recklessness of Indiana Jones in his quest for world domination. He has spent and spent and spent like one of life's lottery winners, with no demand to see a return on his investment like some creepy, rapacious chairmen and general blood-suckers, and Chelsea, to their credit, have answered his call with silverware already.

'The question is: is bigger better? For a while, the Cosmos thought it was. In 1977, they won the so-called Soccer Bowl, the season's ultimate prize, in Pelé's last season, laying on unbeatable performances in honour of the Brazilian's retirement. Pelé won, cried, sang 'All You Need Is Love' to a rapturous crowd and, a few years later, it was all gone.'

Mott's fellow *Daily Telegraph* columnist, John Inverdale, said it was a shame that both Michael and Shevchenko had joined a club that was already star-studded. He said, 'Part of me does wonder whether it wouldn't be nice if, instead of shopping in leafy Surrey during the coming season, Michael and Shevchenko were pushing trolleys round the Metro Centre having committed themselves to Newcastle, or maybe the local Morrisons if they were the new signings at Wigan. It would definitely make the next nine months a lot more interesting. Or is that taking the idea of fantasy football a little too far?'

The *Financial Times*' Jonathan Wilson suggested that 'Red Rom', as Abramovich had been branded by some tabloids, was not only exerting his financial muscles at Chelsea, but that he was also dictating the transfer policy of Jose Mourinho. He substantiated his argument by saying, 'When Mourinho arrived, he made clear that his policy would be to sign the best rising stars, players still hungry enough for success that he could mould into his pattern of play. As it turned out, the majority of his most effective players – John Terry, Claude Makelele, Frank Lampard – were already at the club but, to the extent that none were sated by success, Mourinho's philosophy held firm. Even the much decorated Makelele, after his acrimonious departure from Real Madrid, had a point to prove.

'That is not the case with Shevchenko and Michael. Both will have turned 30 by the end of September, and both have a cupboardful of medals. Neither has a history of being troublemakers but they are without question superstars of the kind Mourinho vowed never to bring to Stamford Bridge. Not surprisingly, it is widely believed that they were signed not by the manager but by Roman Abramovich, the owner. It is one of the surest things in football that when an owner starts buying players against the will of the coach, there is trouble ahead.'

Abramovich's intent was clear – by signing two global superstars in Michael Ballack and Andriy Shevchenko, he was determined to usurp Manchester United and Real Madrid as football's biggest brand. Chelsea were not about to pursue Real Madrid's one-time policy of signing 'galácticos', but their shrewd owner knew that his two new recruits could underpin an assault on global marketing supremacy. Both Michael and Shevchenko had, like other Chelsea players such as John Terry, Joe Cole and Frank Lampard, signed over a percentage of their image rights to the club. Despite Wilson's suspicions, Michael confirmed that he had struck up a friendship with the taciturn Abramovich before signing a deal at Stamford Bridge. The pair exchanged a few words in Russian because Michael had learned the language at school. They were kindred spirits, given that both grew up in the Communist era – Abramovich in the USSR and Michael in Soviet-influenced East Germany. The German also admitted he sought advice from his then national team manager Jürgen Klinsmann before opting for a move to the Premiership. Klinsmann, who had two successful spells as a player at Tottenham, warmly supported his decision to head for England.

Michael said, 'I spoke to him several times about it and he was very enthusiastic about it. He phoned me and congratulated me on this move and my new challenge at Chelsea.'

He was offered further reassurance and endorsement of his choice of club by Klinsmann's former assistant and successor as Germany coach, Joachim Löw. 'I think it is a big benefit for him to play in a different league,' he said. 'He has accomplished everything you can accomplish in Germany. He played on a very high level for the ten years he was here. Chelsea is a new challenge. It is important for every player to play in a lot of matches and I am convinced he [Michael] will be playing.' He added, 'The permanent pressure to perform and the competition at Chelsea is very positive for him.'

So, as he had done throughout his career, Michael Ballack had spectacularly divided football opinion. Some would continue to snipe that he was motivated by financial considerations following his choice of the blue shirt of Chelsea. He himself maintained a powerful argument that the quest for Champions League medals and more silverware are what he desired.

In his heart of hearts, he was always intent on moving abroad, but did not want to sever his ties with Bayern prematurely. This sensitive soul left his decision to the last minute to avoid having his final months in a red shirt sullied by the Munich faithful jeering his every move on the football pitch.

To Chelsea, or not Chelsea, that was the question that preyed on Ballack's mind for many torturous months. Hopefully for him, life at Stamford Bridge would turn out to be dramatic and fulfilling, and a long way from a tragedy on a Shakespearian scale.

8

Bridging the East-West Divide

Being successful in the public relations game is one of the necessary evils that leading footballers are expected to master in addition to excelling on the football pitch. Winning a football match comes naturally for the doyens of the beautiful game, but winning over the public can be an infinitely harder proposition. Great players are, with the possible exception of Pelé, rarely universally adored and generally divide opinion; for instance, David Beckham is a fashion icon for some people, and a pampered prima donna for others. In the case of Michael Ballack, he should, you might think, attract little negative press given his male model looks and polite, personable nature.

To most Germans, Michael is simply an outstanding footballer, adept with both feet as well as his head; in short, he is a midfielder par excellence. He is perhaps the only world-class talent Germany currently has at its disposal and, as such, you would expect him to be fêted and adored wherever he goes in his home country. However, irrespective of what he has achieved on the pitch for Germany, whether it be overcoming cramp to convert a penalty, scoring a crucial winning goal or committing a foul, some Germans will never truly respect and appreciate Michael Ballack. Why? Well, when you are reputed to be the highest-paid footballer in the world, you are bound to induce the very worst emotions – envy, bitterness and anger – in some of your fellow human beings. Furthermore, Michael continues to be viewed with suspicion in some quarters in his homeland due to circumstances beyond his control: his roots and upbringing and their subsequent impact on his personality. Indeed, one of the biggest hurdles Ballack has had to confront is the fact that he is a man of two countries – he was born in the former East Germany and is now part of a united Germany.

While Germany may be, overall, 'united', long-held prejudices continue to be harboured by many Westerners about their Eastern counterparts – despite the fall of the Berlin Wall nearly twenty years ago. The expectation that the potentially potent fusion of ruthless Western organisation, efficiency and winning mentality, and the Eastern two-footedness and socialist team ethic would create an unbeatable German football juggernaut was never quite fulfilled. While players from the East like Michael Ballack have undoubtedly enhanced the German national team, they continue to arouse contrasting reactions in the East and West. In Eastern Germany, he is the local boy made good, a throwback to the communist era in which a hugely successful sporting system, part of which was tainted by allegations of the provision of performance-enhancing drugs, readily churned out highly disciplined and skilled sports stars.

He has become an important symbol for many Easterners throughout the dismal decline of many of their own football clubs – only one East German club currently features in the Bundesliga, Energie Cottbus, while others have struggled to survive without corporate sponsorship and without many of their best players, who are readily snapped up by clubs in the West. One of Michael's former youth coaches, Joachim Müller, revealed as much when he told the *New York Times*, 'For the self-confidence of eastern Germans, which doesn't exist, it is quite important. He grew up here and was educated here and he made it.'

However, for many people who were born and brought up in the West, Ballack's Eastern heritage is anathema; he is what is known somewhat derogatorily as an 'Ossi', an East German, while they are 'Wessis'. The suspicion of some Wessis is that an Ossi like Michael is a greedy, shallow mercenary who moved to the West for the sole benefit of swelling his own wallet after living his early years in bleak impoverishment. When Michael decided to pursue his career in England with Chelsea and become the recipient of an outrageous monthly salary, it was a slap in the face for many trenchant traditionalists in Germany.

'How could someone who truly cared about Germany, who had profited from its riches and luxuries after 1989, leave the country which had nurtured him and catered for his every need in football and life?' they fumed. Michael himself has admitted that he wants more than to be 'a local hero'; in his mind, the lure of international fame and fortune, and the promise of achieving the greatest honours available to a European footballer, necessitated his move from Germany on to a more prestigious, challenging stage.

The opinion of his detractors was expressed in the meeting between the journalist John Doyle, of Globeandmail.com, and a German woman during the World Cup of 2006. He wrote, 'A woman I met here, aged about 50 and a season-ticket holder for Werder Bremen, took ages to answer my question about her opinion of Michael. "He is an Ossi," she said.'

Michael bears other perceived communist traits which are despised by some nit-picking Westerners – he is still a socialist at heart, more intent on playing for the team than leading from the front, and he is regarded as being too quiet and aloof. The cumulative toll of such deficiencies means that, for some harsh Wessi judges, he does not represent a leader like, for instance, the goalkeeper Oliver Kahn, whose huge frame is matched by an imposing personality and fiery temperament.

While Michael is an introverted Mr Nice Guy and a contented family man, Kahn resembles a raging lion with a ferocious temper, someone who has erred in his private life – he deserted his pregnant wife for a waitress. Neither has Michael flicked 'V' signs at his own supporters like the former German midfielder Stefan Effenberg did at the 1994 World Cup in the United States. Nor does he call his troops to order with sharp rebukes à la Effenberg. In summary, Michael Ballack does not fulfil many Germans' template for a football icon – he's not a macho bad boy.

One of his most savage critics has been the former West German midfielder, and now television pundit, Günter Netzer, who has constantly questioned his captaincy credentials. He has said, 'Michael will never be a leader, he has too much of that sense of the collective that comes from the East.'

However, it was a desire to put the team before himself, perhaps borne of his socialist upbringing, in the 2002 World Cup semi-final that saw Ballack championed as a possible captain in Germany. He committed a foul against South Korea which helped prevent a goal, but also resulted in him receiving a booking to rule him out of Germany's appearance in the World Cup Final against Brazil. However, following Germany's subsequent elimination in the first round of the European Championships in 2004, many German commentators, including Netzer, opined that he did not possess the leadership qualities required of a captain. Netzer then went on to castigate the German national team, which has included a number of Eastern German-born players in its side in the 21st century such as Bernd Schneider, Carsten Jancker and Alexander Zickler, for having 'no self-confidence, no courage and no creativity'.

What, if anything, does he make of these accusations? Not a lot, understandably. He is known to be sensitive to criticism, although he has frequently refused to enter into a war of words with Netzer. In one interview, he admitted, 'I was surprised that so celebrated a man could come out with such a thing and I shall leave it at that.'

So is Michael Ballack forever to be faced with the fact of his Eastern upbringing being dredged up and used as a stick with which to beat him? Perhaps not, given the radical effect the 2006 World Cup in Germany had on the German psyche, where long-standing differences between East and West were cast aside and a nation reunited behind a reborn and hugely inspiring German team under Jürgen Klinsmann's management.

From the outset, Michael was his country's leader and captain on the pitch, and his fundamental importance to Germany became evident when injury befell him prior to the opening match against Costa Rica. His calf injury became an entire country's concern – indeed, it was reported as 'the country's calf' in some German newspapers, as a nation prayed for their hero to regain fitness.

'This is a sign of progress,' said Pierre Gottschlich, a political scientist at the University of Rostock, in the *New York Times,* about how the incident changed the perception of Michael. 'Think about it as a game played on certain levels. We've gone from the first level, where everybody thinks of him as East German, to the second level, where some see him as East German and others don't, and we're getting to the next level, where it doesn't matter at all. Probably in another 10 or 20 years, we'll get there.'

He duly became the figurehead of the German football team's extraordinary renaissance under Klinsmann as they powered to an unlikely semi-final appearance through a combination of swashbuckling attacking football and their legendary resolve. Although patently not at his best throughout the competition, he played a stirring captain's part when, despite suffering the ravages of cramp, he stepped up to score a penalty and help his country to a 4–2 victory in the shootout over Argentina in the quarter-finals.

Germany not only included Eastern Germans like Michael, but also two prodigious forwards in Miroslav Klose and Lukas Podolski, who were both born in Poland. Klinsmann was soon being acclaimed a master tactician just months after his decision to base himself in America was heavily criticised by the media and German public alike.

Suddenly, few Germans cared where their heroes were born or brought up, or where they lived; they were merely delighted that their moribund team had been revived and had spectacularly returned to winning ways. The knock-on effect of the national team's World Cup odyssey on Germans' morale and sense of patriotism was profound; the national anthem was sung more lustily than ever before, and black, red and gold flags proliferated and fluttered proudly on balconies and in the hands of frenzied fans. For the first time since 1989 perhaps, Germans unashamedly celebrated their identity and rediscovered all that was good about their country. Scores of visitors to Germany for the World Cup have remarked with a degree of surprise how warm and friendly the Germans' welcome was.

Yet perhaps the most remarkable transformation in Germany during the World Cup was that some sceptical Westerners were suddenly worshipping a man they had previously reviled – Michael Ballack. At long last, he was not derided as a lazy, greedy, good-for-nothing Ossi, but a celebrated German. Ballack had become a tangible success story of German reunification along with Germany's chancellor, Angela Merkel. Merkel had defeated Helmut Kohl and Gerhard Schröder, the formidable duo of West German politics, and acted as Germany's supporter-in-chief during the World Cup.

Meanwhile, in 2005, another East German politician, Matthias Platzeck, became head of Germany's Social

Democrats party, prompting the German tabloid *Bild* to declare: 'THE OSSIS ARE OUR NEW BOSSIS!' A bold statement, which may be seen as crass in the former East Germany, given many Ossis' ongoing financial struggles, although it served to illustrate that Michael Ballack and other Easterners were emblems of the continuing optimism of German reunification. Yet Ballack knows that if he ever lets his standards slip, Ossi references will be wheeled out again by a fickle public.

Some things never change.

9

National Service

As a play-making midfielder in the German national team, Michael Ballack could easily be cowed by the spectres of some legendary footballers of yesteryear who represented his country in the midfield with dash and distinction. Their names readily trip off the tongue – Franz Beckenbauer, Günther Netzer, Paul Breitner, Bernd Schuster, Lothar Matthäus, Andreas Möller, Stefan Effenberg and Matthias Sammer, among others, who all earned national and international renown for their dominance of the middle of the pitch.

Emulating their awe-inspiring achievements would induce panic and fear in most German midfielders, but Ballack is a singular exception. The way he struts around majestically on a football pitch, head held aloft, is finesse personified, evoking comparisons with Franz Beckenbauer and earning him the 'Little Kaiser' alias. Ballack plays as if he has no inferiority complex about his midfield lineage and is undaunted by the brilliance of the luminaries who shone before him; he knows he is good and can do everything required of him with consummate ease, whether it be striding into the penalty box to score with a savage shot or thumping header, the tenacious tackling of a dangerous opponent or splitting a defence with a deft pass. For some people, his immense confidence in his ability borders on arrogance and testifies to a swollen ego; as such, German team-mate Christian Ziege hit out at 'big-headed' Michael during a high-profile feud during the 2000 European Championships. 'He acts like he has nothing left to learn and thinks he's a world champion already,' Ziege allegedly said.

While Michael would refute this, he would surely admit that he is not exactly lacking in self-belief. He may be shy and retiring at heart and does not actively cultivate the media limelight, but he is bold and brash enough to have chosen the number 13 shirt for his country. Most German footballers would be reticent about the 'unlucky' number, never mind the fact that this shirt was once worn by the incomparable German goal-machine Gerd Müller and the languid legend that is Franz Beckenbauer.

However, by virtue of his birthright, Ballack could have been playing for East Germany and avoided comparisons with a myriad of marvellous midfielders from the past, had German reunification not taken place in 1990. By then, the West had started to sit up and take notice of his precocious talents which, when he was 20 and plying his trade for Chemnitzer FC, warranted exposure on the international stage for *Der Nationalmannschaft* (the national team). He was duly picked for the German Under-21s by coach Hannes Löhr on 26 March 1996 and played the full 90 minutes in a 0–0 home draw with Denmark.

A little over a year later and he scored his first goal for the Under-21s on 1 April 1997 in Germany's 4–0 win in Albania. In total, he scored 4 goals in 19 appearances for the Under-21s, starring in Germany's 7–0 thrashing of Lebanon in Beirut, where he scored twice in September 1997.

However, reputations are not carved out in comfortable wins over lowly opposition – they are created in the white-hot atmosphere of meaningful, competitive supremacy. To this end, Ballack's appearance in the UEFA Under-21 European Championship Trophy in May 1998 was a more credible examination of his international credentials. He was part of the Germany squad, which lost 1–0 to Greece in the quarter-finals of the tournament in Bucharest, and made his two final appearances for the Under-21s in their consolation victories over the hosts Romania and Sweden.

It is worth noting that he and Torsten Frings are the only two members of Germany's European Championship squad who are currently regulars in the full German side. While many of the youngsters who represented Germany at this level would fall by the wayside, Ballack's considerable gifts would ensure his national team lifespan would be long and fruitful.

At the age of 22, he had outgrown the Under-21s and was now mature enough and clearly of sufficient ability to represent the full German national side. While at Kaiserslautern, he was brought into the Germany squads of Berti Vogts who, in September 1998, invited Michael and his FC Kaiserslautern team-mate, Marco Reich, to join Germany during their preparations for games against Malta and Romania. However, it was not until 28 April 1999 that he made his début for his country.

It was an inauspicious beginning for him as he replaced the Liverpool midfielder Dietmar Hamann after 60 minutes of Germany's home defeat to Scotland in Bremen. To compound matters, the floodlights failed during the match, although thankfully this has not proved to be a bad omen for the rest of his international career. He would have to wait three months before making another appearance in the white shirt of his country, after sustaining a knee injury, and it was another instantly forgettable occasion for him.

Germany were drubbed 4–0 by Brazil in the Confederations Cup – a competition involving the champions of all six continents, the World Cup hosts and World Cup holders – in Guadalajara, Mexico, with Michael playing the full 90 minutes. In the next match, he replaced the legendary Lothar Matthäus after 71 minutes against New Zealand, which the Germans won 2–0. Thankfully for Michael, he did not feature in Germany's third match in the tournament, a 2–0 defeat to the USA.

He would have to wait until March 2000 for his next taste of international action, when Germany drew 1–1 in Croatia. He was now a well-established international, and was named in Germany's squad for the European Championships taking place in Holland and Belgium. However, Germany were a shadow of the great teams of the past, and heavily reliant on ageing talents such as the 39-year-old Lothar Matthäus and Thomas Hassler. Yet for Michael, this was an excellent opportunity to serve notice of his youthful promise alongside another fledgling midfield talent, Sebastian Deisler.

It was Deisler whom he replaced after 72 minutes of Germany's second group game in the European Championships, against England, for whom Alan Shearer scored the only goal of the match. Michael had not played in Germany's opening game, a 1–1 draw with Romania, but was handed a starting spot against Portugal. However, it was another hugely dispiriting day for both Michael and Germany as the Portuguese, who fielded a second-string side without the likes of Luis Figo, Rui Costa and Vitor Baia, having already qualified for the next round, cantered to a 3–0 victory.

Michael was replaced at half-time by the Brazilian-born Paulo Rink, although was perhaps pleased that he was able to escape further humiliation by watching from the substitutes' bench. All in all, he had only played 63 minutes in the tournament in which a dire Germany achieved their worst performance for 50 years by being eliminated at the first stage. What's more, they had failed to register a single win and scored only one goal. He would later moan that the disastrous tournament had 'brought him nothing' on a personal level which, given Germany's own demise, seemed an egotistical statement at the time. He was further lambasted for the enormity of his ego by team-mate Christian Ziege, at that time a Spurs player, who, according to the *Observer*'s Simon Kuper, hit out at Michael after being scythed down by his heavy challenge during training.

Kuper reported that Ziege had said, '"You can't tell him anything any more. He's already a world champion." Asked about this, Michael said Ziege was just angry because of a tackle at training. "I mowed him down. He said, 'Are you crazy?' I said, 'Shut up, what do you want?'" None of the criticism has unsettled Michael.'

These were dark days indeed for Germany, who had slumped to a nadir in their illustrious history. Not surprisingly, Michael and his team-mates received the proverbial roasting in the German media, with daily newspaper *Bild* refusing to hand out a rating for any player and saying instead, 'Even *Bild* is lost for words.' The paper managed to find enough words, though, to have a go at the team through several stark headlines, including YOU'RE EUROPE'S FOOTBALL TWITS and GERMANY IS ASHAMED OF YOU!'

The tabloid further savaged their under-achieving team by borrowing the scathing English media's comparison of embattled manager Graham Taylor in 1994 to a turnip by publishing a photograph of French maestro Zinedine Zidane alongside a *bratwurst*. '*This is a footballer*' read one caption; the other said: '*This is a German international*'.

According to Rainer Holzschuh, the editor-in-chief of Germany's leading soccer magazine *Kicker*, the entire Germany squad deserved to be dropped, save two or three players, including Michael. He told German television, 'If they don't change something fast, if we don't get completely new players – regardless of whether they can play better football, they have to show more heart – then Germany will for years be a second-rate team or even worse.' Unsurprisingly, German coach Erich Ribbeck acknowledged his part in this sorry mess and resigned, leaving Rudi Völler to administer urgent remedial work on a bruised, battered and below-par squad.

Michael's growth as one of the most influential German

footballers of his generation, and the central role he played in Germany revival – which culminated in a World Cup renaissance in 2002 – is detailed in a later chapter. His heroics in Japan and South Korea had marked him out as pivotal to Germany's strategy in their bid to qualify for the 2004 European Championships, which were held in Portugal. To get there, the Germans faced Lithuania, the Faroe Islands, Scotland and Iceland, a group they were expected to top through without much difficulty. However, they would still not be acclaimed as a great side, according to the *Daily Telegraph*'s Henry Winter, who wrote, 'Germany will doubtless win a lightweight group, but their presence at Number 4 in the world rankings hardly reflects well on global standards. Völler is in charge of the most modest German side in modern memory, who relied on a fortuitous draw and an exceptional goalkeeper to reach last summer's World Cup final. Michael Ballack, when fit, has class. So, to a lesser extent, do Torsten Frings and Kahn (and the absent Dietmar Hamann, Sebastian Deisler, Christian Ziege and Christophe Metzelder) but it is hard to remember many more limited strikers than (Fredi) Bobic, Miroslav Klose and Oliver Neuville, whose collected strengths would not equal one Rummenigge.'

Michael was on target in Germany's opening game, a 2–0 win in Lithuania, and was then rubbing his hands with glee at the prospect of confronting the group minnows, the Faroe Islands, in the Germans' next encounter.

'We really ought to score seven or eight goals,' insisted Bayern Munich chairman and former German striker, Karl-Heinz Rummenigge, who somewhat disdainfully suggested that the Faroes ought to be excluded from the European Championships to avoid embarrassing mismatches. He declared, 'There are no longer any great qualifying moments. When Germany play the Faroe Islands, it's like a bone without meat.'

Most people in Germany were similarly blasé about the threat, or lack of it, that the Faroes were likely to pose. For example, one daily newspaper in Germany printed a photograph of an idyllic village in the Faroes and posed the slightly condescending question: 'WE'RE SUPPOSED TO BE SCARED OF THIS?' This over-confidence also owed much to the fact that the multi-million pound national team would be taking to the field against a part-time outfit comprised of carpenters, ice-cream salesmen and teachers.

Michael, who recovered from a bout of 'flu to play in the match, insisted, 'We will have to work hard for the first goal, but after that the match should run its course.'

When such utterances are made, it is often inevitable that the underdog will be stirred to compete gamely against its crowing rival. The Faroes had recently proved that they were far from being the whipping boys of world football by holding Scotland to a 2–2 draw at home. And they made a mockery of the patronising pre-match sniping by putting up a game struggle against Germany in Hanover, losing only 2–1 – Michael scoring the Germans' first goal from the penalty spot.

A more demanding proposition for the German maestro was his country's trip to Scotland in June 2003. After receiving intensive treatment from three physiotherapists, Ballack recovered from a calf injury which had plagued him for seven weeks, much to the delight of German coach, Rudi Völler, who said, 'Michael has showed with Bayern that he is back to his best and I hope he can put up a great performance for us and maybe score a goal or two. This the most important game of the year for us.'

It was a tussle which had extra spice for Michael, given that the Scots were managed by his former coach at Bayer Leverkusen, the former Germany coach Berti Vogts. Vogts and Michael had become estranged at Leverkusen, with the former branding Michael an under-achiever who ought to do more for the team. Three years on, Vogts was fulsome in his praise of Ballack in an attempt to avoid any recriminations, calling Michael 'the best attacking midfielder in Europe'. But Michael had not forgotten his unhappy period under Vogts' tenure.

He said, 'I don't want to hang out any dirty laundry, but I don't have to keep secret that some Leverkusen players had a problem with him. Some players want to prove something to him – me, too. Working together with him was difficult from the start.'

At least Michael had won the confidence of German manager, Rudi Völler, who showered yet more plaudits on his talisman, enthusing, 'What Zinedine Zidane is for France, Michael is for us. He's developed into a team leader and a deadly scorer.' Yet he was still not able to boss a match as masterfully as Zidane, and was hugely disappointing in the tame 1–1 draw in Scotland, admitting that he and his team-mates had been somewhat intimidated by the famed Hampden Roar.

While he was not stamping his authority enough on the pitch, he was certainly making his presence felt away from it.

He demanded a dramatic improvement in the quality of the team's play after the Scotland match, commenting, 'Some of the players must realise what it means to play for Germany and act accordingly. At the moment, we are not able to dominate our opponents when we're playing away from home. Scotland were one of the weakest teams we played recently and look what happened.'

Meanwhile, Germany's former World Cup-winning captain and coach, Franz Beckenbauer, said Michael and Germany had worryingly regressed after their strong showing at the 2002 World Cup. He commented, 'We're back to where we were before the World Cup. The World Cup was exceptional because Rudi Völler managed to make that team really fit. To me, that was the key to our success.'

Germany could not respond to Michael's clarion call and Beckenbauer's disapproving words, and struggled to beat the Faroe Islands 2–0 away in their next match, before stumbling to a dismal 0–0 draw in Iceland in their next Euro 2004 qualification game. The subsequent virulent media reaction in Germany prompted a furious tirade from German coach Rudi Völler, who warned that he would consider resigning if berated in such a fashion again. He told ARD Television, 'I'm not going to put up with this for long. I can't stand to hear this crap any more about "another low point" and "another lower point" for German football. You are all talking as if we should have come here and blown them away 5–0. I have to defend myself and the team against those who are dragging us into the mud.

'The performance today was not in order... but we didn't lose. We were fortunate to come away with a draw. It was naturally not enough. We're not scoring enough goals, but it's a load of crap the way we're being criticised by the commentators here. I'm not like Erich Ribbeck and Berti Vogts. I'm not going to cling on to my job here. It's not worth it for me.'

Michael's penalty in a 2–1 home win over a plucky Scotland side, who had Maurice Ross sent off in a tempestuous encounter, pushed the Germans nearer a place in the Finals and kept a disgruntled Rudi Völler happy for the time being.

He scored again in Germany's final group game, a comfortable 3–0 win over Iceland, which completed the qualification formality as the Germans progressed as group winners. On a personal level, Ballack could be fairly satisfied with his own performances during the qualification phase, which had been embellished by four goals. In spite of this, Germany's lacklustre qualification form did not bode well for their bid to restore themselves to a championship side of repute in 2004. Michael was also playing down his side's chances of success, saying, 'Of course we want to play a prominent role at the European Championships and challenge for the title if at all possible. But at the moment, I don't see us being one of the top contenders. We are just not at the stage where we can say we are going out on the pitch to become European or world champions. In order to do this, we need to grow together more as a team and also have our top players back from injury.'

It was a fair assessment from him, given that Germany had made heavy going of a fairly easy qualification group which did not comprise any of the world's leading countries. To consolidate his world-class standing, he recognised that he would need to produce the goods against a better standard of opposition. So, when European champions France visited Germany in November 2003, it was a perfect opportunity for the midfielder to measure himself against the world's most accomplished midfield operator, Zinedine Zidane, who had come out of retirement for the French to galvanise the bid to retain their European crown.

However, it was ultimately no contest on both counts – the marvellous French inflicted a 3–0 beating on Germany, which was an emphatic indicator of how far the Germans had plummeted in world football since their last major trophy triumph, at the 1996 European Championships. Michael, too, was largely anonymous, like the rest of his hapless team-mates.

As 2004 began, Germany opted to warm up for the European Championships by taking on perceived lesser opposition. The ploy worked a treat in March, against Belgium, as Michael found the net in Germany's 3–0 stroll in Cologne. He then continued his scoring streak by bagging four goals in a 7–0 mauling of Malta in May.

However, sandwiched in between these hollow victories was a 5–1 drubbing by Romania in Bucharest, although he missed out due to injury, which was Germany's worst defeat since they lost by the same scoreline in 2001 to England.

Germany had responded to this collapse by reaching the World Cup Final of 2002, so no one could accurately predict how they would fare in Euro 2004 given their wildly inconsistent form – good in one game, pitiful the next.

In their two final friendly matches before the tournament kicked off, Switzerland were seen off 2–0 in Basel, before Hungary – managed by the German icon Lothar Matthäus –

triumphed by the same scoreline in Rudi Völler's 50th match in charge of the Germans.

So, how did Michael assess his chances of success in Euro 2004, in which Germany were in the proverbial 'Group of Death' – Group D – along with bitter rivals Holland, championship newcomers Latvia and the ever-dangerous Czech Republic? He told the *Guardian*, 'Our 5–1 defeat by Romania recently was a serious setback to our preparation. I'm sure we can reach at least the quarter-finals, though. There's no point going to Portugal otherwise. The last World Cup showed what we can do if we put our minds to it. But maybe we haven't got the class of a France or an Italy.'

Yet when he was asked in a separate interview about who in the Germany squad could emerge as a possible star of the tournament, himself excepted, his reply of Philipp Lahm, the young Stuttgart full-back, was a damning indictment of the dearth of quality the Germans possessed in a creative sense. The halcyon days of the German national team saw an array of talented, inspiring footballers – men like Jürgen Klinsmann, Karl-Heinz Rumenigge, Gerd Müller and Uwe Seeler – but their names and achievements had been replaced by mediocrity, apart from Michael and a handful of others.

Germany were now pinning their hopes on Kevin Kuranyi, a Brazilian-born striker with a German father, and Fredi Bobic, meaning Michael would be even more important alongside fellow midfielder, the gifted but unpredictable Bastian Schweinsteiger. Hardly reasons to inspire confidence, yet Germany have a habit of surviving on their famed iron will and mental fortitude when their morale is flagging and quality is lacking. And they have an uncanny ability to transform themselves from a stuttering second-hand car to a well-oiled, efficient outfit, capable of gaining momentum as they negotiate the competition stage by stage. The current German side, though, could not always rely on the great strength in depth of yesteryear, as Euro 2000 bore testimony when their lamentable lack of class was brutally exposed. Their opening group game against Holland was either the perfect way to commence a tournament, for some Germans, given the galvanising historical significance the clash has, or the worst possible start, given the sheer class of the brilliant Dutch.

Michael and his men had been given extra incentive to defeat the Dutch after Holland's striker Ruud van Nistelrooy declared, 'This is not just about football history. It's about real history and what happened 60 years ago.'

Many Germans felt that van Nistelrooy had needlessly dredged up the past, referring to the bitter legacy of the Nazi occupation of the Netherlands during World War II. Germany therefore fought tigerishly to secure a richly deserved 1–1 draw with the Dutch, with Michael on top of his game. While the rest of the battling Germans relied on robust tackling and stolid defending to cope with their more talented opponents, Ballack oozed class, sauntering around the pitch with cocksure confidence, exuding effortless grace and immeasurable influence.

'How easily that boy plays,' enthused Holland's Wesley Sneijder afterwards as Michael stole the show in a Man of the Match masterclass. Aleksandrs Starkovs, coach of Germany's next opponents Latvia, was similarly impressed, commenting, 'Michael is a really excellent player and he could be very dangerous. He was the best player on the pitch against the Dutch.'

While in 2002, game by game he had grown in stature in the World Cup. Here he was doing what all world-renowned players should do – displaying his lavish gifts from the outset and laying down the gauntlet to his peers. His personal achievement was less of a priority to the midfielder than team success, though, as he admitted after the Holland match. 'It is nice to be named Man of the Match, but I would have preferred the three points. But it was a team effort and I dedicate this award to all the other players in the German squad.' He admitted that even he was bemused at Germany's innate strength in the cut-and-thrust of competition, adding, 'We know other teams have respect for us. But I cannot explain this tournament team phenomenon. One for all and all for one. The only way we can be successful is if we are a team.'

That team spirit, however, did not materialise in the next match against European Championships débutants, Latvia. Despite laying siege to the Latvian goal, Germany were unable to score against the group outsiders, who battled bravely to secure a 0–0 draw. With Germany coach Rudi Völler attempting to maximise the scoring instincts of Michael by employing him behind strikers Miroslav Klose and Kevin Kuranyi, the Germans should have breached their opponents' rearguard at least once. Yet their inability to find the net meant that a win for Germany was vital against the Czech Republic if they were to advance to the quarter-finals of the tournament.

Fortunately, Ballack had not lost his scoring touch and gave Germany the lead against the Czechs with an outstanding shot with his left foot from 20 yards in the 21st minute. Sadly, the rest of the German team were unable to match his level of performance on the pitch, and Germany crashed to a 2–1 defeat to the under-strength Czechs, who rested most of their first-team squad.

The *Guardian*'s Michael Walker wrote, 'Michael Ballack once again pointed up Germany's general deficiency. They simply lack Ballacks and the glaring inadequacies of those picked to score goals for Germany was exposed here almost as much as against Latvia.' Walker went on to pose a question which preyed on the minds of other football devotees, particularly those of German extraction, after the one-time powerhouse of world football tumbled out of the European Championships at the first hurdle for the second successive time. 'Whatever happened to German football? Less than two years after they reached a World Cup Final against Brazil, Germany were sent home from Euro 2004 by the Czech Republic B team. Germany scored two goals over the course of three games and did not win one of them. Though that is an improvement on Euro 2000 when they scored one in three games, losing to England and, embarrassingly, 3–0 to a weakened Portugal, this defeat provides fresh despair.

'Germany host the next World Cup and their pride is hurt by this. They have now not won a match at the European Finals since beating the Czechs 2–1 at Wembley in Euro '96 and wanted to set down a marker for 2006. But this will be their last competitive fixture until then and that is a long time to reflect.'

At least Ballack had further confirmed his world-class credentials. It did leave you wondering, though, just how much he could achieve if he were surrounded by players of comparable ability and mental strength. He went some way to achieving this, through UEFA's hypothetical all-star Euro 2004 squad, while statistics experts Opta also indulged in some fantasy football and pencilled his name into its dream team of the tournament. Opta included him in a four-man midfield, along with other leading lights of European football: Deco, Zinedine Zidane and Luis Figo. A mouth-watering proposition indeed – some saw it as a pity that Michael Ballack was plying his trade along more prosaic players such as Jens Jeremies. At least he offered the Germans a beacon of hope for the future, which including Germany's hosting of the 2006 World Cup.

He said, 'We have to look to the future. We have to work harder in view of the World Cup at home in 2006. I can't make any accusations against anyone. We all worked hard but it wasn't good enough.'

The fading superpower, Germany – branded 'one of the worst teams in their history' by BBC Sport's Phil McNulty – would have to prepare for the 2006 World Cup with a new coach after Rudi Völler unsurprisingly tendered his resignation just hours after their abysmal showing against the Czechs. At least whoever had the unenviable task of rebuilding a demoralised, ineffectual squad could count on Ballack and be encouraged that a number of youngsters – namely Philipp Lahm, Lukas Podolski and Bastian Schweinsteiger – had international experience under their belts which stood them in excellent stead for the world's premier footballing competition. What Germany desperately needed now was a bright, inspirational figure to herald a fresh, new dawn and consign the all-prevailing feeling of failure to history.

Enter Jürgen Klinsmann.

Germany had reputedly wanted the more experienced and battle-hardened German coaches Otto Rehhagel – he had just led Greece to an astonishing European Championship triumph and had coached Michael at FC Kaiserslautern – or Ottmar Hitzfeld, to assume control of the national team, but both refused the poisoned chalice. Instead, they were left with little option but to gamble on the inexperienced yet effervescent Klinsmann, winner of the World Cup in 1990 and the European Championships in 1996. It was a universally popular choice in Germany as Klinsmann's seemingly perpetual sunny disposition, earning him the nickname 'Grinsi Klinsi', was exactly what a despondent German side, short on confidence and struggling for salvation, needed.

However, in some quarters it was also viewed as an extremely risky and controversial appointment given that Klinsmann had absolutely no coaching experience and was based in California, two apparently insurmountable obstacles, according to some, that would be used as a stick to beat him with whenever Germany lost or struggled before the World Cup. Klinsmann also tested the patience of many critics when he suggested that the best model for Germany and Michael to follow was Holland, their country's greatest rival, apart from England.

On the flip side, Klinsmann was exactly what Germany and its stale and tired régime and brow-beaten players required – he had a radical vision for reform, implemented a modern, attack-minded playing style, preached the benefits of psychological training and introduced innovative fitness programmes. Michael Ballack was particularly enamoured of the German Football Association's choice given that, not long

Ballack is introduced to the media after he signs for Chelsea, May 2006.
© *Cleva*

Above: With his manager Jose Mourinho.   © *Empics*

Below: With the 2006-07 Chelsea team, UEFA Champions League match vs PFC Levski Sofia, December 2006.
                                                           © *Cleva*

Germany's 2006 World Cup campaign.

Above left: Michael Ballack, captain of the German national team, and his teammates Miroslav Klose and Oliver Neuville celebrate their 1–0 win over Poland in the group stages of the World Cup.

© *Cleva*

Above right, and below left and right: The captain battles with all his heart in the World Cup semi-final against Italy – an extremely tightly fought match which Germany ultimately lost 2–0 after goals in the final minutes of extra time.

© *Cleva/Empics*

Michael Ballack is visibly devastated after Germany's defeat in the semi-final of the World Cup.   © Cleva

Above: Michael Ballack at the welcome party for the German football team, Berlin September 2006. Despite scoring no goals in the World Cup, Ballack successfully led his team to third place and was nominated as one of the players of the tournament.

© *Stefan Krempl / WENN*

Below left: In pre-season training with Chelsea in Los Angeles.   © *Empics*

Below right: Andriy Shevchenko and Michael Ballack at the 'Hit the Ground Running Party' which was hosted by Chelsea FC and Adidas clothing to celebrate their new partnership, July 2006.

© *Jody Cortes / WENN*

Above left: Michael Ballack in action in the Champions League match vs Werder Bremen, September 2006.
© Cleva

Above right: Ballack marks Celtic's Evander Sno in a pre-season friendly.
© Cleva

Below: On the bench alongside Chelsea's Frank Lampard and Ashley Cole.
© Empics

Michael Ballack scores his first goal for Chelsea in the Champions League group stage match vs Werder Bremen at Stamford Bridge with a penalty.

© *Cleva*

after he was appointed, Klinsmann bestowed on him the greatest honour in football – the captaincy of his country, a role previously held by goalkeeper Oliver Kahn. The German coach invited Michael into his hotel room prior to Germany's first match after the European Championships, against Austria in August 2004, and informed him of his decision.

'He said that I would be his captain and that he had great confidence in and huge expectations of me,' recalls Michael of one of his proudest moments in football. He was the logical choice for such an esteemed position given that he was Germany's best and most respected player among his peers. Although Oliver Kahn offered a more pugnacious and authoritative presence, his advancing years meant that his international career was coming to an end. Furthermore, there was always the argument that he might often struggle to influence proceedings from his goal line.

Michael, on the other hand, might not lead by clenched-fist exhortations, but he could set an impeccable example through his on-pitch demeanour – cool, calm, collected and invariably stylish and skilful. He was also nearer the age of many of the younger German players, unlike Kahn, making interaction that much easier.

Klinsmann said of the appointment, 'I wanted as the captain an outfield player who was in contact with all members of the team. Michael is exactly the link-man I had imagined. I spoke with both players about this and both accepted the decision. Oliver Kahn will deputise for Michael in future.'

After installing Michael as his captain, Klinsmann set about revamping his predictable team's playing style, advocating a 4-1-3-2 formation with a high defensive line and encouraging high-tempo, aggressive pressing of the ball. Germany were encouraged to attack at every opportunity and pin their opponents in their own half.

Klinsmann said, 'We identified an attacking style, an aggressive style, getting the ball as fast as possible to the strikers and attacking midfielders.'

While the new tactics carried great risk, given that the high-defensive line would make Germany vulnerable to counter-attacks, for Klinsmann they represented the best chance of giving his under-fire strikers an opportunity to score. However, the strategy required great stamina, traditionally one of Germany's great strengths, although this was no longer the case, as Klinsmann discovered when he conducted fitness tests on his squad in the autumn of 2004 and ascertained that his players were struggling to compete with players from other European leagues.

It was clear that he had a serious job on his hands, particularly as there was one other major factor to be considered – the current German team was not richly stocked with fantastic talents like the ones Germany had consistently produced in the past. Ken Early of Ireland's *Village* magazine attempted to rationalise Germany's plight as follows: 'Nobody really knows why this has happened. Some point to Germany's declining birth rate, now the lowest in Europe at 8.5 births per 1,000 inhabitants (the equivalent figure for Ireland is 15.2). Michael's home town, Chemnitz (formerly Karl-Marx-Stadt), has the lowest birth rate of anywhere in the world. However, Germany is still the most populous country in Europe with 82 million people. The DFB claims to be the world's largest sports organisation, with 6.3 million members, including 2 million children. There are still plenty of players, they're just not as good as they used to be.

'Another explanation has been suggested by 1997 Tour de France champion Jan Ullrich and former Olympic swimming star Franziska van Almsick. Like Michael, both Ullrich and van Almsick spent their formative years in Communist East Germany. They believe that German youth is now too plump and pampered to face the pain that is the price of sporting success. 'They go to play soccer but the first time they get kicked in the shins, they quit,' says van Almsick. 'Sport is about fighting back through setbacks, but today's generation is an easy-going generation. No one sticks with it any more.'

In spite of Germany's perceived deficiencies, the Klinsmann era began promisingly, with a 3–1 win over Austria, inspired by a hat-trick from Kevin Kuranyi. A 1–1 draw with Brazil provided further grounds for German optimism, before wins against Iran, Cameroon and Japan were notched up before the end of the year. Klinsmann's winning streak was ended, though, in December when Germany met the team they had beaten in the 2002 World Cup, South Korea.

Ballack repeated his goal of that infamous occasion, although the fired-up South Koreans responded by hitting the net three times to gain revenge for their elimination from their home tournament. He then missed an 85th-minute penalty and the game eventually finished in a 2–2 draw. He was unavailable due to injury for Germany's next two matches, a 5–1 defeat of Thailand and a creditable 2–2 draw with Argentina, although he returned for his country's 1–0 win in Slovenia in March 2005.

Michael said of the latter encounter, 'The match was

chaotic, it wasn't good at all. Our defence wasn't well organised and that shouldn't happen. We should have gone ahead 2–0 and then things would have been easier.' He was then instrumental in Germany's 4–1 dismantling of Northern Ireland in Belfast, in June 2005, scoring twice in a commanding Man of the Match display.

Following this, he was included in the German squad for the Confederations Cup, which was being held in Germany in the summer of 2005 and therefore provided a tantalising precursor to the next year's World Cup. In the self-styled mini-World Cup featuring eight countries in two groups, Germany were paired with Australia, Argentina and Tunisia in Group A, from which two winners would progress to the semi-finals and then a final. A disappointing showing could have been devastating for the World Cup hosts, whose form and organisation of a tournament were under intense scrutiny. Michael, too, knew that he had to raise his game to compete against the likes of Ronaldinho, Robinho and Ronaldo for Brazil and Riquelme, Tevez and Crespo of Argentina.

According to one leading coach taking part in the tournament, he was on a par with the Brazilian participants. Brazil's coach Carlos Alberto Parreira gave the following ringing endorsement: 'In my opinion, only Michael Ballack comes close to having a Brazilian's class. Michael has a marvellous mixture of wonderful skills on the ball and strength in man-against-man situations. Germany won't be in with much of a chance if we shut out Michael Ballack.'

Germany survived a late fightback from Australia in their opening game, which they eventually won 4–3, with Michael scoring a 60th-minute penalty and earning the Man of the

Match award in the process. German tabloid *Bild* was unimpressed, however, commenting, 'We will not win the World Cup with performances such as this. We need to improve a lot just to win the Confederations Cup.' But they had to wait until the 74th-minute of their next game against Tunisia to break the deadlock, thanks to another penalty from Michael, and another two late goals saw them run out 3–0 winners.

'We are very disciplined and patient,' said Michael, of his country's comfortable win. 'It was a hard match. We missed our early chances but we tried to keep the pace quick. Maybe they got tired at the end.'

He was then rested for Germany's final group game, an entertaining 2–2 draw against Argentina, which proved that the Germans could survive without their inspirational skipper. Germany had finished ahead of the Argentinians in their group, but were presented with an equally rigorous examination of their World Cup credentials in the semi-final, where the then holders of the Jules Rimet trophy, Brazil, lay in wait.

Despite the outstanding quality of the opposition, Michael was full of confidence, insisting, 'We want that final on Wednesday. We are in good shape and believe we can beat them. We want this cup. There's a lot of belief in this squad – we are confident, even if the opponent is Brazil.'

Jürgen Klinsmann added that Michael's influence could be pivotal, saying, 'We are hoping for Michael to control our game, to set the pace and to ensure the balance between defence and offence.'

Once again, Germany and Michael appeared inspired by

their home advantage in Nuremberg, twice equalising Brazilian goals in the opening 50 minutes – the second courtesy of another Ballack penalty. However, Brazil proved stronger in the second half of a pulsating encounter and finally emerged 3–2 winners, thanks to Adriano's second goal of the game in the 76th-minute.

A disconsolate Michael believed that Germany's convincing performances in the tournament illustrated that they were narrowing the gap on the leading nations. He said, 'We don't have quite enough at the moment to beat the really big teams in the world. Perhaps we'll never duplicate the class of Argentina and Brazil, but I think we've shown we are very close. We're not lacking very much at all. I think we had a very good match. That the crowd gave us a standing ovation at the end, despite the defeat, shows we did well.'

There would be further evidence of the new gung-ho, entertaining and enterprising Germany in their third-place play-off match against Mexico. Michael's magnificent extra-time free-kick, curled over the wall and beyond goalkeeper Oswaldo Sanchez, not only earned him a deserved Man of the Match award, but also powered Germany to a thrilling 4–3 victory against the gallant Mexicans. The German captain fulfilled his leadership role to perfection, and helped his side shrug off the 54th-minute sending off of Mike Hanke. FIFA Technical Study Group member, Lim Kim Chon, said Michael had just about merited his Anheuser Busche Man of the Match accolade. He commented, 'It was a close call between Michael Ballack and Robert Huth, who was also outstanding for Germany tonight. In the end, I chose Michael for his leadership qualities on the pitch as well as his superb performance. When Germany went down to ten men, his exceptional leadership qualities came through and he was superb at organising his players and keeping them focused. He was always pushing forward and his distribution was excellent. And then, of course, there was his wonderful free-kick that took the score to 4–3. Mexico had numbers in the wall, but Michael got the ball to sail over all of them and into the net. It was a technically brilliant free-kick but it also came in extra time when there were a lot of weary legs.

'After running up and down the pitch for nearly 100 minutes, it took a calm head and real concentration to strike a set-piece that well. He made a superb contribution in a very exciting match.'

Michael was thrilled with his own contribution in the match, which was held in Leipzig, just north of Chemnitz, where he had grown up. He commented, 'This was a great win and should give us an important boost for the months ahead.'

He could also draw immense confidence from his exploits in a competition which is often marginalised. He had finished as joint second-best goalscorer with four goals, one behind Brazil's Adriano, winning the Adidas silver shoe and also the bronze ball for being named the third-best player in the tournament behind Riquelme of Argentina and Adriano. He had scored freely, although most of his contributions had come from the penalty spot, and led from the front as a rejuvenated Germany revelled in Jürgen Klinsmann's promotion of expansive, attacking football.

The Germany coach was full of praise for his main man, remarking, 'Michael was brilliant. He has the potential to take the World Cup by the scruff of the neck like Lothar Matthäus in 1990 or Zinedine Zidane in 1998.'

Germany and their captain could not get carried away given that the World Cup offers, bar Brazil and Argentina, a superior calibre of opponent, but their early progress under their manager was extremely promising and exciting. The orgy of attacking football they had served up was a far cry from their inability to score against European minnows Latvia in the European Championships. The Confederations Cup had successfully emerged from the shadow of the World Cup to prove an appetite-whetting dress rehearsal for the global festival of football. German Chancellor, Gerhard Schröder, was among its many admirers. He said, 'The tournament has been a huge success for world football, for German football, and for the people. The crowds have proved Germany's passion for the game, but even more importantly, our hospitality.'

Two months later, Germany once again showed they were on the right path to progress by earning a 2–2 draw in Holland, fighting back from 2–0 down at half-time through goals from Michael and Gerald Asamoah. A 2–0 defeat in Slovakia in September 2005 halted their winning ways, however, although these were restored for three of the next four games to develop a mini unbeaten run as 2005 came to a close.

South Africa were overcome 4–2 by the Germans in September; Turkey were beaten 2–1 in Istanbul, while China were edged out 1–0 – although Michael did not appear in the last two games due to injury.

Despite these confidence-boosting wins – albeit against

weaker nations – the all-prevailing mood of pessimism among most Germans about the chances of World Cup success had still not completely abated. A poll in Germany revealed that 15 per cent of Germans believed their country would falter at the group stage, while gnawing doubts about Jürgen Klinsmann's coaching capabilities, methods and his decision to remain in the United States for long portions of time, were bones of contention for his football-loving countrymen. The tabloid newspaper *Bild* encapsulated the views of many in Germany when it showed Klinsmann jogging on the beach only a day after Germany's win over China. The message was clear – here is our leader lapping up the sunshine while we Germans are worried sick about our team in the cold and wet.

Concern was also expressed about the eccentric coach's controversial ideas about fitness, psychology, preparing for matches and even the playing style he encouraged, which was yielding goals galore for Germany but conceding plenty, too. Michael admitted that he, like other sceptics in the German camp, had been critical of Klinsmann's idiosyncratic approach, but added, 'He has certainly made decisions that aren't to everyone's liking, but he is very good at arguing his case to get through what he wants. I have rarely had a coach who is so incredibly positive and who can motivate people to such a degree. He has a gift which a lot of other coaches cannot find.'

He returned to help his side earn a morale-boosting 0–0 draw against the French in Paris in November 2005. The early part of 2006 would bring a humbling 4–1 defeat in Italy, before Germany responded admirably by going undefeated, before and during the World Cup, until the Italians ended their heroics in the semi-finals. It would be the end of an era for Germany, given that their engaging coach Klinsmann – despite the passionate pleading of German players, politicians and scores of football devotees – decided enough was enough and ended his two-year association with the national team.

He cited a desire to return to his family in the United States and his exhaustion at the endless pressure of managing his country under persistent media scrutiny. Michael admitted he was disappointed by the news and expressed a desire for Klinsmann's radicalism to be upheld by whoever succeeded the outgoing coach. He was also determined to try and influence the appointment of Klinsmann's successor, commenting in *Stern* magazine, 'Coaches like Juergen Klopp [Mainz 05] and Thomas Doll [SV Hamburg] could do the job.' However, he was satisfied that Klinsmann's legacy would be maintained by his assistant, Joachim Löw, who was eventually named the new coach of Germany.

But he was also wary of over-optimism infecting the German preparations for their next mission: to qualify for the European Championships from a competitive group which contained the Republic of Ireland, Wales, Cyprus, Slovakia and San Marino. Michael warned, 'We have to come down off our World Cup cloud and focus on the hard work. There are a lot of tough games coming up. It is a new chapter and the circumstances are very different from the World Cup. We need to prove ourselves all over again. We have a new coach now. We all miss Jürgen Klinsmann but not that much has changed really as Joachim Löw was connected to the old regime.'

Germany's third place in the World Cup had installed them as the bookmakers' favourites to win Group D which, if achieved, would ignite expectations of even loftier aims, he acknowledged. Michael admitted, 'We want to qualify and then we can set the target of winning the European championships. Away games against Slovakia, Wales or Ireland are not going to be a piece of cake. Once we have achieved that goal, only then can we say we want to win the title.'

After injuring his hip for Chelsea in the Community Shield against Liverpool – a game the Blues lost 2–1 – Michael was denied the chance to step out for Germany in Joachim Löw's first match in charge, a 3–0 home win over Sweden in a friendly.

However, he was restored to the German side for their first Euro 2008 qualification match against the pugnacious the Republic of Ireland. It was the two sides' first meeting since a 1–1 draw in the 2002 World Cup and, once again, it turned out to be a keenly-fought war of attrition. Lukas Podolski's deflected free-kick handed the Germans victory which, although uninspiring, recalled their dogged qualification form of old.

Ballack, who had a quiet game, remarked afterwards, 'The Irish impressed us with their aggressiveness and with offensive strength. We had at first a little luck... however, patience proved. The victory was deserved, we were very well disciplined.'

If Germany's opening game in Group D bore all the hallmarks of a bitter struggle, their second encounter, against one of the world's weakest footballing countries, San Marino, presented them with a hideous mismatch and an opportunity to rack up goals galore.

The old adage that 'there are no easy games any more in

world football' was resoundingly disproved as Germany romped to a 13–0 win in San Marino, the biggest win in European Championship history. The only surprise was that such a potent goal threat as Michael Ballack did not add his name to the scoresheet more than once, while Lukas Podolski helped himself to four goals, and second-half substitute Thomas Hitzlsperger weighed in with two of his own. Such supremacy does little else other than reinforce a team's natural game and inject confidence into the ranks, so Germany's landslide victory was meaningless in the context of what they wanted to achieve.

However, teams can only play the opposition they come up against, focus on the present, and win convincingly – anything less than a resounding win would have been akin to a defeat.

In their next game, a home friendly against Georgia, another satisfactory win, 2–0, was earned and the prolific Michael once again found the net and provided a delightful pass with the outside of his left foot for Bastian Schweinsteiger, who drove a first-time strike into the net from 20 yards. Michael's goal was his 33rd in international football, bringing him level with Fritz Walter – West Germany's World Cup-winning captain in 1954 – in 11th place in his country's top goalscorers' list. It was an extraordinary achievement for a midfielder and surely confirms his standing as one of Germany's all-time greats.

It wasn't all good news for Ballack, though, as he then became involved in a very public feud with Lukas Poldoski, Germany's livewire young striker, who was sent off against Georgia. Michael chastised the youngster in the press, claiming Poldoski ought to work more on his game. Poldoski

– or 'Poldi', as he is known to his team-mates – responded by saying, 'I could also go and speak to 20 newspapers. But I don't do that. If I had a problem with Michael Ballack, then I would speak to him personally – and not through the media. If somebody has a problem, then he should come to me. Michael didn't speak with me.'

The Bayern Munich tyro was supported in his stance by German goalkeeper, Jens Lehmann, who said he disagreed with Michael's decision to criticise a team-mate in public. Michael then hit back by insisting his coach, Joachim Löw, shared his views.

Despite all the needless in-fighting, Germany continued their excellent form under their new coach by powering to a 4–1 win in Slovakia in their latest European Championship qualification game in October 2006. Michael was again central to Germany's success, heading in his 34th goal for his country from left-back Philipp Lahm's cross on 25. He was then instrumental in his country's second goal, firing in a shot that the Slovakian goalkeeper Kamil Contofalský failed to hold, allowing Bastian Schweinsteiger a simple tap-in. His new nemesis, Lukas Poldoski, showed that he thrived on criticism by netting twice to complete a very satisfactory evening's work for *Der Nationalmannschaft*.

Michael said, 'It was a very impressive performance, particularly during the first half. We played very maturely, very serenely and converted our chances cold-bloodedly. There's a good rapport between the old and the new players, both on and off the pitch.' But he went on to warn, 'Yet we mustn't feel too secure. It's a long qualifying campaign, what with seven teams in the group.'

Germany now lay second in Group D on nine points, a point behind the Czech Republic, who had amassed ten points but who had played one game more. The Germans' European Championship journey promised to be a bountiful one, their captain revelling in the attacking ambition instigated by Jürgen Klinsmann and carried on by his former assistant, Joachim Löw. He was scoring regularly and influencing games expertly, to lie eighth in the list of Germany's all-time top goalscorers in November 2006. He had scored a marvellous 35 goals in a list headed by the German goalscorer supreme, Gerd Müller, nicknamed 'Der Bomber', who had rattled in 68 goals in only 7 years as an international.

Many observers would agree that Michael Ballack has already emulated the wondrous achievements of his midfield predecessors, through his courageous captaincy and innate goal-scoring flair on the big occasion. Others believe he must secure major silverware to be unequivocally considered an all-time great midfielder for his country.

With Germany motoring impressively towards the European Championships in 2008 in Austria and Switzerland, their supremely talented Rolls Royce midfielder and captain, Michael Ballack, may very well win over the doubters.

10

World Cup Agony and Ecstasy

In response to a question about the impact of the World Cup on Germany in 2006, Michael Ballack replied tersely, 'I am a footballer, not a social historian.' He has also revealed that he remembers little about Germany's last World Cup triumph, in 1990.

In light of these two statements, you could be forgiven for thinking, if you didn't know about his remarkable history in the tournament, that Ballack does not appreciate nor care about the monumental significance of the World Cup. Yet while he does not profess to be an expert on how the football extravaganza can impact upon a nation, and can scarcely recall the last time Germany became world champions, he could write a full university thesis about the unique agony and ecstasy those competing in a World Cup can experience. In 2002 and 2006, he was a pivotal part of Germany sides that wildly exceeded expectations, before their hopes withered in the bitterness of defeat. His unbridled joy at crucial goals and superlative displays were interspersed with the flowing of many tears, and the resounding echo of 'nearly... but not quite', as injury and suspension cruelly hampered his quest to be a world champion.

A further example of his desire to become a world champion was his response to a question posed by Wolfgang Golz, a leading German journalist, who asked, 'What would you give to score the winning goal in the 2006 World Cup Final, just like Helmut Rahn, Gerd Müller or Andreas Brehme in earlier Finals?'

With uncontained enthusiasm, he replied, 'Oh, quite a lot. I can't put it into words. If you knew you were going to score that goal... There's nothing in the world that can beat that, either as a sportsman or a human being.'

In its simplest terms, football is the pre-eminent global sport... and the World Cup is the pinnacle of any footballer's career – perform well in front of massive global audiences and you can consider yourself an all-time great. The greatest, even. While the likes of Marco van Basten and George Best may be exceptions to this rule, there are a whole host of footballers in the history of the game who never impressed or appeared at the World Cup and can therefore never really be considered 'great'.

Michael's quest to be acclaimed as a legend of the beautiful game began in 2000, after he had inspired Germany to a heroic and, what looked at one stage, wholly unlikely qualification. His hopes of showcasing his skills on the world stage appeared forlorn after Germany stumbled and stuttered in the closing games in Group 9, which paired them with

England, Finland, Greece and Albania. Automatic qualification would be guaranteed for the team that topped the group, while the second-place side would be forced to play in a sudden-death play-off with other runners-up from the European groups.

However, Germany and Michael started out on the World Cup 2002 trail in September 2000 against Greece – whom they had not beaten since 1970 – in buoyant mood. The Germans had never lost their opening game in the World Cup qualifying competition; they had a new head coach in Rudi Völler, who had tasted World Cup success himself as a striker in the German team that triumphed at Italia '90, and they had recently drubbed Spain 4–1 in a friendly.

However, Germany still had much to prove to erase the bitter disappointment of exiting Euro 2000 at the first stage – their worst performance at a major tournament for 50 years. On the positive side, Völler was operating on a clean slate and had at his disposal a clutch of precocious young midfielders in Ballack and the gifted Sebastian Deisler, who were helping to compensate for the loss of Lothar Matthäus, Stefan Effenberg and Ulf Kirsten, who had all retired since Euro 2000. Germany therefore started on the long and winding road to Japan and South Korea with a satisfactory yet unconvincing 2–0 win against Greece in Hamburg.

Goals from Sebastian Deisler, his first for his country, on 17 minutes and a Marinos Ouzounidis' own goal 15 minutes from the end of time, achieved the much-needed three points. Michael played the full 90 minutes in a five-man midfield alongside Deisler, his Bayer Leverkusen team-mate Carsten Ramelow, Marco Bode and Mehmet Scholl. In the win he also picked up a booking. However, there were worrying glimpses of defensive frailty from the Germans' three-man rearguard, which would return to haunt the home side in future encounters in the group.

Rudi Völler acknowledged as much. 'We concentrated on attacking and we left gaps at the back. There are still parts of our game that don't function properly and it's a problem we must tackle, but I'm particularly pleased with the fact that all the guys gave 100 per cent.'

Greece's captain, Theo Zagorakis, predicted England would cause Germany considerable consternation in the clashes to follow between the two. He said, 'They are very predictable. The German defence was struggling every time we got in behind them. We spotted that weakness on match videos, and we knew we could do them with pace. If a team has speedy players, they will cause problems. I can see Owen [Michael] and Bruno [Emile Heskey] going to town at Wembley. England are a much better team all round, and if Germany get heavy with the physical stuff, like they did with us, England will cope comfortably.'

The validity or otherwise of Zagorakis' assertion would be revealed in Germany's next game, a seismic confrontation against the Three Lions at Wembley in October. It was the two old foes' second clash in a matter of months after Alan Shearer's stooping header gave England victory over the Germans in Euro 2000.

On this occasion, Michael and his team-mates were out to gain retribution, and were given extra incentive to do so by the fact that England were playing their last game at Wembley, before the proud old temple of football was knocked down and rebuilt after 77 years of providing an intoxicating cocktail of dreams, drama, tears and triumph. Could the new German outfit succeed on the lush, green grass of England's spiritual home, unlike the unfortunate 1966 German side and like the 1996 European champions?

A dull, dismal day weather-wise heralded a drab and dreary encounter in which Germany's renowned organisation and dour efficiency stifled an England side hamstrung by Kevin Keegan's tactical naïveté. The occasion assumed a funereal rather than a celebratory flavour for English fans when Paul Scholes was adjudged to have fouled Michael some 30 yards from goal after only 13 minutes of play.

Dietmar Hamann sent a low shot skidding beyond David Seaman's despairing dive, the only goal of a clash utterly unworthy of the old Wembley's final farewell.

While England mourned and Kevin Keegan resigned, Michael Ballack and his team-mates celebrated stealing a significant advantage in the march for World Cup qualification. In the long term it was to prove a false dawn, however, rather than a springboard for bigger and better things, although Germany's winning ways initially continued. Michael did not feature in their next match in March 2001, a 2–1 home win over Albania, which matched England's victory over Finland. He was, though, included in Germany's midfield for the away trip to Athens a few days later, in a high-scoring affair which the Germans edged 4–2. Michael was also on target in that game, converting a penalty after 25 minutes after he was hauled down in the penalty box by Grigoris Georgatos. It was the midfielder's first international goal and would be the first of many memorable strikes. Germany then had Miroslav Klose, playing his second international, and

Marco Bode to thank for scoring late goals to confirm a hard-earned victory in front of 55,000 passionate Greeks.

While the journey to Japan and South Korea had been somewhat rocky thus far, Germany were grinding out victories in time-honoured fashion despite under-performing and Michael was, slowly but surely, beginning to prove his worth as an international player. The Germans now had 12 points from 4 games, 5 clear of England, making their impending contest in September 2002 crucial. However, a perfect start to qualification was ruined when Finland held Germany to a 2–2 draw in Helsinki in June. The Germans fell 2–0 behind during a torrid first-half, but their legendary battling qualities were in evidence again when they mounted a second-half recovery to restore parity.

Michael led the comeback on 69 minutes with a penalty, before the lanky Carsten Jancker secured a scarcely deserved draw 3 minutes later. It was an underwhelming display from him, despite his goal, as he had failed to shine in tandem with Borussia Dortmund's Lars Ricken in central midfield. More worrying for the Germans, however, was the fragility of their defence, something that would be devastatingly exposed in the ensuing months.

Then came a welcome clean sheet and another win was secured in Germany's next game, a 2–0 away victory against Albania, in which Michael scored the second goal. Partnering fellow creative inspiration Sebastian Deisler, he struck on 68 minutes after Carsten Jancker had put Germany out in front. He could now savour a summer holiday, although this would probably be cut short, as it seemed likely that Germany would be involved in World Cup duty. However, so confident – and presumptuous as it transpired – were Germany of topping their group and securing qualification, that they had scheduled friendly matches for November when the second-place teams would battle it out in play-offs.

The Germans were six points ahead of England, who had a game in hand and could virtually seal their place in Japan and South Korea with a victory over their long-standing rivals on 1 September 2001. Michael nearly missed the showdown with England due to a broken toe, although he may now regret that injury did not prevent him avoiding one of Germany's most humbling defeats in their proud history. Rampant England, inspired by a scintillating hat-trick from Michael Owen, massacred the Germans 5–1 in Munich – the first time they had won in Germany since 1965.

Prior to the game, Germany had lost just one of their previous 60 World Cup qualifying games, while they had not been beaten in the Olympic Stadium since 1973.

But they produced a gutless, guileless and utterly ghastly performance, and suffered accordingly. Michael was fairly anonymous for much of a shambolic German display, slicing a wild volley wide on 58 minutes when it appeared easier to score. He was substituted after 67 minutes to be replaced by Miroslav Klose, but it was defensive strength rather than attacking threat which Germany needed to stem the English waves of lightning quick, rapier thrusts. A cacophony of boos from the disgruntled Olympic Stadium faithful rained down on him and his team-mates long before the final whistle of a game which former German legend Karl-Heinz Rummenigge described as his country's worst-ever defeat. He lamented,

'This was a new Waterloo for us. What really disturbed me was that we seemed to give up halfway through the match.'

To compound the despair for Germany, coach Rudi Völler had to flee the Olympic Stadium before the end of the match to be at the bedside of his father, who had suffered a heart-attack. After such a potentially cataclysmic blow to the morale of the notoriously assured Germans and their fledgling talents such as Michael, huge question marks remained. Could they flourish in adversity and still cement World Cup qualification, or would the Germans suffer an unusual crisis of confidence? And would Ballack be able to keep Germany's challenge for the ultimate prize in world football on track?

A win over Finland at home was essential for Germany, although they were now reliant on England slipping up against Albania and Greece at home – a futile hope, it seemed, given England's swash-buckling revival under Sven-Göran Eriksson. England duly beat Albania, albeit unconvincingly, but then seemed destined to slip up at the final hurdle when they went 2–1 down to Greece at home to give Germany renewed hope. However, an unforgettable goal from David Beckham – a glorious, whipped free-kick that arced into the top corner in the dying minutes – broke the hearts of Michael and Germany, who laboured to a 0–0 draw with Finland in Gelsenkirchen.

Michael's hopes of measuring himself against the world's élite now depended on success in a play-off game against the ever-unpredictable Ukraine, who featured his future Chelsea team-mate Andriy Shevchenko in attack. Not only would Germany have to face the daunting prospect of a hostile crowd in Kiev, but Michael's fellow midfielders Mehmet

Scholl, Sebastian Deisler, Jorg Heinrich and Jens Jeremies were also injured for the trip to Ukraine. Furthermore, his Bayer Leverkusen team-mate, striker Oliver Neuville, was forced to miss the first leg due to suspension. Michael later recalled that, 'The pressure we had to cope with in the build-up to the game was unbelievable. If it was like that all the time, it would be unbearable.'

When the chips are down, though, the Germans normally respond positively and their dreams were kept alive by two immense performances by their magnificent midfielder. Michael proved beyond question that he was an international player of renown, who thrived on the big occasion by firstly cancelling out Gennadi Zubov's opener for Ukraine in the first leg in Kiev. He stole in at the far post to score his fourth international goal from Bernd Schneider's free-kick on 18 minutes, giving Germany a crucial away-goal advantage for the return match in Dortmund a few days later.

The second leg in Dortmund will go down in history as one of Ballack's proudest nights in a German shirt as he produced a virtuoso display, crowned by two sublime headers, which silenced those critics who believed he was an inconsistent player of wasted potential. Germany were soon back on course for Japan and South Korea after Michael, Oliver Neuville and Marko Rehmer swept them into a three-goal lead. Michael rose imperiously in the Ukrainian box to meet Bernd Schneider's wonderful cross from the right and powered an emphatic header beyond Maxim Levintsky. Roared on by 52,000-plus within the cauldron of the Westfalenstadion, noted as German football's most intense and noisy bastion of football, Germany, and their midfield maestro in particular, were simply irresistible.

The second half was heralded by euphoric German fans singing out 'You'll Never Walk Alone', and their side responded by cantering into the World Cup final stages, thanks again to a towering contribution from Michael. Germany's latest national hero delivered another impressive header, this time from Oliver Neuville's cross on 50 minutes, reducing the rest of the game to a training session as Germany ran out surprisingly easy 4–1 victors.

Michael later dedicated his goals to his baby son, Louis, commenting, 'My goals are for him. When he grows up, he can watch the video and I hope he will be proud of his dad.' It was a marvellous personal performance from him and one of rousing passion and pride from Germany as a collective unit, a far cry from the ineptitude which had characterised their recent run of miserable displays and depressing scorelines.

Two goals in a 4–1 rout confirmed that Ballack was now a talismanic figure for the Germans, one who would be invested with his country's hopes in the full glare of world football's prestige tournament. In the past, he had been guilty of sporadic contributions for Germany, rather than the sustained excellence that his abilities warranted. But, thankfully, he was now beginning to consistently translate his coruscating form for Bayer, in their assault on both the Bundesliga championship and the Champions League in 2001/02, into the international arena, prompting his club manager, Klaus Toppmöller, to declare, 'I shudder to think what could happen to Germany if Michael is injured, because with him would go a vital source of goals [he top-scored for Germany with six in the qualifiers] and the vision in the side. He has a chance to be the best German player ever. I've played against Beckenbauer,

Günter Netzer and Wolfgang Overath and, you name them, but Michael is the most complete player.' Rich praise indeed, although football devotees outside of Germany would find it hard to agree with such lofty claims given that he had only seen fleeting glimpses of Michael at his best.

Prior to his rise to prominence with the national team and his inspirational input into Bayer Leverkusen's marvellous season, Michael Ballack had reached the age of 25 largely unnoticed by football observers abroad. But slowly and surely, he was seeping into the consciousness of every football fan and pundit in the world. For instance, when Michel Platini was asked in 2002 by German journalists about his knowledge of Michael Ballack, he was initially hesitant. 'I really don't know much about him,' confessed the Frenchman. But then Platini had a sudden flash of recognition, recalling Michael's two goals for Bayer Leverkusen against Liverpool, remarking with admiration, 'They were two different goals – that's important.'

While his heroics in qualifying and domestic excellence had helped establish him as an international player of renown, he still faced a battle to rid himself of a reputation of being egotistical and overly laidback. *Spiegel* magazine dedicated a whole feature to his alleged arrogance, a claim his father dismissed as 'rubbish with sauce'. A sports magazine in Germany further fuelled the anti-Michael campaign by ranking him as third in a list of footballers most disliked by their peers in 2002. While a younger and more sensitive Michael might have gone into his shell when being savaged by his critics, the new, more mature version was confident that his rich vein of form would help him reverse this unattractive portrayal. He was now imbued with greater self-confidence following his recent footballing feats and felt more able to withstand those who scoffed at his swaggering gait, perpetually spotless shirt and male model looks.

'I can't help it – I was just born with that style,' he protested. 'I've always been criticised but I can live with it. I've played well before but the difference now is I'm consistent, that's the secret. I think it's just maturity, experience you get after years of playing in the Bundesliga, Champions League and national team. I am pleased with all the nice things that have been said about me, but I know from experience that you go through highs and lows in this game. What I have to do is keep working hard and giving my best while not putting too much pressure on myself.'

While Michael was majestically soaring towards stardom, his once-mighty country approached the World Cup with significantly lowered expectations after the poverty of their displays during the closing stages of the qualification campaign and Euro 2000. They had failed to progress beyond the quarter-finals of the last two tournaments, with their title-winning triumphs of 1990 and final appearances in 1982 and 1986 both dim and distant memories. As such, Franz Beckenbauer was among those ruling out a return to the glory days of old for the Germans. He said, 'What can we hope for after a 4–1 win against the Ukraine? Not the title. France and Argentina are clearly ahead of us.'

The Germans' World Cup warm-up games did little to alter Beckenbauer's view as although Israel were brushed aside 7–1 in February 2002, and the USA were easily disposed of 4–2, with Michael scoring the fourth goal, when

Germany faced a genuine world-class outfit in Argentina in their final warm-up match, they suffered a 1–0 home defeat and chastening reality check.

Gerhard-Mayer Vorfelder, the president of the German Football Association, echoed Beckenbauer's downbeat assessment of his nation's chances. 'I will consider our campaign successful if we reach the quarter-finals,' he announced.

Contrary to this pessimistic view, two of Germany's leading players – Oliver Kahn and Oliver Bierhoff – were both of the belief that they could emulate the heroes of the past and win the tournament, and duly negotiated a financial incentive with their president. They successfully agreed a €92,000 bonus per player with Mayer-Vorfelder if Germany won the title, although their manager, Rudi Völler, refused to entertain such towering ambitions. He said, 'Firstly, we have to survive the first round. Then we'll see. To put it bluntly, we are not among the favourites.' As for Michael, he preferred to share the management's view of Germany's prospects, rather than that of his fellow players. He confessed, 'We are not a great team yet – we are still developing, even if we do have many good players in our squad.'

At least Rudi Völler could console himself that, while his squad lacked the threat of old, it was a more cohesive unit than the one that had embarrassed a nation both at Euro 2000 and in the horrific capitulation to England during the World Cup qualifying campaign. Furthermore, the Germans' World Cup group – which paired them with Cameroon, the Republic of Ireland and Saudi Arabia – offered Völler, Michael and his compatriots even greater optimism as it looked an eminently 'winnable' section. However, as the showpiece loomed, Germany were thrown into turmoil by injuries to key players in their already impoverished reservoir of talent. Völler's midfield was decimated by the withdrawals of Joerg Heinrich, Sebastian Deisler and Mehmet Scholl, while their persistent defensive worries were aggravated by the absences of Jens Nowotny and Christian Wörns. Suddenly, any ambitions that Germany had of making an impact were swiftly and brutally eroded, but at least they could count on the reassuring presence of their midfield inspiration, Michael Ballack.

Or could they? After sustaining a foot injury against Liverpool in the Champions League in April, Michael's own participation in the World Cup was thrown into temporary doubt. However, Rudi Völler was not prepared to entertain the unthinkable scenario of him failing to regain fitness, insisting in May, 'The injury is not so bad that he won't be able to play.' The German coach added that he expected his player to be back in training well before Germany's first match against Saudi Arabia on 1 June. For his part, Michael was prepared to go through the pain barrier for his country's cause. He said, 'It's getting better and I assume I will be playing. If it hurts, I can take pills and I'll be fine.'

Meanwhile, Rudi Völler attempted to play down suggestions that his weakened squad was destined to fail. 'We do lack strength in depth but I believe if we can take all the 23 players I consider to be the best in Germany, then we will be a match for anyone as we showed against Ukraine, who are not exactly lightweights in European football,' he said. He then added that he had every faith that his midfield general could shoulder the burden of increased expectations coming his way. 'Michael is the type of player who can take over the leadership role. I think he will cope well with the situation.'

Fifaworldcup.com suggested that Michael, who had endured a season of heartache with Bayer Leverkusen losing the championship on the final day after his own-goal against SpVgg Unterhaching and failing against Real Madrid in the Champions League Final, could shake off his perennial loser's tag and become a winner in the same vein as Zinedine Zidane. The website recalled that the French maestro had suffered a succession of disappointments for club and country before earning a winner's medal and legendary status for his two goals in France's World Cup Final victory over Brazil in 1998. He then went on to win the European Championships with his country in 2000 and the Champions League two years later, and was named FIFA World Footballer of the Year in 1998 and 2000.

The FIFA website said, 'Michael is still a way off success of this nature, but the midfielder seems somehow destined to follow a similar path. After some outstanding displays and vital goals for both club and country, Michael is already a certainty for the title of German Footballer of the Year. Numerous top clubs at home and abroad, including Zidane's Real Madrid, were lining up to obtain the model professional's services, but in the end he chose to stay in Germany and is on his way to Bayern Munich.'

While Germany's midfield boasted an outstanding performer in Michael, who provided a glimmer of true class alongside the tough-tackling Jens Jeremies and the reliable Dietmar Hamann, they remained suspect defensively. However, goalkeeper Oliver Kahn was a formidable barrier and the 6ft 5in Christian Metzelder had emerged as an imposing defensive bulwork at centre-back, while in the striker's department, Oliver Neuville had only scored 2 goals in 29 internationals, Oliver Bierhoff looked a shadow of his former self, and Miroslav Klose and Ghana-born Gerald Asamoah were unproven in a major tournament.

Any lingering doubts surrounding the quality, or lack of it, of Germany's threadbare squad were temporarily banished by a resounding 8–0 win in their opening game against potential danger side Saudi Arabia. And Michael Ballack cast aside any concerns about his fitness by playing the full 90 minutes and scoring Germany's third goal in the romp, which featured a hat-trick from Miroslav Klose. In trademark fashion Michael bulleted home a header from Christian Ziege's sumptuous left-foot cross five minutes before half-time, and also provided assists for two of Klose's three goals.

After an easier-than-expected start to the World Cup, Michael and his inexperienced team were cheered further by the news that Ireland's 1–1 draw with Cameroon meant his country topped the table after the first round of matches. Yet he acknowledged that Germany could not get carried away by their thumping triumph, the biggest scoreline in the World Cup since Hungary's 10–1 rout of El Salvador in 1982. He said, 'I'm sure many club sides could have beaten Saudi Arabia. There is a feeling of euphoria but we now have to prove ourselves against Ireland, which will be a very different game.'

While Germany strived to eschew over-confidence, their hapless victims were given the proverbial roasting by the unforgiving Saudi media. 'COME BACK, IT'S A SCANDAL,' bellowed *Al-Youm*'s front page. 'No defence, no midfield, no attack, not even goalkeeping,' it went on to lament. The *Ar-Riyadiyah* sports daily was similarly vicious in its description of the Saudi's humiliating defeat, calling it a 'giant earthquake that tarnished the Greens' reputation'.

Meanwhile, the English media were slightly more generous when acknowledging the Germans' legendary 'bounce-back-ability' and Michael's highly influential role. The *Daily Telegraph*'s Alan Smith wrote, 'With one or two exceptions, the names stay the same. Yet, just when it mattered, this much-criticised Germany side lifted their game several notches. An 8–0 thumping of Saudi Arabia in their opening match has brought fervent hope that this World Cup may actually turn out to be a lot better than anticipated.

'I suppose we should have known. Germany, the princes of perseverance, can never be discounted, even with a squad that falls well short of previous standards. Great things have long been expected of Michael Ballack and, over recent months – for club and for country – the midfielder has delivered in impressive fashion. Manchester United and, to a lesser extent, Arsenal, can heartily vouch for his dominance in a Bayer Leverkusen shirt (soon to be a Bayern Munich one) as the German side marched to the Champions League final. Confidence has never been a problem for this cocky 25-year-old with an ability to put team-mates' noses out of joint. But another goal against Saudi Arabia will further boost his belief that he can be a force to be reckoned with, and perhaps the team's leader, in the upcoming weeks.'

Once again Michael and Germany initially impressed in their next match against Ireland, with his left-wing cross headed home by the irrepressible, in-form Miroslav Klose on 19 minutes for his fourth goal of the tournament. However, the profligate Germans were unable to put their plucky opponents to the sword, and were left to regret Robbie Keane's 92nd-minute equaliser.

Germany's hopes of qualifying for the next stage now rested on their final match, against Cameroon. The Indomitable Lions would, it was predicted, again live up to their nickname – although their showing was to be more feisty and fiery than anyone had expected. The African Nations Cup champions had two men sent off, while Germany's Carsten Ramelow was dismissed by what many observers felt had been an over-zealous referee in Spain's Antonio Lopez Nieto.

Germany prevailed, though, in a stormy encounter with Marco Bode with the Ballack-Klose axis reaping another goal for the latter and Michael crossing for his team-mate to head in his fifth World Cup goal. It was a case of mission accomplished for the Germans, who had won Group E without really ever having to over-exert themselves. For his part, Michael had provided fleeting glimpses of the form which had secured Germany's qualification, but it was clear that he had much, much more to offer. Despite not really hitting fifth gear, he had demonstrated his ability to play for the team by topping the World Cup assists' table, with four.

The knock-out stages, and the pressure and increased quality which they bring, are a more accurate barometer of a player's standing in world football. Waiting in the second round for Germany were Paraguay, who had established themselves in recent years as a stubborn and gritty outfit. However, Michael emerged as a doubt for the game after suffering a calf injury during the Cameroon match. He was provided with intensive physiotherapy reflecting his worth to the squad, made all the more important because Germany were already without Dietmar Hamann, Carsten Ramelow and Christian Ziege due to suspension.

Germany's goalkeeper Oliver Kahn said that if Michael were to be unavailable for the match, 'it would almost be fatal because he's enormously important, especially as a creative player. I can't really imagine him not playing because, during World Cup games, pain doesn't come into it, does it?'

Thankfully, Michael recovered and now it was time for him and his cohorts to grind out an unspectacular, but efficient victory, in true German style. They edged out the South Americans with an Oliver Neuville goal and suddenly their prospects of capturing the Jules Rimet trophy did not appear as fanciful or as laughable as they had before the tournament started, as BBC Sport's Stuart Roach noted. He wrote, 'The demise of France, Argentina and Portugal and Italy's failure to win their group leaves Germany's road ahead relatively obstacle-free. They will face Mexico or the USA in the quarter-finals and, with coach Rudi Völler welcoming back his trio of suspended stars, the Germans suddenly look a reasonable bet for a semi-final place.

'That is a far cry from the shambles Völler looked out on last autumn. Thrashed 5–1 by England and forced to qualify through the play-offs, Völler would have bitten the hand that offered him a place in the last eight of this World Cup. For Germany, it is a case of back to the good old, bad old days, when they were winning games by sacrificing style for ruthless efficiency. "This is how championship teams are born," laughed one German journalist after the dire but desirable win over Paraguay.'

Yet while Germany and their stand-out performers, such as the excellent Oliver Kahn and the free-scoring Miroslav Klose, captured the headlines, Michael Ballack was going about his business quietly yet effectively. His time in the spotlight would come. In fact, perhaps realising that star players must prove their mettle in the decisive stages of tournaments, he seized the chance to make a telling impact in Germany's quarter-final with the United States. In a disappointing game from which Germany barely deserved victory, Michael's goal – a header from Christian Ziege's curling cross – was the decisive moment. Germany survived a second-half onslaught from the gutsy Americans to scrape into the semi-finals – but performances in major tournaments do not always get teams through to the next stage. Victory is the only thing that counts.

A relieved Michael admitted afterwards that Germany had ridden their luck. 'The Americans were on top, fit and kept trying for 90 minutes, putting us under a lot of pressure. They proved their presence in the quarter-finals was no accident. They deserved to be at that stage. We knew that set pieces were one of our strengths. I'm happy that it worked out well but it was a lot of hard work and we also had a bit of luck.'

Seasoned World Cup campaigners Germany were now in familiar territory – the semi-finals – and in days past, they would have been heavily tipped to cruise into the final, given their immense mental strength and resilience in the final throes of a tournament. Michael said, 'I wasn't really bothered who we played in the semi-final, either Spain or Korea, as both teams had shown themselves to be great survivors. Playing against the hosts, though, will be good... it will be a rare opportunity to play in such a big, big game.'

However, the surprise outfit of the World Cup – the co-hosts, South Korea – promised to offer an exacting test of Germany's World Cup-winning credentials.

Not only were the spirited Koreans playing at home in front of a frenzied, electrifying support, but they had also disproved the suggestion that they were fortunate to have progressed so far by first ousting Italy and then Spain in successive rounds of the tournament.

The last four of a football competition is where dreams can be realised and football legends created. On the other hand, there are always two losers, and often villains or ill-fated players are remembered for all the wrong reasons. Which would Michael Ballack turn out to be? Could he and Germany realise the impossible dream and continue their remarkable, Phoenix-from-the-flames resurrection from the nightmare of Munich, the previous year, when England had wreaked havoc and left a proud football nation on its knees?

Few could have predicted the drama that was about to unfold and the fluctuating fortunes of the protagonist in that match, Michael Ballack. The semi-final transpired to be a classic encounter, matching Germanic grit and organisation against South Korean effervescence, pace and passion in front of 60,000 screaming fans. The Koreans' twin attacking threats of Cha Bum-Kun and Hwang Sun-Hong gave the German rearguard a torrid time in the opening period through tidal wave after tidal wave of Asian attack, forcing Oliver Kahn to display again the superlative shot-stopping skills that had characterised his tournament. Eventually the Germans responded by pumping in high balls to Miroslav Klose and Marco Bode in a bid to exploit the South Koreans' supposed deficiencies in the air. The Asian adventurers gamely tried to break down the watertight German defence in the second half and, in the 70th minute nearly succeeded – but for Michael Ballack. It was the first of his two crucial interventions in the match – a bittersweet, iconic moment which will define him when his career comes to an end.

The lively Lee Chun-Soo skipped past several German defenders on the edge of the box and was about to make a dangerous incursion into the area when Michael hacked him down and was promptly yellow-carded by Swiss referee Urs Meier. It was his second booking of the knock-out stage of the World Cup and it meant that he would be cruelly denied the chance to compete for football's greatest prize. Anyone continuing to accuse him of being a selfish narcissist would do well to recall this incident. Faced with the agonising realisation that they might be deprived of a coveted World Cup final appearance, quite understandably most footballers would avoid putting themselves in the firing line for the rest of the match. Who could forget Paul Gascoigne's weeping after his ill-timed lunge on, ironically, a German – Thomas Berthold – resulting in him being ruled out of a possible World Cup Final place in 1990 as England played West Germany?

But there were no tears or tantrums from Ballack; just an extraordinary manifestation of stunning stoicism, unflinching tenacity and match-winning drive as the agony and ecstasy of football were encapsulated within a matter of minutes. Just three minutes after his fateful foul, he strode forward imperiously, striking a powerful first-time, right-foot shot that the South Korean goalkeeper Lee Woon Jae blocked, but there was Germany's saviour following up to calmly knock home the rebound with his left foot. It was quite an act of redemption. Never can a goalscorer have felt such mixed emotions at having scored what proved to be his side's winning goal in a game of such magnitude. Perhaps only Denis Law's cheeky backheel flick for Manchester City in 1974, which condemned his former side, Manchester United, to relegation to the Second Division, comes close.

While pleased that he had propelled his country into a completely unexpected World Cup Final, he was also left contemplating another enormous disappointment to add to his litany of personal misery in 2002 – an *annus horribilis* indeed. For a distraught Michael, missing the biggest game in world football had been preceded by him losing in the German Cup Final, finishing second in the Bundesliga and runner-up in the Champions League Final.

He was understandably beginning to wonder if he was a jinxed nearly-man.

'Perhaps the fact that I will not be in the Final is a good sign,' he pondered. Later he confessed to *Spiegel* magazine that if he ever found himself in a similar situation again, where he might be on the brink of making a tackle that would elicit a yellow card in a World Cup semi-final, thereby risking suspension, he would 'act differently'. He remarked, 'Last time, I did think about talking to the referee before the semi-final and pointing out that I would miss the final, but I didn't speak to him. I was given yellow and was out against Brazil. This time I would talk to the referee.'

Not surprisingly, he wept inconsolably in the dressing room

as he contemplated the devastating fate that had befallen him, although he received some comforting words from his coach, Rudi Völler, who said, 'Him up there saw that and one of these days you'll get something back for it.' Divine intervention could not rewrite history, sadly, and the heartbroken German was left to regret his decision to transgress and become the fourth player – after Argentina's Claudio Caniggia in 1990, Alessandro Costacurta of Italy in 1994 and France's Laurent Blanc in 1998 – to be suspended for the Final. He admitted, 'It is a very stupid situation for me personally, because my dream had been to play in a World Cup Final – but now it is not to be. My first thoughts are bitterness. Four years ago, the same thing happened to Laurent Blanc [the French defender] and I felt for him when I watched him on TV. It's difficult to say how I feel now because I can't really imagine what it will be like only to sit on the bench for the Final. Maybe only later it will really sink in what I'm going to miss.

'Obviously, I wish my team-mates every success in the Final and I'll be with the team on the pitch in my heart even if I won't be out there with them.'

Michael would not allow his individual suffering to completely take the gloss off his country's extraordinary achievement, however. He added, 'The team as a whole has managed to accomplish an incredible feat. We can definitely be proud of ourselves. As a footballer, you always have faith in your ability – but you have to be realistic as well. We did not believe we would get this far, but we have done it. We believed in ourselves throughout. Tonight's game really proved to the world that we are here to get something.'

However, he was lionised rather than maligned by his country for his part in firing Germany into their seventh World Cup Final in what was their 50th win in the competition. Rudi Völler said of his tragic hero, 'Even though he knew with another yellow card he would miss the Final, he still committed that tactical foul which was utterly necessary. He placed himself at the service not only of the team but the whole of Germany. The entire country will understand him and applaud him.'

Team-mate Dietmar Hamann also focused on Michael's match-winning contribution rather than his tactical foul, and pledged that Germany would try to win the final for their suspended colleague, declaring, 'He has scored two winning goals in the last two games and it's a pity he can't play on Sunday. We have to go out on Sunday and try and win the Cup for him. Everybody knew he had been booked going into the game and that a second booking would mean he couldn't play on Sunday. When he got booked, it was 0–0 and he had the power and stamina to keep on playing and score the winning goal. He's a strong player. He's had a fantastic season and unfortunately he will miss the World Cup Final, which is very disappointing.'

There were some observers that found it crass and distasteful that Michael was applauded for what he did. Yet he says he only did what any other footballer would do when faced with an onrushing, speedy attacker who looked likely to threaten the German goal. And who could argue with him? The *Scotsman* newspaper, for one. It carried the following condemnation of his action: 'If the Bayer Leverkusen star is swept home on a wave of support as Germany's saviour, he will surely be heckled and bullied whenever he crosses the confines of the border. There is no worse place to reveal your nasty side than at the World Cup, and the Germans are not known for their gentlemanly conduct on the football pitch.

'Remember Harald Schumacher, the German goalkeeper who gave in to his demons and lashed out at Patrick Battiston to stop him scoring in the 1982 semi-final?

'Lee Chun-Soo might not have scored if he hadn't been felled on the edge of the box, nor even completed the obvious ball to an unmarked colleague at the far post. But we shall never know. The overriding impression had already formed that Germany have unearthed another unflappable machine which will stop at nothing in pursuit of its goal. Michael will require all of his resolve to get through this agonising phase.'

The *Daily Telegraph*'s Giles Smith preferred to compare favourably Michael's response to his suspension to Paul Gascoigne's tearful reaction to his own suspension from the World Cup Final of 1990. He wrote, 'Here's how it works – an English footballer and a German footballer receive yellow cards in separate World Cup semi-finals and realise that they will be suspended for the respective finals, should their side reach them. The English player weeps in self-pity and is still being encouraged to talk about those tears on television 12 years later; the German player scores the goal which takes his team into the Final. To consider the implications of these alternative attitudes is to understand with abrupt clarity why the poorest German side in living memory are this tournament's runners-up, while the best English side for a generation have been home for a week.'

Now not only Germany but also the whole world was wondering how Michael, the irreplaceable, could be replaced in the World Cup Final. His prodigious work-rate, exquisite passing, lung-busting runs from midfield into the box and his uncanny ability to score decisive goals and provide vital assists made him indispensable for the Germans, one of their few world-class players. 'The only more serious loss would be the alien abduction of Oliver Kahn, but he will keep goal against Ronaldo and friends in Yokohama,' wrote *Scotland on Sunday* about Michael's self-inflicted removal from the showpiece occasion. Rudi Völler agreed with these sentiments, albeit less colourfully. He confessed, 'It's almost impossible to replace Michael Ballack adequately. If the team gets into a bad situation, he can turn the match around by scoring a goal or providing an assist. It's going to be nigh on impossible to replace him.'

The man charged with the impossible task of filling his shoes was Jens Jeremies, a terrier-like midfielder from Bayern Munich. Jeremies would certainly provide the work-rate, but he was not a match-winner nor a cultured creator in the vein of Ballack. However, he would be deployed in a different way, hopefully to nullify the luminous Brazilian talents of Rivaldo, Ronaldinho and Ronaldo, who had tormented defences in the World Cup in an inexorable march to the Final. But after the tournament Germany had had, who was to say that they could not stifle Brazilian flair and conjure up a goal for Miroslav Klose?

'Never write off the Germans' is a chilling cliché that is all too true for many English football fans' liking; one that had assumed an even greater significance during their unimaginable journey to the World Cup Final. It was a remarkable transformation from pathetic no-hopers, who had wilted in their own backyard against England, to courageous battlers with a ferocious will to win, who had ridden a Michael Ballack-inspired wave to the verge of success.

Rudi Völler drew much of the credit for the German revival, showing unwavering belief in his players during good times and bad. He had been rewarded in kind with a marvellous team spirit and unity, developing great respect among players, many of whom referred to him in the familiar German 'Du' form. Apart from Völler, perhaps the happiest man at Germany's reversal of fortunes was Oliver Kahn, the German captain. He would be proudly leading out his country in a World Cup Final in Yokohama less than a year after letting in five goals against England and subsequently banging his fist in frustration on the Olympic Stadium turf. This was certainly Germany's unlikeliest World Cup Final, but perhaps their most satisfying for that very reason. Negotiating a tricky play-off game and coping with a raft of injuries to key players made the going tough for Germany but, in the words of American crooner Billy Ocean, 'the tough got going'. For their absent hero, Michael Ballack, missing the final was simply excruciating.

Later he spoke of his torture and torment at watching the most prestigious game in world football from the sidelines. 'Before the game, I had to leave the changing room because I didn't want to participate in the preparations,' he admitted. 'During the Final, I was 1,000 times more nervous than if I had been out there on the pitch, because I was unable to help my team-mates.' As it turned out, bereft of their inspiration, no amount of German guts and determination could overcome Brazilian style and skill, as two Ronaldo goals brought the Jules Rimet trophy back to South America for the fifth time.

After the disappointment had dissipated, Germany could reflect on the fact that reaching the Final was a phenomenal achievement for what was, in comparison with formidable German sides of the past, a fairly average bunch of players – Michael, Kahn and Klose excepted. The class of 2002 could still not have expected the warmth of the rapturous reception they received on returning to Germany. More than 50,000 supporters turned out at Frankfurt Airport to show their appreciation for the endeavours of Michael Ballack and his team-mates, cheering them all the way to the Römerberg square in the heart of the city. Even in the midst of the jubilation at the Frankfurt town hall, German Football Association (DFB) president Gerhard Mayer-Vorfelder was looking ahead to the next World Cup, declaring, 'I have never known a side with such team spirit. I said to Rudi Völler, "You're runners-up now, and in 2006 in your own country, you'll be world champions."' So, Michael's first taste of the fury and frenzy of the World Cup had ended in disappointment.

He had proved, though, that he unquestionably had the ability to deliver on the grand stage, obtaining six votes to finish ninth in the list of players proposed as the best player of the competition, the Golden Ball, won by German goalkeeper Oliver Kahn. The World Cup in 2006 in Germany, would be an altogether different story, however.

11

Cup Fever on Home Soil

Michael Ballack would no longer be the new kid on the block. In the 2006 World Cup tournament, he would be expected to impose himself even more, to seize the chance to be his country's leader and to inspire Germany to World Cup glory on home soil.

The Germans had won the chance to host the World Cup in July 2000 by performing the ultimate act of brinkmanship and stealing victory from South Africa by only one vote after an abstention from one of the voters. The man given the task of leading the German national team into the promised land of the World Cup was a former winner of the trophy, Jürgen Klinsmann. He was the surprise choice to succeed Rudi Völler, who stood down after Euro 2004, given that he had never coached any team at any level. Yet his ebullience and relentless striving for perfection – as well as the fact that he had been one of Germany's most adored and talented strikers –

mitigated against any lack of coaching experience, as far as German fans were concerned.

Klinsmann revolutionised Germany's ponderous and predictable style of play, encouraging his players to attack at speed when they had possession. He replaced Germany's traditional 3-5-2 formation with a 4-4-2 system, employing a four-man defence, a four-man or a diamond formation in midfield in and two forwards.

Integral to Klinsmann's plans was, of course, his playmaker Michael Ballack, to whom he gave the captain's armband, previously the property of Oliver Kahn. In an interview with CNN World Sport's Don Riddell, Klinsmann described Michael's talents. 'He is basically a perfect player because he is both-footed, and he is incredibly strong in the air... he has wonderful body language, his movements are very smooth and he is a great communicator within the team... that is why we made him the captain, because he looks after the young players, he is very balanced, very calm... he's the right player at the right time but he needs that stage of the World Cup to prove it to everybody.

'Michael Ballack is our leader, and we're looking forward to the World Cup because that's his stage... the dawn of Zidane, of Shearer, Shevchenko, is the World Cup... and whatever you do in your club team and winning European Championships, it's nice, it's great, but the real stage is the World Cup, so we have big hopes in Michael that the timing is the right one.'

But he still had much to prove before being declared a world great, according to Brazilian legend Pelé. 'I am sorry, but Michael is not a top player,' Pelé told *Welt am Sonntag*. 'He has been playing at the same level for a number of years now and that level is not good enough. He has highs and lows but, in truth, he has hardly improved over the past few years.'

What Michael had improved as he neared his 30th birthday was his willingness to embrace the captaincy of his country. Who would have thought that the shy, young East German who shunned the leadership mantle in his early career in the Bundesliga would now feel so at ease about being his country's leading light? He outlined his role by saying, 'As captain, I'm aware that many of the young players in our team will be looking to me for an example, listening to what I say and watching what I do. When they have problems, they speak to me... my role is to lead the way, to be an example to them, but also to guide them tactically and by my performances on the field. The most important thing is to win their confidence, their trust; if we were able to reach the Final of the last World Cup, it was largely down to our solidarity and I'm sure that will be key to our success this time.'

While having the World Cup staged on home soil affords the hosts the luxury of not having to qualify, continual non-competitive fixtures can blunt a country's sharpness and take the edge off their desire. On the other hand, friendly fixtures allow a coach to tamper with selection and experiment with different systems without needing to grind out a result at the expense of the performance. Yet even in friendly matches, the unforgiving German media demands results – especially against the leading nations, over whom Germany had not won since 2000 when England were defeated at Wembley. So, when Italy comprehensively beat Germany 4–1 in Florence in

March 2006, just months before the start of the World Cup, the vicious press backlash was inevitable.

One German newspaper suggested Klinsmann should consult his country's women's team for advice, while *Bild* lambasted him for 'whooping it up in sunny California', where he was living. Indeed, the latter charge was repeatedly levied at him throughout his tenure, and would only be dropped once the German team started producing results on the pitch during the World Cup. The former Tottenham player at the time was only staying one week a month in Germany, spending the rest of the time with his family in Los Angeles.

'If Bayern are playing for the title, the Germany coach should be sitting in the stadium, not watching delayed coverage of the game on ESPN in California,' remarked Bayern Munich chief executive, Uli Hoeness, voicing the sentiments of many within the German footballing fraternity.

Klinsmann's decision to miss a workshop for World Cup coaches in Germany a few months before the tournament was also roundly condemned in his homeland, with German legend Franz Beckenbauer branding his absence 'incredible'. His critics were not even placated by his explanation that the conference took place on the first anniversary of his father's death and that his mother had flown to visit him in the United States. The malcontents in the German press pack were also on Klinsmann's back because of his decision to leave Borussia Dortmund defender, Christian Wörns, out of the Italy game, a decision that appeared misguided given the way Germany's rearguard was ripped to shreds by the Italians. Wörns was the first name on the team sheet in the back four until Germany slumped to a defeat against Slovakia near the end of 2005, prompting Klinsmann to reveal that he favoured Hannover's Per Mertesacker and Cologne's Lukas Sinkiewicz. He insisted Wörns did not 'fit with our philosophy', but Michael Ballack was quick to denounce the decision, commenting, 'I'll certainly talk to the coach about it. Christian was always an important part of our team.'

When most players question their manager's judgement, they can expect to be severely rebuked or even summarily jettisoned into the international wilderness.

Not Michael Ballack – when you are your country's symbol and heartbeat, you can speak your mind quite freely without censure. The beleaguered Klinsmann would have been risking the wrath of the German nation and perhaps might have even jeopardised his own job had he clashed with Michael – although he still stood by his contentious decision to axe Wörns. This would not be the first time that the two men had differing opinions during their brief working relationship. But the mutual respect they shared and their common goal of transforming Germany into unlikely World Cup winners prevented their relationship from becoming overly destructive. But petty personal squabbles were the least of their worries – the morale and form of the German national team were infinitely more vexing. When it came to the crunch, Michael was standing by his manager in the face of unrelenting criticism. The German captain enthused, 'Jürgen has some good ideas and his methods make you feel a real wind of change, something fresh. The criticism he has got has been exaggerated, but then the national coach, along with the Chancellor, is the most important person in the country!'

Michael said that he knew when to keep his mouth shut,

adding, 'I do try to speak my mind but we have to stick to the rules. The coach is the boss and everybody has to follow him. If everybody spoke out in public it would be chaotic, especially at crucial moments.' He and his team-mates appreciated the fact that Klinsmann was, despite the scepticism of the media, succeeding in fostering a camaraderie and *joie de vivre* in the German camp. Rather than demand that his players were cooped up in an isolated mountain retreat, he believed that team outings and city centre hotel bases suited his team better.

While British players enjoy keeping themselves entertained with a PlayStation or by playing snooker, Klinsmann introduced novel ways of occupying his players between matches. For instance, at a Swiss training camp before the World Cup, Michael and the rest of the German squad learnt how to make a watch. Team manager Oliver Bierhoff explained, 'They learnt how to take a watch apart and put it back together again. It's something a bit different.' The German management also asked Ballack and co to read a treatise on etiquette and human relations written by the 18th-Century nobleman Adolphe Knigges. Oliver Bierhott explained that the thinking behind the bizarre request was to try and develop players' personalities both on and off the football pitch.

Klinsmann explained the rationale for his idiosyncratic approach to the *Observer*'s Amy Lawrence, saying, 'Nobody wants to stay outside somewhere in the suburbs. After three days walking up and down their hotel rooms, they are bumping against the walls. We asked them and they wanted to go out, to buy some CDs, to visit Starbuck's. Today, we have a sports psychology session, then they have to sign some shirts for an hour and then they're free. They go for dinner by themselves and they've got to be back by 11.30pm. They are self-responsible for what they do and they need to go out, they need to hear what people think, and they love it. It is a new generation. It's hip-hop.'

He also explored innovative ways of preparing the Germans for matches, including showing his team a video of Costa Rica prior to Germany's meeting with the South Americans in the first game of the World Cup. In an initiative described by Michael as 'highly educational', Klinsmann believed that gaining an insight into the Costa Ricans' culture and lifestyle would provide clues as to their character and likely playing style.

Not everything Klinsmann subscribed to fell into the 'innovative' category, though; he was a great believer in the benefit of good, old-fashioned toil on the training ground, particularly important during a tournament where successive matches can take their toll on both mind and body. To that end, he brought in Mark Verstegen, an American fitness coach who led intensive training sessions designed to aid endurance and speed – key facets of Germany's new, high-tempo playing style. Under Verstegen's gruelling régime, Michael and his fellow Germans were forced to drag heavy weights around a pitch, although there were also one-to-one sessions tailored to individual needs. Klinsmann also employed his staff to work on his players' psychology, promoting positive thinking at all times.

Then there was the issuing of… homework. Michael and his team-mates were each given a particular assignment to complete after hours to sharpen up their concentration. For instance, in his house in Bremen, Miroslav Klose's assignment involved trying to turn the light switches off by kicking a ball at them. As news of this unconventional approach prior to the World Cup leaked out, Klinsmann's stock fell to such a low that he was viewed more as a strict schoolmaster, floundering in his teaching methods, than a genius professor, heartily acclaimed for his inspirational coaching style.

There was an urgent need for Klinsmann, Michael and their team-mates to arrest the plummeting confidence the German people had in their national team and its chances of success in the World Cup. A survey conducted after the Italy defeat revealed that fewer than 10 per cent of Germans thought their team was capable of succeeding in their quest for silverware. In the fallout from the disastrous loss to the Italians, Michael said it was imperative that Germany enjoyed a swift upturn in fortunes as the World Cup rapidly approached. He commented, 'Thank God the next match is only three weeks away, when we play another friendly against the USA. You will see a different German team then. It's a decisive game. Not just for us but also for the mood of the country. It's important going into the World Cup that we get a successful result.'

Cometh the hour and cometh Michael and Germany, who recorded a 4–1 victory over the ever-improving Americans in their next World Cup warm-up match in Dortmund, which was dubbed 'das Spiel der Wahrheit' – the game of truth. Michael was on target with a header, although only the most optimistic of German supporters would accept that everything was now rosy in the World Cup hosts' garden.

It had to be borne in mind that the USA had fielded a

weakened side and were not among the world's élite. Yet with Luxembourg, Japan and Colombia remaining for Germany in their build-up games to the football extravaganza, there would not be the opportunity for Michael *et al* to show that they could match the world's best. They just had to rely on gaining confidence from more wins and to savour the World Cup fever that was beginning to build.

So what could Germany and a fired-up Michael Ballack – intent on erasing the depressing memories of his enforced absence from the World Cup final four years earlier – realistically expect from their date with destiny in their own country? Michael was cautiously optimistic when asked to discuss Germany's chances in an interview with the journalist, Wolfgang Golz. He admitted, 'Of course, I'm the captain and we are aiming high. But it will be difficult. Sometimes you have to rise to the challenge even if that doesn't appear realistic at first. In 2002, hardly anybody thought we had a chance and we got to the Final. This time we are at home and we will have our fantastic fans behind us. That will motivate every player of the team to go beyond his limits.'

What excited Michael, a man with an innate instinct to attack, was Jürgen Klinsmann's desire to surge forward in numbers when the opportunity presented itself. The dour defensiveness of the Rudi Völler reign was no more; in Miroslav Klose, who scored five goals at the 2002 World Cup, and Lukas Podolski, Germany had two vibrant young attackers who could profit from Ballack's creativity in central midfield. Michael said, 'In the past, Germany had a reputation for having an impermeable defence and for waiting for opponents to make a mistake before trying to score. These days, we are a more attacking side but we must be careful to track back and not leave ourselves too exposed.'

Germany's talismanic captain was also salivating at the promising clutch of youngsters they had at their disposal – marauding left-back Philipp Lahm, who was only 22, 21-year-old centre-back Per Mertesacker, talented midfielder Bastian Schweinsteiger, also 21, and the highly-rated Lukas Poldoski, who turned 21 just before the World Cup. He commented, 'We have a lot of hugely talented youngsters... all they're lacking is experience. Eight or nine are still young enough to play in the Under-21s. When they are 25 or 26 and have that experience and have confirmed the hopes placed in them, Germany will be extremely strong. You can feel that a great generation is coming through.'

It remained to be seen whether Jürgen Klinsmann's decision to favour youthful promise over seasoned campaigners, such as Didi Hamann of Liverpool and Christian Wörns, was a wise decision. However, a win in the opening match against Costa Rica would imbue his country with the confidence that would compensate for any inexperience and nerves as the home advantage factor came into effect. Michael added, 'It's a delicate thing to play the opening match of the World Cup with a young side and you only have to look at opening matches of the past to see that favourites often run into difficulties. But it's up to the more experienced players to show we are ready and competitive. We have this great advantage of playing at home – but we just don't know how we will deal with any difficulties once they come.' He went on to admit to Wolfgang Golz that he was revelling in the intensifying media spotlight as the World Cup loomed large on the horizon. 'There are constant profiles in the media where players' form is rated for the World Cup,' he remarked. 'At the moment, it is just based on the performance of a particular day. However, every aspect of a player's performance will be evaluated as the tournament gets closer. People are already stopping me in the street and wishing us well for the World Cup. That makes you feel good.'

So what were his opinions on Germany's group, a section they were expected to coast through? 'Poland will be tough to beat. They finished only one point behind a very strong England team in their qualifying group. With supposedly smaller nations such as Ecuador and Costa Rica, there is always the danger that you don't show them enough respect. It's a trap we must not fall into. I'd go as far as to say we'll find it easier against the top teams.'

When asked by *Spiegel* magazine to summarise his thoughts on whether the World Cup would serve up a more palatable feast of football than the European Championships in 2004, the German captain responded, 'Hopefully, yes, particularly with the South American teams taking part. Their natural game is dynamic, keeping things in constant motion. Then you have the Africans who play so freely, move differently, such agile athletes. But at tournaments like this, you tend to see novel, unanticipated trends coming through, with everyone watching each other like hawks and immediately copying anything new. What is really important for every team is to be aware of its own capabilities and find a style which plays to one's own strengths.'

Yet just two weeks before the World Cup, in an unpleasant echo of four years earlier, Michael's participation in the tournament was thrown into doubt when he injured his ankle in a practice match in Geneva. Just as England prayed for the recovery of their talisman Wayne Rooney, who had broken his foot in April, Germany sweated on the fitness of their spearhead, with the German media inducing panic with hyperbolic comment and speculation about Michael, whose popularity had reached messianic levels.

The *Guardian*'s Luke Harding wrote, 'The German press has wasted little time in indulging in overblown speculation as to what might happen should Germany's talismanic captain fail to return to full fitness. As Berlin's *BZ* newspaper put it on Saturday: "Our destiny hangs by this foot."'

Shorn of Michael's presence, with Tim Borowski taking over the central role in midfield, Germany had little trouble in beating Luxembourg by the morale-boosting margin of 7–0 at the end of May. Michael recovered to take his place in the team for their penultimate warm-up game against Japan, held at his old stomping ground, the BayArena – home of Bayer Leverkusen. He was unable to inspire a lacklustre Germany to victory, however, as the Germans snatched a 2–2 draw with the Japanese through two late goals from Miroslav Klose and Bastian Schweinsteiger.

The indifferent display enraged Michael, who fumed, 'The weaknesses of the past two years have not been solved. We play with too much risk. We always have to think defence. Every player has to have this all the time on his mind and not wait for the instructions from the coach. He added 'It's important for us players to have the certainty, to know who is playing next to me. It's good to know who is playing and how we are playing. That gives us players a secure feeling. The coach knows my opinion. We agree on most points but sometimes we have different opinions.'

Once again, given his significance within the German team, he knew his outburst would not be viewed too harshly by Klinsmann and his management team. He insisted he was merely fulfilling his duty as captain and was not seeking to undermine his coach. Later he defended his outspoken comments by insisting, 'There were some deficiencies which I simply had to address. That is what he [Klinsmann] expects from me. The team needs to understand that a good defence will be the key to success. The coach knows what I think as well as what other players think. We have already spoken about this but it's up to him to make the final decisions.' Klinsmann, meanwhile, said he appreciated a player like Michael voicing his thoughts. And Germany seemed to be galvanised by their skipper's scathing words when they defeated Colombia 3–0 in their final game before the World Cup opener against Costa Rica.

Michael scored the opening goal in the win, although he still harboured doubts about his team-mates – and also sustained a calf strain, which was to be the subject of frenzied debate in the days before the World Cup kicked off. He told the German daily newspaper *Handelsblatt*, 'We have players that have been on the pitch only sporadically with their club teams. We don't have the choice of players we had in the 1990 World Cup or in the 1996 European Championship. As a result, the team makes mistakes and is not fixed. For that reason, I think there is a little uncertainty as we head into the tournament.'

He confessed that his injury was 'nagging' rather than serious and German assistant coach Joachim Löw said that such ailments were common for a committed and combative player of his calibre. Löw remarked, 'He goes into a lot of tackles and is tightly marked by his opponents. Very often he can only be stopped by fouls. I don't expect it to be a serious issue. It is just a normal bruise.'

But how wrong he was. Michael's injury, which soon materialised as more serious than was first expected, and his ever-decreasing chances of being fit for Germany's World Cup opener were soon dominating the news headlines in his homeland. And so 'the country's calf muscle' was born. Of particular interest to the voracious newshounds reporting on the biggest sporting event in the world was Michael's choice of treatment for his calf strain – a healer by the name of Kurt Schweinberger. *Bild* carried a photograph on its front cover of him leaving the office of Herr Schweinberger carrying a bottle of water; apparently, the '*Naturheiler*' was trying to speed up his recovery by undertaking bioenergy, using oscillating water and electrodes to fend off negative energy caused by the injury.

Bild hailed the technique '*Wunderwasser*' or 'wonder water', although a degree of scepticism about its effect was still retained as Michael Walker of the *Guardian* reported, 'In England, the idea would bring ridicule, plus the ghost of Eileen Drewery [Glenn Hoddle's spiritual healer]. *Bild* did ask whether this was "hokus-pocus" but Klose and other Germany players – Jens Lehmann and Robert Huth among them – have also visited Schweinberger, who works occasionally with Werder Bremen, where Klose plays. Torsten Frings, also of Werder, said that after ten Schweinberger visits, Werder lost only once. Klose was earnest when he added, "We have top doctors and physios, but if a player, psychologically speaking, has trust in other people – call them healers or whatever – that is up to them. If that is someone's key to success, then that is his choice.'"

Meanwhile, Jürgen Klinsmann was said to be privately unhappy that Michael had underestimated the extent of his injury, although he was perfectly satisfied with his decision to seek alternative healing methods. Michael, too, was aggrieved about the fuss created by his untimely injury and the fact that he was accused of waiting two days before announcing it. He therefore decided to release a media statement saying, 'I completely reject all allegations this was handled unprofessionally. Such claims are an affront. It's almost a slur on my reputation.' In the meantime, Borussia Dortmund's Sebastian Kehl and Tim Borowski of Werder Bremen were the two men lined up to replace Germany's great white hope.

But the German nation and Michael refused to contemplate his likely absence from the opening game. In an Internet blog for BBC Sport, reporter Celina Hinchliffe described the fraying nerves and tear-stained, ashen faces in Munich the day before the big game as Germans contemplated the impending absence of their leader. She said, 'Grown German men in my hotel are on the verge of tears with the news that Michael Ballack may be out of the opening match' (though until the team sheet is published, no one really knows). I spotted two men hugging and consoling each other over the biggest glass of beer I have ever seen in my life. If you think Rooney has fans in Britain hanging by his metatarsal tissue, Michael's calf strain is the talk of Munich and Germany as a whole.'

Michael, meanwhile, was defiant. Just a day after Jürgen

Klinsmann ruled him out of the clash, there was another twist to the extraordinary 'is he… isn't he?' saga – he astonishingly pronounced himself fit. He told *Bild*, 'I am fit, I want to play. I am ready and without problems. Whether I will be playing or not is up to the national team coach. I have had intensive treatment. I feel fit and I'm not feeling pain any more. I want to play.'

Imagine Wayne Rooney openly disagreeing with the combustible Sir Alex Ferguson? Here was further evidence both of Michael's ego, his standing within the game, and his burning desire to represent his country. Yet in the battle for supremacy Klinsmann would not back down and reasserted his authority by adhering to his original decision to omit Michael from his team to face the Costa Ricans. 'We wanted Michael on board as he is our captain and leader but it is important that he recovers,' he said. 'We want him to get back to full fitness so that he can be fit for the other games in the competition.'

Michael now reluctantly had to resign himself to missing the eagerly-awaited opening match of the host country in the greatest football competition on earth. It was a savage blow to a man who had to sit out Germany's last game in a World Cup – the Final. Reflecting on his statistics during Klinsmann's tenure showed the massive void his absence would leave in the German team. He had scored 31 goals in 65 internationals, a phenomenal return for a midfielder, and he was now regarded as the sole German world-class player. He had also missed just 6 of Klinsmann's 27 games in charge, although Germany could comfort themselves with the knowledge that they had lost just once without Michael, in a 2–1 defeat to Turkey in October 2005.

Another East German-born player, Bernd Schneider, assumed Michael's captaincy duties, while the angular Tim Borowski of Werder Bremen took his place in the line-up against Costa Rica. And Germany responded to being without their totem in magnificent style, in a 4–2 win which epitomised Jürgen Klinsmann's free-spirited and flamboyant attacking philosophy. It was the ideal start to a major tournament and, what's more, the refreshing manner of Germany's play and, more importantly, the three points, had consigned the Michael 'scandal' to the back of an expectant nation's minds.

Thankfully, any hint of a feud between Klinsmann and Michael was also removed when the pair openly aired their respective viewpoints about the injury drama. Klinsmann had been vindicated by his decision to start without Michael, and rationalised his argument as follows: 'It's the World Cup opening match, at home. But I also told him, "What if something happens to you? What will then go on in the nation?" We had to tell him we were responsible for the whole team and responsible for his health. We'd be devoid of responsibility if we let him go on. It's not a problem if a player says he wants to play – I hope all my players are like that... He was raring to go, champing at the bit. It's a tough decision for a coach. Michael said he was ready, he could definitely play, but we had a scan and it still showed some kind of problem, so we'd never take the risk. We'll build him up slowly but surely.'

Michael responded by reiterating his intransigence in the whole affair was borne of a keenness to play. He said, 'We were of different opinions... he had to stop me. I simply wanted to play. I didn't have any pain, but the doctors were against it.' Nevertheless, he was impressed by Germany's performance without him. He went on to say, 'I am really pleased by the way the team did it. It's always difficult in the opening match. We scored two sensational goals – four goals – that's always strong.'

Once the euphoria had subsided after Germany's stunning win, media attention returned to Michael's anatomy – or, more precisely, his suspect calf. Was the most famous leg in Germany fully recovered and able to take the field against Poland? Thankfully, after all the furore, he was passed fully fit and was the only change from the Germany side that beat Costa Rica, replacing Tim Borowski.

Yet his reintroduction into the fold would not be without hitches and he was again at the centre of a media storm due to his choice of attire during a training session before the Poland game. He made the mistake of wearing a T-shirt bearing the name of one of Germany's sworn enemies, Italy, anathema to the patriots in the media who wanted to whip up a feeling of national identity to underpin their country's bid to win the World Cup. When the reporters asked him why he had chosen to wear the T-shirt, he simply answered, 'I have had it for one year now, and I really like to wear it. It's my favourite T-shirt.'

Doubts over his choice of T-shirt aside, for Michael, the game against Poland carried extra significance given that he had been born in the old East Germany, near the Polish border. He called the showdown between the neighbours 'an emotional affair', and said that the Poles would be in belligerent mood given their loss to Ecuador in the opening game. Driven on by an estimated 25,000 pumped-up Polish fans, Germany's opponents were set to be a dangerous test for the host nation, he warned. 'Their country has grown nervous and they will be highly motivated. Their backs are against the wall and it will be a heated battle because, for them, it is all or nothing and that is something we need to be prepared for.'

Indeed, Germany had to wait until the closing stages of a dour struggle to snatch a winner through Oliver Neuville. This was Germany at their ruthless best, grinding out a victory through sheer force of will, while Michael's first match in the World Cup 2006 was satisfactory as he dictated play from midfield. He displayed his usual range of assured passing and commitment to the cause and was also denied a goal when his shot cannoned off the bar.

Of slight concern to Germany was a booking Michael picked up which, like 2002, could come back to haunt him if the hosts progressed in the tournament. Nevertheless, Jürgen Klinsmann was not about to protect his key man; the horrific experience of missing the World Cup Final through accumulative yellow cards was surely enough to prevent him from picking up any rash bookings in Germany's final Group A match against Ecuador. Michael admitted, 'It is always difficult to scale back in a World Cup match. There are a few situations where you start to hesitate and to second-guess your moves, but I am experienced enough to deal with it.' He successfully escaped the wrath of the referee and avoided entering the official's notebook as Germany comfortably disposed of the South Americans 3–0.

Michael – who was named Man of the Match for his endeavours – provided a delightful chipped pass for Miroslav Klose to score the second goal, but was hampered in the second half of the contest when a forceful tackle left him with a nasty bruise.

After securing such a trouble-free passage into the second round, Germany and their captain could breathe a collective sigh of relief and focus on more demanding challenges to come. Suddenly, everyone was smiling with Grinsi Klinsi rather than scowling at his every tactical decision or disagreement with Michael, as joy and optimism spread throughout the nation. Germany had been transformed from a dour and slightly colourless European state into a land buzzing and bubbling with electric expectancy and football fervour. Its cities were crammed with flag-waving fanatics sporting Michael Ballack shirts, clamouring around big screens and joyfully thronging the streets whenever their country was playing. An entirely new era of public pride in the country and a delight in the success of the football team was gradually displayed and celebrated in a way that had not been seen since the aftermath of World War II. Germans felt comfortable now expressing pride in their homeland, for the first time in half a century, and other nations felt comfortable in seeing them do it.

Surely, if unheralded Germany could reach the Final on Asian soil in 2002, their dizzying momentum and inspirational support could carry them one step further in their own land? In the knock-out stages, four years previously, Michael Ballack had come of age, so why could he not replicate the achievement and instigate a successful push for glory this time? Of course, there were several reasons why Germany might fail to deliver the ultimate prize for the legion of fans – one major factor was the quality of the likes of Argentina, Brazil, France and England, who had all successfully negotiated the group stages and had now stepped into the maelstrom of the winner-takes-all second phase games.

Germany's second-round opponents, though – Sweden – were ideal opponents for the hosts; the Scandinavians may be obdurate, plucky combatants with an impressive World Cup pedigree, but on paper they did not pose a significant threat to an upwardly-mobile country playing in front of its adoring faithful. Germany seemed to have read this script as they tore into their opponents with verve and gusto, storming into a two-goal lead within 12 minutes, thanks to a brace from Lukas Poldolski. It was an explosive display of unrelenting pace and power, which recalled the Germany of old and exemplified the new gung-ho attacking spirit encouraged by Jürgen Klinsmann. Michael was simply immense, strutting about imperiously, spraying probing and precise passes all over the Stadion München pitch, and firing speculative shots from distance with either foot – the Germans had an astonishing 26 shots on target – as Germany poured forward with abandon, as if released from the burdening shackles of expectation. Sweden could muster little in response and the only decent chance they had – a penalty taken by Henrik Larsson in his final international – was thumped into the stands.

After such a convincing display, Germany had hammered out an emphatic message of intent that they had become genuine World Cup contenders. The aftermath of this exhilarating victory over the Swedes, though, brought yet more worries for Michael on the injury front. He was forced to miss training with a sore foot, although he was subsequently passed fit for Germany's quarter-final against Argentina.

Not many people gave Germany a chance against the South Americans, citing the fact again that the hosts had not beaten a top-quality international side since their 1–0 win against England at Wembley in 2000. The Argentinians had also been installed as World Cup favourites after weaving a mesmerising route to the last eight with some sumptuous football.

It was a game of two playmakers – Michael versus the languid conductor of the Argentine orchestra, Juan Román Riquelme – both of whom were eminently capable of exerting a stranglehold on the game with their supreme ability and authoritative command of the pitch. Victory in this pivotal personal battle would be one of the keys to the outcome of what promised to be a fascinating collision of styles and tactics, as Gordon Strachan outlined in the *Guardian*: 'The battle for supremacy between Michael and Riquelme will be intriguing. They play the same sort of playmaker position but in very different styles. Riquelme slows things down and is very cunning, whereas Michael is all action, gets shots at goal and is much more of a goalscorer.

'Michael is a huge presence for Germany, physically and as a personality. He can play the ball short or hit 45- or 50-yard diagonal passes. If you watch the Germany midfielders, when he receives the ball on the left, one of them will stay wide on the right because they know he can reach them, but I am sure Argentina will be round him so quickly it's not true and I can't imagine they will let him have as many shots as Sweden did.'

Yet a confident Michael refused to acknowledge that Riquelme's threat was as potent as many pundits such as Strachan suggested. He insisted Germany would not 'stoop so low' as to man-mark the Argentinian maestro, which could be interpreted as a sign of cockiness or merely burgeoning confidence at his country's ability to impose themselves on the game without needing to worry unduly about stifling their opponents. He said, 'We are not afraid, even though the opponent is Argentina and, besides Brazil, have been the best team in this tournament. But after our most recent performances, we do not need to hide ourselves. The team is in very confident mood and we know we have a big chance to defeat them. We have the hunger to play three more matches and that is why our chances are 60:40. We are not worried.'

While he preferred to focus on his own and his countrymen's talents, the football world was excitedly analysing the respective merits of two great footballing nations. It was the classic match of contrasts – red-blooded Latins against ice-cool Europeans, artists versus artisans and underdog versus favourites – the team who prevailed in this eagerly-anticipated encounter could undoubtedly then go all the way to the Final and become World Champions.

The game, though – as is often the case when a game is prone to such hype – failed to live up to expectations. Germany v Argentina was an angst-ridden affair as both countries appeared weighed down by the inhibiting pressure of the occasion. There was little to excite the neutrals or, more pertinently, the German fans, as Argentina dominated possession, caressing the ball around for 60 per cent of the time in the first-half without carving out any clear-cut opportunities.

Michael was seen exhorting his troops to even greater efforts and led by example when he sent a flashing header wide on 16 minutes after bursting through into the box from midfield and meeting Bernd Schneider's right-wing outswinger. It was a golden chance spurned and, in a tight contest which would be decided by the narrowest of margins, he was hoping he would not live to regret his profligacy. Indeed, it was Argentina who drew first blood, finally piercing the German defence on 48 minutes, when Roberto Ayala rose unchallenged in the box to head home.

How could the Germans, hitherto ineffectual and second-best, contemplate victory when their opponents were able to fend them off with slick possession play to dictate the tempo and therefore their own destiny? The first glimmer of hope came through the Argentinan coach, Jose Pekerman, who seriously undermined his country's chances of maintaining or extending their lead by confining his creative geniuses, Lionel Messi and Javier Saviola, to the bench. He further weakened his side's vice-like grip on the game by committing the cardinal sin of withdrawing Michael's equal in the midfield, Riquelme. The sullen-faced schemer may have been having an off day, but he was still the pivot around which Argentina's attacks revolved; he was also, like Michael, capable of a moment of genius that could decide a match at any given moment

Michael nearly drew his side level with 20 minutes remaining when he pounced on a loose ball in a penalty box scramble, but mis-hit a volley into the ground which was blocked by Ayala and then hacked clear. Five minutes later, Germany's concerted pressure paid off when Miroslav Klose headed in his fifth goal of the World Cup and Michael, almost inevitably, was involved in the build-up. He swung the ball in from the right, and Borowski headed the ball into the path of Klose, who dispatched a low header into the bottom left-hand corner of the Argentinian net.

The hosts had now surged into the ascendancy. Their chances of ousting the favourites were accelerated when the match entered extra time, after which the German footballer's favourite pastime – converting penalties with cool aplomb under unbearable pressure – followed. As a master of penalty-taking, Michael was an obvious choice for one of the crucial kicks, but the fickle hand of fate is never far away, and this time it was felt in the gut-wrenching pain experienced by all sportsmen and women from time to time – cramp. Towards the end of the extra time period, Michael suffered dreadfully from the condition, and would surely not have even been on the pitch had Jürgen Klinsmann not already employed his three substitutes.

But when extra-time ended and the nerve-shredding match decider – the penalty shootout – arrived, most spectators expected the hobbling Michael Ballack to sit out the ordeal, watching from the sidelines, rubbing his aching limbs. He was barely able to walk properly, let alone kick a ball with any conviction; this would be virtually impossible in normal circumstances, never mind the all-consuming pressure of penalties. However, as we have seen, Michael is not one to withdraw in times of difficulty, nor shirk his responsibilities – he was determined that he, as Germany's captain, was going to fulfil his duty to his country and dispatch a penalty. He was second to walk, or in his case, hobble, up football's equivalent of the Green Mile after Oliver Neuville and Julio Cruz had both successfully slotted home from 12 yards. No one would have blamed him if he had come out second-best in his own personal duel with Argentinian substitute goalkeeper Leonardo Franco, who had replaced the injured Roberto Abbondanzieri after 71 minutes.

Yet Germans, even those suffering from spasmodic muscle cramps, do not miss penalties, and Michael drove his kick confidently into the heart of the goal. It was a decisive, psychological boost to Germany and a demoralising hammer-blow to Argentina. If an ailing Michael could withstand the palpable tension in Munich, surely his weary team-mates could muster every last ounce of effort and courage to emulate their skipper's heroics. Lukas Podolski and Tim Borowski followed the impeccable example of their Captain Marvel and Jens Lehmann also covered himself in glory by saving the penalties of Esteban Cambiasso and Roberto Ayala.

Resurgent Germany had once again prevailed in the ultimate test of nerve, defeating Argentina 4–2 on penalties and, implausibly, they had reached the semi-final stage of the World Cup. German players and officials celebrated victory with joyful abandon on the pitch, although their delirium was interrupted by petulance, punches and kicks from angry Argentinians, who claimed their opponents had gloated about their triumph and goaded them. It was an unsightly mêlèe and a wholly unsavoury end to what turned out to be pulsating finish to a very ordinary game. Michael was insistent that the Argentinians were entirely culpable for the shameful scenes, which prompted a FIFA investigation.

'The first provocation came from Argentina,' he said. 'They were shouting at our players as they were going to the penalty spot. They shouted something in Spanish and we didn't understand what they were saying. But they were definitely trying to influence our strikers. After Tim Borowski scored, he put his finger to his lips to tell them to shut up. They were a bit mad at that. After that, I didn't see much but I saw one or two lying on the ground. I didn't see what happened.'

However, for Michael Ballack and Germany, nothing could darken the afterglow of success that they were basking in. He was once again his nation's hero in the dénouement of the World Cup and this time, unlike in 2002, his heroism would not be tempered with bitter disappointment. He was deservedly given the Man of the Match award, and the acclaim of his team-mates, manager and euphoric supporters. Then, with the eyes of the world on him, he delivered a perfect spot-kick – his second for Germany. 'Michael was the Budweiser Man of the Match for his commitment and leadership,' said FIFA Technical Study Group member Kim Chon Lim. 'He led the team in the fight to find the equaliser, and he had an important part in the play that tied the score. There were other very good players, like Philipp Lahm and Torsten Frings, but Michael was the spirit of the team, and he converted his penalty despite not being 100 per cent fit.'

He later reflected on his battle with injury, remarking, 'I got a kick from Juan Román Riquelme and that was possibly why I got cramp so early. We'd already used the three substitutes but I wanted to play to the end. It was tough but we fought to the end.' He was now more than ever convinced that Germany could continue their dogged pursuit of the Jules Rimet trophy. 'We've got over a huge obstacle now,' he said. 'We've beaten one of the favourites and we have great self-confidence. We have a great dream and we want to live it.'

Meanwhile, Jürgen Klinsmann said he had never doubted his captain's ability to take a penalty kick, despite his obvious discomfort. He remarked, 'My only question was whether he would take the penalty with his left or right foot. The match was a thriller, like a Hitchcock movie. Obviously, you're the happiest person in the world if you win it, and the saddest if you lose.'

Germany's march to their record eighth World Cup Final now looked as if it had been pre-ordained, but what did fate have in store for Michael Ballack in his second successive semi-final? Nothing could match the vacillating emotions of his exploits in the last four of the 2002 tournament, that much was clear. This time, only the gut-wrenching agony of defeat or the heady euphoria of victory would be experienced by Germany's inspirational captain.

Germany's opponents in the semi-final in Dortmund were Italy, another country that had enjoyed an unexpected renaissance in the World Cup, seemingly spurred on by a corruption scandal that was brewing back home. Their meeting came only months after Italy had humbled Germany 4–1 in a friendly in Florence, but ever since then, Jürgen Klinsmann's embattled side had not lost another game – yet they still had not beaten one of the world's leading nations in 90 minutes for almost six years. However, the team suffered an untimely blow ahead of the match when FIFA banned Michael's midfield partner Torsten Frings. Frings, who was replaced in Germany's line-up by Sebastian Kehl, had been caught on television throwing a punch at Argentina striker Julio Cruz during the fracas that had erupted at the end of the quarter-final.

In what turned out to be a typically tense, tight and cautious semi-final in the first-half, Michael seemed to be suffering from the cramp he had sustained in the quarter-final as he was unable to exert his usual influence on the game. He looked a shadow of the player he had proved himself to be, fouling Italy's industrious midfield warrior Gennaro Gattuso on three successive occasions as he became increasingly frustrated at his inability to assert himself. He was outshone by Andrea Pirlo in the Italian engine room, who fashioned a succession of chances for Italy, who were playing with an attacking abandon which flew in the face of their reputation for miserly defending and dogged conservatism. Germany survived the Italians' best efforts and entered extra-time happy in the knowledge that if the match remained goalless, they would be favourites to outperform the Italians in the penalty shootout.

However, just as Germany were steeling themselves for another test of their resolve in the impending shootout, Italy broke their hearts by striking a minute before the end of extra-time through Fabio Grosso. The Italians duly completed their thoroughly deserved 2–0 triumph through a delightful finish from Alessandro Del Piero. Germany and Michael were dumbstruck – surely their dreamlike World Cup odyssey was not meant to end in such a painful defeat?

As Michael knew only too well, football is a capricious, unsentimental beast, not a fairytale film. Tears streamed down his cheeks at the final whistle in a distressing echo of 2002, although, perhaps this time, his misery was even more deep-rooted, given that this defeat had come on German soil. Unlike four years earlier, however, there would be no World Cup Final for Germany and Michael could not console himself that he had been his country's hero and match-winner. He was now facing up to the depressing realisation that his last chance of lifting the World Cup had disappeared.

Speaking to the *Welt am Sonntag* newspaper, he lamented, 'It is very bitter for us to get eliminated like this, one minute from time. It is bitter but not undeserved. We started out rather slowly but did a much better job in the second half. The game was well balanced. The Italians had the better chances in extra-time as they hit woodwork twice. But we also had some good opportunities afterwards, with the header [from Lukas Podolski]. I will be almost 34 [by the time of the next World Cup] and at that age there is no guarantee I will be there. I realised this could be my last chance to be a world champion. It is just not meant to be for me.'

He was also deprived any further action in the 2006 tournament when a minor knee injury ruled him out of Germany's third-place play-off with Portugal, which the hosts won comfortably 3–1.

When Michael reflects on his performances during the 2006 World Cup, he will probably do so with a degree of regret and disappointment. He was troubled with injury throughout and was never able to consistently produce the displays which have marked him out as one of the greatest footballers of his generation. Yet he can still look back with some satisfaction on his Man of the Match performances against Ecuador and Argentina. Jürgen Klinsmann offered an accurate and glowing summary of his captain's tournament, by commenting, 'Michael Ballack has a very important role. He has literally filled out his role of captain at the World Cup. He has great strength and we speak of him with the greatest respect. He didn't play in the first game against Costa Rica and didn't train for a week, and he was trying to find his rhythm. I think the Argentina game was the best possible example of the character of Michael Ballack. He was plagued by cramp and left the pitch, but he wouldn't be substituted and only left the field after the game was decided.'

Michael returned the compliment when asked to discuss Klinsmann's involvement in the rebirth of Germany's football team after the former Tottenham striker decided to call it a day as manager, despite being implored to remain by an entire country. In an article in *Stern* magazine, Michael admitted that he had initially had his doubts about Klinsmann's methods. 'I am not thrilled, simply because something is new. I was a bit hesitant, maybe even sceptical, for instance concerning training methods.' But he went on to add that the World Cup had showed that Klinsmann had been 'right' in his adopting a new policy of exuberant attacking, which the captain felt should be maintained in the future.

The revival of the national team had certainly been embraced enthusiastically by the German public, who turned out in force with their flags, replica shirts and banners at Berlin's Brandenburg Gate to pay tribute to their heroes on the day after the third-place play-off. Some 500,000 fans held placards bearing congratulatory messages such as 'You are the world champions of our hearts' and 'We're proud of you' as Michael and the rest of the German squad lapped up their acclaim under clear blue skies and brilliant sunshine. The players – who wore T-shirts bearing the message 'Thank you, Germany' – stepped out individually to receive applause and, when Michael's turn came, he shouted to the legions below, 'Many, many thanks... you're the greatest!'

The Germany team received further reward for their endeavours during the World Cup when they were presented with silver laurels – the country's highest decoration for sporting achievement and excellence – by German president Horst Köhler in August 2006. Sadly, Michael missed the ceremony, after picking up an injury in Chelsea's Community Shield loss to Liverpool, as did Jürgen Klinsmann, who was in America at the time. Yet he was provided with a further chance to celebrate Germany's achievements when he attended the Berlin première of director Soenke Wortmann's film documentary of the World Cup entitled *Germany: A Summer Fairytale*. Wortmann had been given exclusive access to Jürgen Klinsmann's squad throughout the festival of football, and used a hand-held camera to film fly-on-the-wall footage of various stages of Germany's World Cup journey, including motivational team-talks and shower-room scenes.

One fascinating moment in the film sees Italy defender Marco Materazzi, the man who provoked Zinedine Zidane into a vicious head-butt in the World Cup final, waiting for Michael in the tunnel after Germany's semi-final loss. Materazzi is shown trying to hug and kiss Michael in a bid to console him. Michael is also prominent towards the end of the film when he voices his objection to holding a massive farewell and thank-you party for supporters in Berlin after Germany's win in the third place match in Stuttgart.

Some of his team-mates agree with Michael, suggesting they are eager to go on holiday, although others oppose him and a vote is taken – which results in Germany lapping up the ardour of their jubilant fans. Michael admits he is glad that he was outvoted on this occasion, as he may never get the chance to revel in such unfettered joy and passionate expression of patriotism as a result of his country's World Cup feats ever again.

So, if he never again appears in the World Cup arena, what will be his legacy to the tournament? He cannot be considered a World Cup great, as he has never won the Jules Rimet trophy nor dominated the tournament à la Diego Maradona or Pelé. Neither can he claim to have scored a glorious, tournament-defining goal or have performed a sublime piece of skill, comparable to Johan Cruyff's breathtaking turn in 1974, for example. Yet, having said all that, Michael Ballack displayed moments of greatness – his match-winning goals in the 2002 competition and the courageous way in which he shrugged off cramp to slot home a penalty in 2006, for example. He will also be forever remembered for his incredible transformation from villain to hero in a matter of minutes during the 2002 World Cup semi-final, where he picked up a yellow card, knowing it would preclude him from the Final, and promptly scored the winning goal for his country.

But what also needs to be borne in mind is that Michael was central to the resurgence of two Germany teams which had looked anything but World Cup winners prior to the tournaments. He was the enigmatic tyro who secured Germany's qualification to the contest in 2002 by almost single-handedly seeing off Ukraine in the two-legged play-off match.

Four years later, he was the world-class talent and lynchpin of his country's football team, who was fundamental to Germany's revival under Jürgen Klinsmann. If he does withstand the test of time and make South Africa 2010 at the age of nearly 34, he would be part of a team which would, given its youthful promise at the moment, theoretically be at its peak. And if he plays – well or otherwise – the third instalment of his World Cup adventure will, in view of his past involvement with the tournament, undoubtedly be another roller-coaster ride for the former East German, who has yet to give up completely on his dream of lifting the most prestigious trophy in global football.

12

Market Leader

Footballers have long been willing pawns in the marketing men's money-making schemes. Their global popularity means they are deluged with requests to endorse all manner of weird and wonderful products – all for considerable cash sums which can, in some cases, outstrip their earnings from football. And if a practitioner of the beautiful game is blessed with good looks and an unsullied character, the rewards they can reap are that much more extravagant.

Step forward Michael Ballack, the epitome of the modern footballer-cum-promotional vehicle. He is young, talented, famous, stylish and handsome, ticking all the boxes of the fat cats of world-renowned corporations such as Adidas, Coca Cola, McDonald's, Sony and PlayStation – all of whom employ him in lucrative advertising contracts.

Even his current club, Chelsea, has to pay £25,000 a week out of his estimated £130,000 salary to protect the German star's image rights, a deal his agent Dr Michael Becker helped broker. Chief executive of Chelsea's kit sponsors Adidas, Herbert Hainer, confirmed the fact that Michael met certain image criteria to make him an ideal advertising figurehead for his company after being asked the following question by Germany's *Spiegel* magazine: 'If Michael played soccer just as well, but looked like a cross between the House of Horrors and Quasimodo, would you sponsor him?'

Hainer replied, 'It would be tougher for him, because fans today don't only care about achievement, but about good looks, good public appearance and good lifestyle.'

Little wonder, then, that Michael is tied to Adidas until 2012, promoting the sportswear giant, along with the likes of other leading world football icons such as David Beckham, Raul and Kaka. He has taken centre stage in the sports firm's numerous marketing drives, perhaps the most striking and ambitious of which saw him elevated into football heaven, metaphorically at least, when his image was incorporated into a fresco similar to Michaelangelo's legendary artwork in the Sistine Chapel. The 20 x 40 metre fresco was installed in Cologne's main train station during the 2006 World Cup and featured Michael and fellow German Lukas Podolski, and a clutch of other Adidas-sponsored luminaries of world football – Zinedine Zidane, Lionel Messi and David Beckham, to name but three – captured in an impressive piece of art created by illustrator Felix Reidenbach.

He was also part of another Adidas World Cup 2006 commercial called 'The Impossible Team', designed to fire the imagination of young and impressionable football fans – and ultimately sell shedloads of products. The aspirational advert showed Michael, other renowned world footballers and a handful of past masters of the beautiful game – such as Franz Beckenbauer and Michel Platini – form two dream teams and do battle in a hotly-contested football match.

Technological giant Sony has also acknowledged the merit of having Michael's name associated with its products. Once again, World Cup 2006 provided the impetus for Sony's campaign in which Michael showcased 13 of its products, including a laptop and a camcorder. Lucky 13 indeed for Sony and Michael Ballack.

As if further proof of his commercial appeal were needed, Michael can now also play with his own 'Kick-o-Mania' action figure. Meanwhile fast-food chain McDonald's might not automatically spring to mind when considering the image of a super-fit, world-class footballer. However, McDonald's have put considerable thought and energy into launching a new healthy-eating range, and has worked hard to woo back many of its hardcore opponents by allying itself to worthy causes, such as Children's Homes in the UK, and other charitable enterprises around the world. Football then, and the mass appeal of its world stars, such as Michael Ballack, offered the resurgent fast-food chain an opportunity it couldn't refuse.

In particular, McDonald's initiative for the World Cup – Player Escorts – was something that attracted Michael Ballack and their co-operation appeared to be a marriage made in heaven. During the 2006 tournament, McDonald's offered 1,182 children aged 6–10 years from all over Germany the once-in-a-lifetime chance to walk on to the pitch hand-in-hand with the best footballers in the world at every match.

The lucky escorts were those who demonstrated the greatest creativity in in-store drawing, writing and sculpting competitions. Michael agreed to be a patron of the programme, and enthused, 'It's a pity that there wasn't a McDonald's Player Escort Programme when I was this age. I would have done anything to be part of this once-in-a-lifetime experience.'

His profile in his home country is naturally stratospheric; he is unarguably the most popular advertising personality there. You only have to spend half an hour flicking from one television channel to the next or browse through a few magazines in his homeland to be assured of that.

The 2006 World Cup merely consolidated his billboard-blazing omnipresence in all things advertising. For example, Germany's technological magazine *SFT* dedicated 13 pages to Michael promoting televisions, laptops and all things digital during the tournament. Newspaper column inches were filled with gossip about him, while billboards and cinema screens were adorned with his brooding, square-jawed features. A Hamburg hotel even covered its façade with a massive, 1,500 square metre poster of the German icon during the festival of football.

It was no surprise, therefore, when he was announced as the most popular football advertising star in Germany, leaving contemporaries such as Oliver Kahn and Miroslav Klose trailing in his wake. The revelation was made by Thomson Media Control, a company surveying the scope and the impact of advertising in the various media in 2006, after it was confirmed that Michael Ballack had earned €15.3 million (£10.2 million) from advertising contracts.

Given all this exposure, there was perhaps the insidious danger that Germany would soon become sick and tired of Ballack, and that his omnipresence could destroy his marketability. Ralf Zilligen, Creative Director at BBDO Campaign Düsseldorf, certainly thought so. In an interview with *Spiegel* magazine, he remarked, 'Consumers see Michael Ballack appearing in ads for four or five companies on a single day. With that kind of exposure, who can tell what he's promoting any more?'

Spiegel revealed evidence that corroborated Zilligen's view. The magazine went on to say, 'The [Cologne Sports & Market Institute's] market research discovered 83 per cent of consumers believe that advertising with soccer stars lacks credibility. Besides, consumers hardly even notice whoever happens to be appearing in ads for any given product at any given moment. Not even 10 per cent of those surveyed could say that Michael is a spokesman for sporting goods maker Adidas. So is the use of such stars nothing but money wasted?'

Perhaps realising that over-exposure in an over-abundance of ephemeral advertisements is detrimental to his self-image, Michael has often leapt at the chance to use his fame to benefit more worthy campaigns. He was delighted to promote FIFA's anti-racism message at the World Cup, for instance, saying, 'Football has no room for racism of any kind... especially at the World Cup. We footballers always want to win, but we always treat our opponents with respect and fairness, no matter what the colour of their skin or their religious convictions. I hope the fans who travel to Germany from all over the world for the 2006 FIFA World Cup will act in exactly the same way and, in spite of all the footballing rivalry, will join together for one giant party both inside and outside the stadium.' True to the World Cup motto: 'A time to make friends'. Michael also backed the Germany city of Leipzig's ultimately unsuccessful bid to stage the 2012 Olympic Games.

In May 2006, he signed up for something with more longevity and credibility when he was appointed a Special Representative for the Joint United Nations Programme on HIV/AIDS (UNAIDS). His prestigious role involves him raising awareness on HIV and AIDS with an emphasis on youth and sport. 'I am proud to have Michael Ballack on board as a UNAIDS Special Representative,' said Dr Peter Piot, UNAIDS Executive Director. 'Through his dedication and eagerness to make a difference, I know he will be a strong voice on HIV and AIDS. Mr Ballack's talent and commitment will inspire young people to be smart about HIV.'

Michael added, 'AIDS is everyone's business. Sport and especially football can help break social barriers and fight stigma and HIV. Through sport, young people can become more self-confident and protect themselves from HIV. I want today's youth to know the facts about HIV and AIDS. In my new role as UNAIDS Special Representative, I will help save lives by engaging the sports world to take action against AIDS.'

He was keen to promote the safe-sex cause, then, but was not so willing to ally himself with other issues relating to sex or promiscuity. Therefore, when the German erotic retail store Beate Uhse thought it would launch a Michael Ballack sex toy during the 2006 World Cup, the Chelsea star was none too impressed. Beate Uhse wanted to capitalise on women's obsession with football icons by marketing its own line of vibrators apparently named after Michael Ballack, Oliver Kahn and David Beckham.

The red 'Michael B' model was 16 centimetres long (6.3 inches), cost £50 and came with the message: 'The players' muscular torsos arouse women's fantasies. They dream about spending an hour between the sheets with their fantasy man'. Both Michael and Oliver Kahn were distinctly turned off at the prospect of being used to titillate women, however, and successfully banned sales of the vibrator after serving injunctions. A lawyer for Michael claimed that the sex toy was 'an objection to my client's honour'.

Michael was sending out a clear message that while he accedes to many demands for his name to be used in advertising campaigns, he isn't desperate and eschews lending his name to anything that he believes would damage his unblemished reputation. Beate Uhse spokesman Assia Tsernookoff rather unconvincingly protested the company's innocence in the whole affair. She insisted, 'We never had any intention to make a connection between the vibrators on sale in our shops with the names of "Olli K" and "Michael B" and the footballers.'

Michael's avowed dislike of being portrayed as a sex symbol has also seen him reject the chance to pose with a top model and display his naked torso for the front cover of *Vogue* magazine. But his reluctance to fulfil the fantasy male role and the fact that he has a long-term girlfriend, Simone Lambe, and three children have not doused German women's ardour for their handsome star.

His athletic physique – he is a statuesque 6-foot 2-and-a-half inches tall – and his 1950s French film-star good looks, jet-black hair and dark skin have made him one of the most revered male pin-ups in his home country. Women's magazines in Germany have regularly nominated him the most handsome footballer in the country, while the daily newspaper *Bild* put him on its front cover twice in the space of a week following the 2002 World Cup. One headline summed up his universal appeal perfectly: 'EVERYBODY LOVES MICHAEL, ESPECIALLY WOMEN'.

Perhaps the sense of mystique surrounding Michael, given his aversion to the public glare, have added to his magnetic allure. While living in Germany, he successfully maintained his image as a clean-cut, family man and devoted father, fiercely guarding his privacy in a lavish home on the banks of the Starnberger Lake just south of Munich. He also only agreed to a biography before the World Cup on the condition that the book did not explore his private life.

It remains to be seen whether he can be as adept at shielding himself and his nearest and dearest from the intrusion of the notoriously invasive English media, however. His cause has not been helped by the fact that he is engaged to Simone Lambe, a stunningly attractive woman – manna from heaven for tabloids who crave a good-looking celebrity couple to adorn the gossip columns and supply great images, and who will happily castigate them when it suits their purposes.

Could Michael and Simone – voted the ninth most attractive couple in German football in 2005 behind Rafael van der Vaart and his wife Sylvie by the German newspaper *Bild* – become the German Posh and Becks while in England, then? Highly unlikely if Michael gets his way, while Simone has

shown absolutely no desire to conform to the *Footballers'
Wives* ideal – the entirely different styles of English and
German players' wives and girlfriends (WAGs) during the
World Cup irrefutably proved that. The English brigade –
including Victoria Beckham and Wayne Rooney's girlfriend
Colleen McLoughlin – went on publicly rampant shopping
sprees while in Germany and then ostentatiously paraded their
wares while watching their men in action. The German
women, in stark contrast, were portrayed as being more
interested in the football, arriving at matches in national team
shirts and remaining more low-key in their approach. Being
on public display and judged for her fashion sense and looks
is, in complete contrast to Victoria Beckham, for example,
anathema to Simone Lambe. She shares Michael's desire for
privacy, and rarely attends the paparazzi photo-fests that her
English counterparts seem to frequent.

The pair met in the late 1990s when Michael was at
Kaiserslautern and Simone was working as a waitress in the
Café am Markt. Michael admits that their meeting was love at
first sight but Simone decided to play hard to get and only
agreed to a date after they had known each other for six
months. Four years later and the lovestruck pair had their first
baby together – Louis – on 16 August 2001. Proud father
Michael watched the birth and described the experience as the
most amazing feeling ever. A second son, Emilio, followed on
19 September 2002, reflecting Michael and Simone's penchant
for Latin names. Jordi, Michael's third child, was born on 17
March 2005.

As an archetypal family man, Michael greatly appreciates
the sanctuary of home while not involved in the pressure-

cooker environment of football. He admits that not seeing his family while flitting from match to match is 'horrible'. So when he is not involved in playing football, rather than frequent pubs and clubs like some superstar footballers, he prefers to 'chill out' at home with his children, girlfriend and dog, Sancho. Curiously, in view of such a stable and committed family unit, he and Simone have continued to postpone any wedding plans, citing their perpetually busy schedules.

It's maybe no surprise that Michael has not yet popped the question. He is, by his own admission, not romantic. Muck-raking sections of English media have therefore found it difficult to unearth salacious revelations about him away from the pitch, as he is as ordinary and as down-to-earth a guy as you could wish to meet. Flashy and stylish on the pitch, he is comfortable and predictable in the comfort of his own home.

One footballer's stereotype Michael conforms to is his love of golf, playing off a creditable handicap of 22. He joined Chelsea team-mates Andriy Shevchenko and John Terry at the Wentworth Golf Course in Surrey in September 2006 to watch the best golf player in the world, Tiger Woods, playing in a pro-am event ahead of the HSBC World Match Play tournament. Sadly, his visit was followed by a rare off-day from the phenomenally consistent Woods, who suffered a surprising loss in the first round of the tournament to fellow American, Shaun Micheel.

Woods was no lucky charm for Michael, either. When he agreed to an offer from Andriy Shevchenko to come and watch Chelsea in action against Liverpool at Stamford Bridge three days later, the German was shown his first straight red card in his football career.

Apart from golf, Michael is fond of other traditional leisure pursuits, like listening to music, reading and watching television and films. His favourite musical genre is R&B, and he is a fan of the group Destiny's Child and the American singer Kelly Rowland. He proved his own worth as a singer during Chelsea's pre-season initiation ceremony which involved the club's new players having to sing a song in front of their guffawing team-mates. His German song was well received by Chelsea manager, Jose Mourinho, who said, 'It was fantastic. I've no idea what it was, but it had a lot of rhythm.' For his part, Michael chortled with some satisfaction that he was glad that his new team-mates did not understand the ditty, whose title he could, perhaps conveniently, not recall.

He confesses that he is by no means a bookworm, but particularly enjoyed a biography about the singer Robbie Williams. He is also a devotee of the German comic, *Werner*, which details the amusing exploits of a mad-cap motorcycle rider. His friends and colleagues remark that Michael can be an extremely witty and entertaining raconteur and teller of jokes, debunking the notion that Germans have no sense of humour. The German is also a film *aficionado*, citing *The Godfather* trilogy as his favourite movies and the Americans Al Pacino and Ben Stiller as the actors he most admires. For all his massive wealth, he is by no means materialistic, unimpressed by the latest gizmos and gadgets – although he admits to being a regular visitor to the Internet auction site eBay, spending several hours a week in front of his PC.

On his official website he reveals that he is more concerned with health than wealth, remarking, 'The most valuable good is primarily health. As it goes without saying, a healthy body is particularly indispensable for professional athletes.'

With such a health-conscious outlook and professional attitude, it's unlikely that Michael will be spending his first season in England going out on boozy benders with his team-mates. For starters, he has an aversion to beer, although he is partial to the odd glass of wine. He likes Italian, Spanish and Japanese food, particularly sushi and pasta – and soon after arriving in England, he developed a taste for the traditional British delicacy that is fish, chips and mushy peas.

Fashion-wise, he exudes the same understated class as he displays on the football field; he's keen on a handful of designer labels – Dolce et Gabbana, Gucci and Donna Karan – to make him sartorially chic. Michael says he is most comfortable wearing smart-casualwear, and a black T-shirt and jeans. Even here, in the apparently uncontroversial world of high street fashion, a footballing superstar can make inadvertent column inches. And it was the love of his favourite T-shirt, the one he wore during the 2006 World Cup, bearing name of Italy, that caused so much trivial fuss at the time.

His love of fashion has proved costly, too, as during the summer of 2006, he was fined €70,000 (£47,000) after going through the 'Nothing to Declare' channel at Munich Airport. Michael had failed to pay £260 duty on a £1,200 Fendi handbag for Simone in Dubai. He initially refused to settle the fine and asked his lawyers to appeal against it, claiming Italian handbags were exempt from duty and that, in any case, he had bought the bag in the duty-free shop. However, he eventually relented to avoid a court case. €65,000 (£43,800) of his fine was donated to good causes and €5,000 (£3,370) covered the administrative costs.

Like his former manager at national team level, Jürgen Klinsmann, who negotiated his way around the perpetually congested streets of London in an unpretentious 1967 Volkswagen Beetle while playing for Spurs, Michael is not overly concerned about fast cars. One of his friends, and a former team-mate at Kaiserslautern, Olaf Marschall, recalls in Michael's 2006 biography, 'Some players come to a new club and ask, "Where's my Porsche?" When they have their first setbacks, they can't understand the world any more. Michael was not that type.'

However, while he was at Bayern Munich, he profited from the club's sponsorship agreement with Audi and, like goalkeeper Oliver Kahn, he drove a complimentary RS6 Plus Avant 4.2 quattro, the most powerful car the manufacturer produces.

Shortly after joining Chelsea, Michael admitted he had begun to yearn for a speed machine. He told the German daily newspaper *Bild*, 'Maybe I'll treat myself to another car for my 30th birthday. Experts like Torsten Frings, who has had a Ferrari for a while now, have made the Italian racer quite alluring to me.'

However, he also confessed that he was wary of stamping on the accelerator too zealously, given the plethora of speed cameras in and around London, although he insisted, 'Luckily, I have found out where they all are near me.'

Appendix 1
Ballack Factfile

NAME: Michael Ballack

DATE OF BIRTH: 29/9/76

PLACE OF BIRTH: Chemnitz, Germany

HEIGHT: 6'2.5" (189cm)

WEIGHT: 12st 8lbs (80kg)

MARITAL STATUS: Partner, Simone Lambe

CHILDREN: Louis, Emilio and Jordi

NICKNAMES: Micha, Balla, the little Kaiser

PROFESSIONAL CLUBS: Chemnitzer FC (1995–1997), Kaiserslautern FC (1997– 1999), Bayer Leverkusen (1999–2002), Bayern Munich (2002–2006), Chelsea (2006–)

POSITION: Midfielder

INTERNATIONAL CAREER:
- 75 full international caps for Germany, 35 goals between 1999 and 2007
- Debut v Scotland in April 1999.
- 19 Germany Under-21 caps, 4 goals.

INTERNATIONAL HONOURS:
- World Cup runner-up, 2002
- Confederations Cup third place, 2005
- World Cup third place, 2006

CLUB HONOURS:
- German championship winner 1998, 2003, 2005, 2006
- German cup winner 2003, 2005, 2006
- UEFA Champions League runner-up 2002
- Bundesliga: 75 goals in 232 games played
- English Premier League: 4 goals in 7 games played

PERSONAL HONOURS:
- German Player of the Year 2002, 2003, 2005
- UEFA Midfielder of the Year 2002
- *Soccer Digest* Player of the Year 2002
- Named in FIFA's 100 Greatest Living Players list.

APPENDIX 1 BALLACK FACTFILE

FOOTBALL CAREER

Club	Season	League		Domestic Cup		League Cup		European Competition		Total	
		Apps	Goals	Apps	Goals	Apps	Goals	Apps	Goals	Apps	Goals
Chelsea	06-07	19	3	3	0	4	0	2	1	32	4
Total		19	3	3	0	4	0	2	1	32	4
Bayern Munich	05-06	26	14	5	1	–	–	6	1	37	16
	04-05	27	13	4	3	–	–	9	2	40	18
	03-04	28	7	3	2	–	–	8	0	39	9
	02-03	26	10	5	4	–	–	7	1	38	15
Total		107	44	17	10	–	–	30	4	153	57
Bayer Leverkusen	01-02	29	17	4	0	–	–	15	6	48	23
	00-01	27	7	2	0	–	–	5	1	34	8
	99-00	23	3	0	0	–	–	2	2	25	5
Total		79	27	6	0	–	–	22	9	107	36
Kaiserslation	98-99	30	4	2	0	–	–	5	0	37	4
	97-98	16	0	2	0	–	–	0	0	18	0
Total		46	4	4	0	–	–	5	0	55	4
Career Totals		251	77	27	10	4	0	58	14	347	101